CPAexcel
CPA Review

Regulation - Workbook

Gregory Carnes, Ph.D., CPA
Marianne Jennings, J.D.
Robert Prentice, J.D.

EFFICIENT LEARNING SYSTEMS™

PO Box 4223 Sedona, AZ 86340-4223
888.884.5669 N.America | 928.204.1066 International

www.cpaexcel.com

Edward Foley, Chairman and Founder
Rahul Srivastava, CEO and President
Nigel Snow, VP Content Development
Gun Granath, Editor

Efficient Learning Systems, Inc.
1120 W. SR 89A, Suite D9
Sedona, AZ 86336 U.S.A.
www.cpaexcel.com

ISBN 978-0-6156422-6-0
Edition 7.8.1

Printed in the United States of America

USING THE CPAexcel WORKBOOK

The CPAexcel workbook is designed for following along with the video lectures and taking notes.

ORGANIZATION

Workbooks compile all the CPAexcel lecture slides in the same order as the table of contents in your textbook and software. However, workbooks include some further organization to facilitate live classroom instruction.

Each of the four sections of CPAexcel are first divided into ***Modules*** that require 3.5 to 4 hours to complete – about the same time as many college classes. Modules contain ***Assignments***[1] which are in turn made up of smaller lesson level ***lectures.***

Each assignment is followed by several past exam questions selected because they illustrate important concepts you should have learned in the preceding material. Your workbook does NOT include the solutions for these questions as they are intended to be worked in class with your instructor.

For example, the Regulation section contains 10 modules. Module 1 contains 3 Assignments. The first assigment (REG 1-1) contains 2 lectures: Treasury Department Circular 230 and Statements on Standards for Tax Services It also contains three multiple choice questions. The table of contents will have the following entry:

> **MODULE 1**
> **REG 1-1: ETHICS AND RESPONSIBILITY IN TAX PRACTICE 1**
> Treasury Department Circular 230 (14:36)
> Statements on Standards for Tax Services (12:29)
> Selected Questions (3)

The structure of the four sections of CPAexcel is as follows.

	Modules	Assignments	Lectures
Auditing	5	29	118
Business	5	32	137
Financial	10	70	271
Regulation	10	49	119

---

[1] The Assignments in your workbook correspond to the assignments in the Exam Plan you will create in the CPAexcel software. However, software assignments differ from workbook assignments in the following way. Workbook assignments consist of video lectures, slides and end of assignment questions. Software assignments include many other types of material and therefore take longer to complete.

FLOW

Each page contains six slides that flow in the following manner:

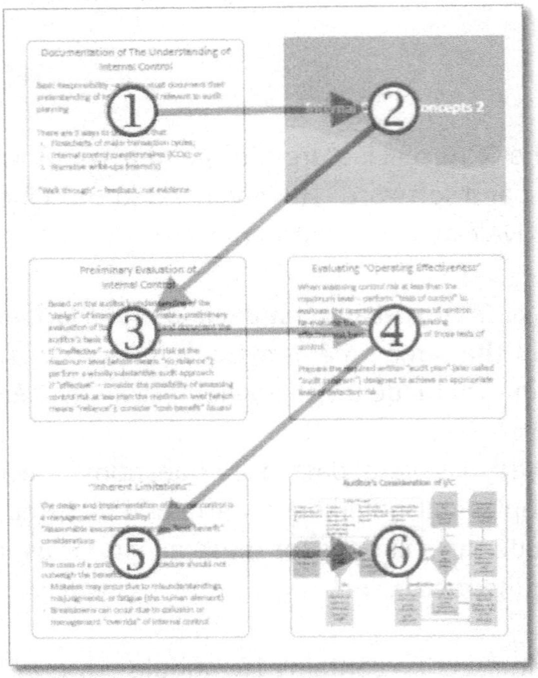

EXCLUDED MATERIAL

Though rare, there are lessons in the CPAexcel review course that do not include a video lecture (e.g. The lesson on Dodd-Frank in Regulation and the Attribute Standards lesson in BEC). These lessons are therefore not included in your workbook. For a complete and current list of items not covered included in this book, visit the "Updates to the Course Material" area in your online software.

TABLE OF CONTENTS

MODULE 1

REG 1-1: ETHICS AND RESPONSIBILITY IN TAX PRACTICE 1 — 16

Treasury Department Circular 230

Statements on Standards for Tax Services

Selected Questions (3)

REG 1-2: ETHICS AND RESPONSIBILITY IN TAX PRACTICE 2 — 27

Internal Revenue Code of 1986 (TRP)

Licensing and Disciplinary Systems

Selected Questions (1)

REG 1-3: LEGAL DUTIES AND RESPONSIBILITIES — 33

Malpractice Liability

Federal Statutory Liability

Privileged Communications, Confidentiality & Privacy Acts

Selected Questions (3)

MODULE 2

REG 2-1: CONTRACTS 1 — 41

Introduction and Classification

Formation – Offer and Acceptance

Selected Questions (6)

REG 2-2: CONTRACTS 2 48

Consideration

Selected Questions (1)

REG 2-3: CONTRACTS 3 52

Contract Form - Statute of Frauds and Records

Selected Questions (1)

REG 2-4: CONTRACTS 4 56

Defenses to Formation

Performance and Remedies

Third Party Rights

Selected Questions (6)

MODULE 3

REG 3-1: UCC ARTICLE 2 - SALES 1 69

Application and Formation of Article 2 Contracts (AFTPDT formula)

Title and Risk of Loss

Selected Questions (2)

REG 3-2: UCC ARTICLE 2 - SALES 2 78

Terms: Warranties and Product Liability

Selected Questions (1)

REG 3-3: UCC ARTICLE 2 - SALES 3 82

Performance

Remedies Under Article 2

Selected Questions (3)

REG 3-4: UCC ARTICLE 3 - NEGOTIABLE INSTRUMENTS 1 87

Introduction to Negotiable Instruments and Negotiability

Selected Questions (2)

REG 3-5: UCC ARTICLE 3 - NEGOTIABLE INSTRUMENTS 2 93

Transfer of Instruments and Holder in Due Course (HDC)

Presentment, Dishonor, and Payment of Negotiable Instruments

Liabilities and Discharge of Duties

Selected Questions (3)

REG 3-6: UCC ARTICLE 5 & 7 102

Purposes, Requirements and Payment

Definitions, Forms, Negotiation, and Rights

Selected Questions (2)

MODULE 4

REG 4-1: UCC ARTICLE 9 - SECURED TRANSACTIONS 108

Introduction and Creation of Security Interests

Perfection of Security Interests

Priorities in Security Interests

Rights of Secured Parties and Debtors

Selected Questions (6)

REG 4-2: DEBTOR-CREDITOR RELATIONSHIPS 120

Suretyship: Introduction, Creation, and Types

Suretyship: Rights of Parties

Selected Questions (4)

REG 4-3: REAL PROPERTY 128

Real Property

Selected Questions (2)

REG 4-4: BANKRUPTCY 134

Prebankruptcy Options, Introduction to and Declaration of Bankruptcy

Bankruptcy Process

Distribution of Debtor's Estate

Discharge and Reaffirmation Agreements

Selected Questions (8)

REG 4-5: AGENCY 153

Types of Agency Relationships and Creation

Duties of Agents and Principals

Contract Liability of Agents and Principals

Tort Liability of Agents and Principals

Selected Questions (6)

MODULE 5

REG 5-1: FEDERAL SECURITIES REGULATION 165

Defining a "Security"

The Registration Process

Exempt Transactions and Securities
Liability Provisions: 1933 Act
Purposes, Requirements and Provisions of the 1934 Act
Criminal Liability
Selected Questions (3)

REG 5-2: OTHER FEDERAL LAWS AND REGULATION 1 — 174

Anti-Discrimination
Employee Welfare
Federal Unemployment Tax Act (FUTA)
Fair Labor Standards Act (FLSA)
Employee Benefits
Selected Questions (2)

REG 5-3: OTHER FEDERAL LAWS AND REGULATION 2 — 181

Health and Safety
Union and Employee Relations
Antitrust
Copyright
Patents
Money Laundering
Selected Questions (3)

REG 5-4: BUSINESS STRUCTURE 1 — 193

Selection of a Business Entity
Formation
Operations
Termination
Financial Structure
Selected Questions (3)

REG 5-5: BUSINESS STRUCTURE 2

Rights & Duties

Authority of Owners & Managers

Selected Questions (1)

MODULE 6

REG 6-1: PROPERTY TRANSACTIONS 1

Introduction to Tax Review

Sales and Dispositions of Assets

Capital Gains and Losses

Selected Questions (4)

REG 6-2: PROPERTY TRANSACTIONS 2

Section 1231 Assets

Sections 1231 Assets - Cost Recovery

Selected Questions (3)

REG 6-3: PROPERTY TRANSACTIONS 3

Like-Kind Exchanges and Involuntary Conversions

Other Nonrecognition Transactions

Selected Questions (2)

REG 6-4: INCOME 1

Gross Income - Concepts, Interest and Dividends

Gross Income - Other Inclusions

Selected Questions (4)

REG 6-5: INCOME 2

Gross Income: Exclusions

Accounting Methods and Periods

Selected Questions (3)

REG 6-6: INCOME 3

Taxation of Employee Benefits

Taxation of Retirement Plans

Selected Questions (3)

MODULE 7

REG 7-1: DEDUCTIONS 1

Deductions: Basic Principles

Deductions for AGI

Selected Questions (2)

REG 7-2: DEDUCTIONS 2

Itemized Deductions - Medical, Taxes, Interest

Itemized Deductions - Other

Selected Questions (3)

REG 7-3: DEDUCTIONS 3

Employee Business Expenses

Selected Questions (1)

REG 7-4: DEDUCTIONS 4

Deductions - Losses and Bad Debts
Limitations on Business Deductions
Selected Questions (2)

REG 7-5: INDIVIDUAL TAX ISSUES

Personal and Dependency Exemptions
Filing Status
Alternative Minimum Tax and Other Taxes
Selected Questions (4)

MODULE 8

REG 8-1: TAX CREDITS

Personal Tax Credits
Business and Energy Tax Credits
Selected Questions (2)

REG 8-2: CORPORATE TAXATION 1

Formation of a Corporation
Corporate Income
Special Corporate Deductions
Selected Questions (4)

REG 8-3: CORPORATE TAXATION 2

Corporate Alternative Minimum Tax
Penalty Taxes
Taxation of Related Corporations
Selected Questions (3)

REG 8-4: CORPORATE TAXATION 3

Distributions from a Corporation

Corporate Redemptions and Liquidations

Corporate Reorganizations

Selected Questions (4)

MODULE 9

REG 9-1: MULTIJURISDICTIONAL TAX ISSUES

State and Local Taxation

Taxation of Foreign Income

Selected Questions (3)

REG 9-2: TAX-EXEMPT ENTITIES

Tax-Exempt Organizations

Selected Questions (2)

REG 9-3: PARTNERSHIP TAXATION 1

Formation and Basis

Selected Questions (3)

REG 9-4: PARTNERSHIP TAXATION 2

Flow-Through of Income and Losses

Transactions with Partners

Selected Questions (4)

REG 9-5: PARTNERSHIP TAXATION 3

Distributions

Sales and Terminations

Selected Questions (4)

MODULE 10

REG 10-1: S CORPORATION TAXATION

Eligibility, Elections, Terminations

Income and Basis

Distributions and Special Taxes

Selected Questions (2)

REG 10-2: ESTATE AND GIFT TAXATION

Federal Gift Tax

Federal Estate Tax

Selected Questions (1)

REG 10-3: FIDUCIARY TAXATION

Income Taxation of Fiduciaries

Selected Questions (1)

REG 10-4: TAX RESEARCH AND PRACTICE 1

Sources of Tax Authority and Research

Selected Questions (1)

REG 10-5: TAX RESEARCH AND PRACTICE 2

Tax Practice and Procedure

Compliance Responsibilities

Selected Questions (1)

REG 10-6: OTHER TAX ISSUES

Tax Planning

Business Entity Choice

Tax Forms and Schedules

Selected Questions (1)

REG 1-1

ETHICS AND RESPONSIBILITY IN TAX PRACTICE 1

Treasury Department Circular 230

Statements on Standards for Tax Services

Selected Questions (3)

TREASURY DEPARTMENT CIRCULAR 230

Introduction

Circular 230: IRS's rules of practice. The government may censure, fine, suspend, or disbar tax advisors from practice before the IRS if they violate Circular 230's standards of conduct

Focus: Part B of Circular 230 which contains its substantive provisions; other portions contain procedural rules and potential punishments

Selected Substantive Provisions

Furnishing Information: A practitioner must promptly submit to the IRS any records or information that its agents and officers request properly and lawfully

"***unless*** *the practitioner believes in good faith and on reasonable grounds that the records or information are privileged*"

Selected Substantive Provisions

Client's Omission: Section 10.21 requires the practitioner, upon discovering an error or omission in a previous return, to promptly notify the client, but the practitioner need not notify the IRS of the error and may not without the client's permission

Due Diligence and Reliance on Others: Practitioners must exercise due diligence in all aspects of their tax practice, including preparing tax returns and making representations to the IRS

Selected Substantive Provisions

With the exception of situations involving aggressive tax shelters, **Section 10.22** allows a practitioner to rely upon the work product of others if the practitioner used reasonable care in engaging, supervising, training, and evaluating them

Delays and Unconscionable Fees

Practitioners may not unreasonably delay the prompt disposition of any matters before the Service (10.23)

No practitioner may charge an unconscionable fee for representing a client before the IRS

Contingent Fees

A practitioner may not charge a contingent fee for providing services before the IRS, with three exceptions where substantive examination is likely and therefore it is unlikely the practitioner and client will play the "audit lottery"

1. A contingent fee may be charged for services rendered in connection with an IRS examination of or challenge to either
   a) an original tax return or
   b) an amended return or claim for refund when they were filed within 120 days of receiving a written notice of examination or written challenge to the original exam

Contingent Fees

A practitioner may not charge a contingent fee for providing services before the IRS, with three exceptions where substantive examination is likely and therefore it is unlikely the practitioner and client will play the "audit lottery"

2. Where a claim for refund is filed solely in connection with determination of statutory interest or penalties

3. When the accountant is representing the client in judicial proceedings

Return of Client Records

Section 10.28 instructs the practitioner, upon the client's request, to promptly return any and all records needed for the client to comply with Federal tax obligations

If applicable state law permits retention in the case of a fee dispute, the practitioner need return only those records that **must be attached to the taxpayer's return**

Conflicts of Interest

Section 10.20 provides that practitioners should not represent a client before the IRS if to do so would create a conflict of interest

1. Such a conflict exists if the representation of one client would be adverse to that of another or if there is a significant risk that the representation of one client would be materially limited by the practitioner's responsibilities to another client

Conflicts of Interest

Section 10.20 provides that practitioners should not represent a client before the IRS if to do so would create a conflict of interest

2. Notwithstanding the existence of a conflict of interest, however, practitioners may represent a client if they:
   a. Reasonably believe that they can provide competent and diligent representation to the client
   b. The representation is not prohibited by law, and
   c. The affected client gives informed consent in writing

--Practitioners should keep the consents on file for at least three years

Best Practices

Section 10.33 sets forth "best practices" for tax advisors, including:

1. Communicating clearly with the client regarding the terms of the engagement, including the purpose, use, scope, and form of the advice

2. Establishing the facts, determining which facts are relevant, evaluating the reasonableness of assumptions or representations, relating the applicable law to the relevant facts, and arriving at a conclusion supported by the law and the facts

Best Practices

3. Advising the client regarding the import of the conclusions reached, including whether taxpayers may avoid accuracy-related penalties if they rely on the advice

4. Acting fairly and with integrity when practicing before the IRS

5. Exercising any firm supervisory powers to ensure that firm employees act in accordance with best practices

Tax Return Standards

Section 10.34 instructs practitioners not to advise clients to take positions that are frivolous and to inform clients of any penalties that are reasonably likely to apply with positions taken on tax returns

"Covered Opinions"

Tax shelter scandals caused the IRS to rewrite some provisions of Circular 230 to raise performance standards for certain types of "covered opinions:"

1. First, is a transaction that is the same or substantially similar to a transaction that the IRS has already determined to be a "tax avoidance transaction"
2. Second, is any partnership or other entity, any investment plan or arrangement, or any other plan or arrangement, the **principal purpose** of which is to avoid or evade income tax obligations

"Covered Opinions"

Third are transactions where tax avoidance is not the principal purpose of the arrangement but is nonetheless a **significant purpose**. Four categories of these opinions are deemed "covered opinions" by §10.35:

I. **Reliance opinions**, which conclude at a confidence level of more likely than not (more than 50% likelihood) that significant tax issues would be resolved in the taxpayer's favor

"Covered Opinions"

II. **Marketed opinions**, where the practitioner has reason to know that written advice will be used or referred to by other persons in promoting tax shelters to taxpayers

Practitioners can avoid having opinions treated as marketed opinions by prominently disclosing in written advice that the advice is not intended to be used and cannot be used by any taxpayer for the purpose of avoiding penalties

"Covered Opinions"

III. Opinions issued under **conditions of confidentiality**, where the practitioner requires recipients of tax advice to keep it confidential; and

IV. Opinions issued subject to **contractual protection**, where the taxpayer has the right to a full or partial refund if all or part of the intended tax consequences are not sustained, or if fees paid are contingent upon success

"Covered Opinions"

Minimum standards for "covered opinions:"

a. Use reasonable efforts to identify and ascertain relevant facts and not basing opinions on unreasonable factual assumptions or representations

b. Relate the applicable law to the relevant facts, not basing opinions on unreasonable legal conclusions, and not basing advice on internally inconsistent legal analyses or conclusions

"Covered Opinions"

Minimum standards for "covered opinions:"

c. Evaluate all significant Federal tax issues (unless it is a "limited scope" opinion explicitly addressing only selected issues), explaining reasons for conclusions reached (including an inability to reach a conclusion or a failure to reach the required confidence level), and provide an overall conclusion

d. Be knowledgeable about Federal tax law so as to provide a competent opinion and disclose any reliance upon the opinion of another tax practitioner

"Covered Opinions"

e. Disclose, among other things:

- Any relationships between the practitioner and a tax shelter promoter
- That an opinion failing to reach a more likely than not conclusion cannot be relied upon by the taxpayer for purposes of avoiding a penalty

"Covered Opinions"

f. Section 10.36 provides that practitioners who have or share principal authority and responsibility for overseeing a firm's tax practice may be sanctioned if they either:
   - Willfully, recklessly, or through gross incompetence fail to take reasonable steps to assure that the firm has adequate procedures in place to ensure that all members and employees are complying with 10.35, or
   - Know or should know that a member or employee is not complying with 10.35, but through willfulness, recklessness or gross incompetence fail to take prompt corrective action

STATEMENTS ON STANDARDS FOR TAX SERVICES

SSTS No. 1: Tax Return Positions

May not recommend a position be taken with respect to tax treatment of any item on a return unless member has a good-faith belief that the position has at least a realistic possibility [*generally regarded as a 33% likelihood*] of being sustained if challenged

SSTS No. 1: Tax Return Positions

Even if there is not a realistic possibility of a position being sustained, a member may recommend a tax return position or prepare or sign a return if he or she concludes that

1. There is a reasonable basis [*generally regarded as a 20-33% likelihood*] for the position, and
2. The position is disclosed to the IRS so it can be reviewed

SSTS No. 1: Tax Return Positions

However, a member must comply with standards, if any, imposed by applicable taxing authorities, and Congress

26 U.S.C. Sec. 6694 provides that a tax return preparer who takes an unreasonable position may be punished

A position is unreasonable unless there is substantial authority (at least a 40% chance of being sustained) supporting it

SSTS No. 1: Tax Return Positions

If a tax position relates to a tax shelter, then it is unreasonable under 6694 unless it is "more likely than not" (>50%) to be sustained on its merits

1. For most federal income tax matters: >40% (*not unreasonable/substantial authority*)
2. For tax shelters: >50% (*more likely than not*)
3. For other tax matters: >33% (*realistic possibility*), or
4. Other tax matters disclosed: 20-33% (*reasonable basis*)

Authority

Internal Revenue Code §6672 is very narrow in what it recognizes as valid authority, but the AICPA allows members to consider:

- A well-reasoned construction of the applicable statute
- Well-reasoned articles or treatises, and
- Pronouncements issued by the applicable taxing authority

SSTS No. 1 : Tax Return Positions

Must: Inform client of consequences if tax return position is rejected and of opportunity to avoid penalties through disclosure

Have right and responsibility to act as advocate for client with respect to proper positions

SSTS No. 1 : Tax Return Positions

Should never recommend a position that:

- Exploits the IRS audit selection process, or
- Serves as a mere "arguing position" to gain leverage in negotiations with IRS

Should make reasonable effort to obtain and provide appropriate answers to all questions on a tax return

SSTS No. 2: Answers to Questions on Return

Why?

- A question may be important in determining taxable income or loss, or the tax liability so that its omission would detract from the return's quality
- A request for information may require a disclosure necessary for a complete return or to avoid penalties; and
- A member often must sign a preparer's declarations stating that the return is true, correct, and complete

SSTS No. 2: Answers to Questions on Return

Reasonable grounds for omitting an answer, which need not be explained, include:

- The information is not readily available **and** the answer is not significant in terms of the tax liability
- Genuine uncertainty exists as to the meaning of the question in relation to the particular return
- The answer is voluminous and the return states that data will be supplied upon examination

SSTS No. 3: Procedural Aspects

CPA may in good faith rely without verification upon information furnished by clients or third parties

SSTS No. 3: Procedural Aspects

But:

1. Should not ignore "red flags," such as inconsistencies in client records
2. Should make reasonable inquiries if information furnished appears incorrect, incomplete, or inconsistent either on its face or on the basis of other facts known to the CPA; and
3. Should where feasible, refer to client's past returns
4. Where a tax law imposes conditions for qualification for a deduction or other tax treatment, such as production of substantiating documentation, a member should make "*appropriate inquiries*" to determine whether the conditions are met

SSTS No. 4 : Use of Estimates

Use of estimates generally need not be disclosed, but should be when certain unusual circumstances exist to avoid misleading IRS regarding reliability, including where:

1. A taxpayer has died or is ill at the time the return must be filed
2. A taxpayer has not received a Schedule K-1 for a pass-through entity at the time the tax return is to be filed
3. There is litigation pending (e.g., a bankruptcy proceeding) that bears on the return
4. Fire, computer failure, or natural disaster has destroyed the relevant records

SSTS No. 5: Departure From a Position

When a tax return position is determined in an administrative proceeding or court decision, a member may still recommend a different position in a later year—unless the taxpayer is bound (such as by a formal closing agreement) to a specified treatment in the later year

SSTS No. 6: Knowledge of Error

When a CPA becomes aware of a material error in a previous return or a return subject to an administrative proceeding, the CPA should:

1. Promptly inform the client
2. Not inform the IRS, absent client permission
3. Consider ending the professional relationship if the client declines to inform the IRS of the error
4. Ensure the error is not repeated in the future

SSTS No. 7: Form and Content of Advice to Client

CPAs need not update clients regarding changes in the law unless:

1. The CPA has agreed to do so, or
2. The CPA is assisting in implementing procedures or plans associated with advice based on rules that have now changed

Written communications are preferable for complicated or important matters, but not required

Which of the following is true?

- [ ] A. **Client Tim told CPA Cho that he wished to take a particular deduction that Cho knows must be documented. Cho should ask Tim whether he has kept, or could obtain, the relevant documents.**
- [ ] B. **CPA Harris asked Client Shavell why the rental income, that she had enjoyed in the previous three years when Harris had done her taxes, was not reflected in this year's records. Shavell's answer was evasive and incomplete. Harris need not inquire further.**
- [ ] C. **CPA Seyhun is preparing Manne's tax return when he notices that Manne was claiming only $20,000 in income from the LMN partnership. Seyhun also does the individual tax return for Noll, an equal one-third partner in the partnership, and recalls that Noll claimed twice as much income from the partnership. Seyhun has always found Manne to be reliable, so he need not inquire further.**
- [ ] D. **B and C.**

In May 2009, CPA Loveland gave tax advice to client Pingleton regarding a tax-free transfer to her children. Pingleton executed the transfer in October 2009 in the form suggested by Loveland. In 2010, the IRS changed its interpretation of the applicable law, rendering this form of transaction ineffective for its intended purpose. In December 2011, without consulting Loveland again, Pingleton repeated the transaction. This time, the IRS challenged the tax consequences and Pingleton lost the challenge. Pingleton sued Loveland for failing to tell her of the change in tax law. Assuming state malpractice laws would be roughly consonant with SSTS rules, which of the following is true?

- [ ] **A. Loveland is liable, because he should have updated Pingleton regarding the change in the law.**
- [ ] **B. Loveland is not liable because no duty to update applied.**
- [ ] **C. A and B.**
- [ ] **D. None of the above.**

John is a tax accountant for PWC and is working on Jane's personal taxes. Jane has provided John with all of her relevant tax information, which seems to be complete and accurate. Which of the following is a required duty of John prior to submitting Jane's taxes?

- ☐ **A. John must verify all data provided by Jane or a third party.**
- ☐ **B. John must inform the IRS when a material error in a previously filed tax return comes to light.**
- ☐ **C. John must inform Jane when a material error in a previously filed tax return comes to light.**
- ☐ **D. John must notify Jane of legislative changes in the tax law affecting previous advice offered.**

REG 1-2

ETHICS AND RESPONSIBILITY IN TAX PRACTICE 2

Internal Revenue Code of 1986 (TRP)

Licensing and Disciplinary Systems

Selected Questions (1)

INTERNAL REVENUE CODE OF 1986 (TRP)

Introduction

The Internal Revenue Code (IRC) has many provisions that relate solely or largely to Tax Return Preparers (TRPs)

This lesson surveys those provisions, both civil and criminal

Who Is a Tax Return Preparer?

Any person who prepares for compensation, or who employs one or more persons to prepare for compensation, all or a substantial portion of any tax return or any claim for refund of tax under the Internal Revenue Code

Thus, people are TRPs if they:

1. Are paid
2. To prepare, or retain employees to prepare
3. A substantial portion
4. Of any federal tax return or refund claim

Subtypes

Signing TRPs are individual TRPs who bear "primary responsibility" for the overall accuracy of the return or claim for refund

Nonsigning TRPs are those other than the signing TRP who prepare all or a *substantial portion* of a return or claim for refund

Substantial Portion

Nonsigning TRPs, who, for example, give advice regarding just one large deduction on a return, may be liable for a "substantial proportion" unless the deduction involves either:

1. Less than $10,000, or

2. Less than $400,000, which is also less than 20% of the gross income indicated on the return

Safe Harbors

One is not a TRP merely because he or she:

1. Furnishes typing, reproducing, or other mechanical assistance

2. Prepares a return for his or her employer, or

3. Prepares as a fiduciary a return or claim for refund for any person

TRPs

1. A firm that employs a TRP is treated as the sole **signing** TRP
2. When there are multiple people working on a return, the one who is primarily responsible for the position giving rise to an understatement is the TRP who will be punished
3. If it is unclear who is responsible, the one with overall supervisory responsibility for the return or for the position will be the TRP

IRC Code Civil Provisions

Understatement of Taxpayer's Liability. Sec. 6694(a) imposes a penalty against a TRP when an "unreasonable" position causes an understatement of tax liability

Guidelines

A position is unreasonable if there is no substantial authority (<40% chance of being sustained) for the position

A position is unreasonable if it is disclosed yet there is no reasonable basis (<20% chance of being sustained) for it

If the position relates to a tax shelter, it is unreasonable unless it is more likely than not (MLTN) (<50% chance) that the position will be sustained

Guidelines

Whereas subsection

1. Focuses on **negligent** conduct, subsection
2. Of 6694 imposes a larger penalty if the understatement is due to **willful or reckless** conduct

Disclosure Provisions

Section 6695 punishes TRPS for, among other things:

1. Failure to furnish copy of return to taxpayer
2. Failure to sign return and show own identity
3. Failure to furnish preparer's identifying number to the IRS; and
4. Failure to keep copy of return

Other Civil Provisions

Other Civil Provisions punish TRPs and others for:

1. Organizing and promoting abusive tax shelters
2. Aiding and abetting understatements of tax liability; and
3. Disclosing a client's confidential tax information or using it for any purpose other than to prepare a return

IRC Code - Criminal Provisions

Tax Evasion. Sec. 7201 punishes "tax evasion," including: failure to file a return, falsifying income, and falsifying amounts that reduce taxable income

Elements:

1. An affirmative act constituting an attempt to evade or defeat payment of a tax
2. Willfulness; and
3. Existence of a tax deficiency

Ex: lottery ticket case

IRC Code - Criminal Provisions

Tax Fraud. Sec. 7206 punishes fraud and false statements, criminalizing:

1. Willfully making and subscribing to any document made under penalty of perjury, which the accountant does not believe to be true as to every material matter
2. Willfully aiding the preparation of any tax related matter which is fraudulent as to any material matter; and
3. Concealing client's property with intent to defeat taxes

Ex: domesticated beaver purchase contract

IRC Code - Criminal Provisions

Other criminal provisions punish, among other acts:

1. Willful failure to file return, supply information, or pay tax
2. Willful failure to collect or pay over tax
3. Attempts to interfere with administration of the Internal Revenue laws, such as threatening IRS agents or misleading them
4. Willful disclosure or use of confidential information learned while preparing a tax return

LICENSING AND DISCIPLINARY SYSTEMS

State Boards of Accountancy

1. Authority: State boards of accountancy license CPAs and can prohibit non-CPAs from performing attest functions

2. It is only state boards that can grant CPA licenses and only state boards that can take them away

State Boards of Accountancy

3. Licensing: To qualify to be licensed as a "certified public accountant," one must meet several requirements. In most states, three steps are the key and may be accomplished in any order:
   1. Education
   2. 'BA + 30' (150 hours of college education)
      - Professional ethics course (required by many states)
      - CPE: Once certification is gained, there are also continuing professional education requirements

State Boards of Accountancy

3. Examination

4. Experience
   - **How long?** One year of professional experience (but at least 2,000 hours)
   - **In what areas?** In accounting, attest, management advisory, financial advisory, tax or consulting areas and may be while working for any employer (accounting firm, corporation, government agency, etc.)

State Boards of Accountancy

4. One needs a CPA license to perform attest-related functions:
   - Any audit or other engagement to be performed in accordance with SAS (Statements on Auditing Standards)
   - Any review of a financial statement to be performed in accordance with SSARS (Statements on Standards on Accounting and Review Services)
   - Any examination of prospective financial information to be performed in accordance with SSAE (Statements on Standards for Attest Engagements); and
   - Any engagement to be perfomed in accordance with the standards of the PCAOB

State Boards of Accountancy

5. One does not need a CPA license to perform such nonattest services as:
   - Preparation of tax returns
   - Management advisory services (consulting); or
   - Preparing financial statements without issuing a report thereon

State Boards of Accountancy

6. Discipline: State boards may revoke CPA licenses and impose other penalties (such as fines) for such acts as:
   - Fraud or deceit in obtaining a certificate
   - Cancellation of a certificate in any other state for disciplinary reasons
   - Failure to comply with requirements for renewal
   - Revocation of the right to practice before any state or federal agency, including the PCAOB
   - Dishonesty, fraud or gross negligence in performance of services or failure to file one's own income tax returns
   - Violation of professional standards; and
   - Conviction of a felony or any crime involving fraud or dishonesty

AICPA Disciplinary Mechanisms

1. **Professional Ethics Division**: investigates violations and sanctions minor cases
2. **Joint Trial Board** hears more serious cases and has power to admonish, suspend, or expel
3. Joint Ethics Enforcement Program (JEEP): AICPA and most state societies split ethics complaints where states handle many cases, but the AICPA handles matters:
   - Of national concern
   - Involving more than one state; and
   - In litigation

AICPA Disciplinary Mechanisms

4. Remember: While the AICPA and state societies can punish CPAs in various ways, **only state accounting boards** can grant and take away the license to practice as a CPA.

CPA Randall has had a run-in with the law. The AICPA may expulse Randall *without a hearing* under which of the following circumstances?

- [ ] A. **Randall has pled guilty to bank robbery.**
- [ ] B. **A jury has convicted Randall of securities fraud.**
- [ ] C. **Randall has been found guilty by a judge following a trial of willfully failing to file a tax return.**
- [ ] D. **All of the above.**

REG 1-3

LEGAL DUTIES AND RESPONSIBILITIES

Malpractice Liability

Federal Statutory Liability

Privileged Communications, Confidentiality & Privacy Acts

Selected Questions (3)

MALPRACTICE LIABILITY

Breach of Contract

Clients may recover from accountant for breach of contract if they show:

- Accountant agreed to perform services professionally
- Accountant breached agreement
- Client suffered damages, and
- Damages were proximately caused by the breach

If an accountant breaches, yet wishes to recover fee:

- No fee if breach was major
- If breach was minor, can recover fee reduced by damages to client caused by breach

Negligence Liability to Clients

Clients may recover from accountant for negligence if they show:

- Accountant owed a duty of due care
- Accountant breached the duty
- Client suffered damages, and
- Breach proximately caused the damages

Negligence Liability to Clients

Accountants are not expected to be perfect and breach their duty of care only if they fail to meet professional standards

In proper circumstances, clients' misconduct may reduce recovery or bar it altogether

Fraud Liability

Accountants may be held liable for fraud to clients or third parties who can show:

- The accountant misrepresented a fact (or failed to disclose when he owed a duty to do so)
- The accountant acted with intent (rather than mere negligence)
- The plaintiff relied on the false statement or omission
- The plaintiff suffered damages; and
- The fraud proximately caused plaintiff' s loss

Actual vs. Constructive Fraud

Actual fraud occurs when an accountant makes a statement s/he knows is false

Constructive fraud occurs when an accountant makes a statement that they have no reasonable grounds to believe is true

Fraud Liability

Unlike plaintiffs in breach of contract and negligence suits, fraud plaintiffs may recover punitive damages in addition to compensatory damages

Negligence Liability to Third Parties

Auditors are often sued by third-parties (typically investors or creditors of audit clients) who lost money by relying upon audited F/S that were carelessly certified by the accountant

Negligence Liability to Third Parties

The majority view (known as the 'Restatement' view) provides that careless auditors may be liable to non-clients where the accountant knows:

1. The information being supplied to the client will be given to or is for the benefit of a **limited group** of third persons, and
2. The information will influence those third persons in a specific transaction or type of transaction

FEDERAL STATUTORY LIABILITY

Foreign Corrupt Practices Act Liability

FCPA has two key provisions:
1. Anti-bribery
2. Books & Records and Internal accounting controls

The internal accounting controls have now been supplemented by Sarbanes-Oxley's "internal financial controls"

- IACs focus on: asset accountability
- IFCs focus on: F/S integrity

Racketeer Influenced Corrupt Organizations Act

RICO has two sides:
1. Criminal
2. Civil

Sec. 1962(c) punishes those who:
1. Conduct or participate in the conduct...
2. ...of an enterprise...
3. ...through a pattern...
4. ...of Racketeering activity

Mail and Wire Fraud

If use of the mails or wires (telephones, telegraphs, internet, etc.) is an essential part of a fraudulent scheme, then perpetrators may be guilty of:

- Mail Fraud
- Wire Fraud

It is not required for guilt that:

1. A lie was told in the communication, or that
2. D sent the communication

Sarbanes-Oxley Act

Among other provisions relevant to accountants, SOX makes it a crime to:

1. Alter, destroy, mutilate, etc. records involved in any federal government matter or bankruptcy with the intent to impede, obstruct or influence the investigation
2. Willfully fail to retain audit and review workpapers, which should be preserved for 7 years after the audit
3. Corruptly
   - Alter, destroy, mutilate, or conceal records, documents or other objects with the intent to impair its integrity or availability for use in an official proceeding, or
   - Otherwise obstruct, influence or impede any official proceeding

Sarbanes-Oxley Act

SOX also:

- Adds a new securities fraud crime
- Punishes those who retaliate against whistleblowers

PRIVILEGED COMMUNICATIONS, CONFIDENTIALITY AND PRIVACY ACTS

Privileged Communications, Confidentiality and Privacy Acts

In today's high-tech information age, safeguarding client confidential information must be an extremely high priority for all CPAs.

This lesson examines three aspects of that subject matter:

1. Privileged communications
2. Confidentiality responsibilities
3. Privacy statutes

Privileged Communications

Testimonial Privileges: Classic privileged communications include attorney-client, doctor-patient, and priest-penitent

Where applicable the protected party (client, patient, penitent) can prevent the party who received the protected communications (attorney, doctor, priest) from testifying

Neither the federal courts nor the state courts at common law recognized an accountant-client privilege

Privileged Communications

Nonetheless, approximately 15 states have statutorily recognized an accountant-client privilege. In those states, remember:

1. The privilege belongs to the client, not to the accountant;
2. The privilege can be waived by the client, either expressly or through voluntary and knowing disclosure of the relevant information
3. Waiver of the privilege as to part of the communication is waiver as to all; and
4. The privilege applies only in state court, where state procedural rules apply

Privileged Communications

Additionally, Congress enacted the "tax practitioner's privilege" in 26 USC Sec. 7525. It extends a modest testimonial privilege to clients of all tax advisers (not just lawyers) authorized to practice before the IRS

Privileged Communications

However, 7525 applies only in noncriminal tax matters

1. Before the IRS or
2. In federal court in actions brought by or against the United States

And it exempts written advice in connection with promotion of a tax shelter

Privileged Communications

Most courts have construed 7525 narrowly, holding:

1. It does not apply to information communicated to the practitioner solely for the purposes of facilitating tax return preparation
2. It merely extends to tax practitioners the same privilege accorded in the attorney-client relationship
3. Legal advice is protected, but not general accounting advice

Privacy Statutes

AICPA has proposed, but not yet adopted, Generally Accepted Privacy Principles (GAPP)

Many states are enacting or considering statutes requiring professionals like accountants to:

- Protect clients' SSN #s
- Encrypt e-mails containing sensitive client info

Vee learned that the IRS was getting ready to launch an investigation of one of his firm's corporate tax clients. Vee knew that he had recommended to the client some very aggressive tax positions and some questionable tax shelters. Vee e-mailed his subordinates, ordering them to destroy some records and to falsify some others. Which of the following is true?

- ☐ **A. Vee might be criminally convicted of destruction of records under SOX.**
- ☐ **B. Vee might be criminally convicted of willful failure to retain audit and review work papers under SOX.**
- ☐ **C. Vee might be criminally convicted of tampering with documents to be used in an official proceeding.**
- ☐ **D. A and C.**

Which of the following is the best defense a CPA firm can assert in a suit for common law fraud based on its unqualified opinion on materially false financial statements?

- [ ] **A. Contributory negligence on the part of the client.**
- [ ] **B. A disclaimer contained in the engagement letter.**
- [ ] **C. Lack of privity.**
- [ ] **D. Lack of scienter.**

CPA Fatjo agreed to prepare Tacko's individual tax return. However, two months before the return was due, Fatjo had the opportunity to take an around-the-world cruise with a rich uncle. Fatjo called up Tacko and said: "Keep your fee and find yourself another accountant. I'm going to cruise the world." Tacko found another accountant who would prepare his tax return, but would charge $300 more than Fatjo. Tacko was extraordinarily upset that Fatjo intentionally breached a signed contract contained in their engagement letter and added a punitive damages claim for $5,000. Tacko sued Fatjo for breach of contract. Which of the following is true?

- [ ] A. **Tacko will probably lose.**
- [ ] B. **Tacko will probably win $300.**
- [ ] C. **Tacko will probably win $10,000.**
- [ ] D. **Tacko will probably win $10,300.**

REG 2-1

CONTRACTS 1

Introduction and Classification

Formation – Offer and Acceptance

Selected Questions (6)

INTRODUCTION AND CLASSIFICATION

Sources of Contract Law

Common Law
- Real estate
- Services (employment)

Uniform Commercial Code (UCC) (Article 2)
- Sales of goods
- Goods and services combined: Intent and breakdown of cost of goods vs. cost of services

CAUTION: Be sure to ask this question first: Am I under UCC or am I under common law?

LAW OF CONTRACTS

UCC	Common Law
Uniform Commercial Code	Restatement of Contracts
Goods – Tangible Personal Property	Real estate
	Services

What are the differences between UCC and Common Law?

UCC is codified and common law is body of cases decisions (majority view of the states is found in the Restatement of Contracts)

Common law requires much more detail for valid contracts

UCC has goal of moving commerce along efficiently and quickly

Types of Contracts

- Express contracts
- Implied or Implied-in-fact contracts
- Quasi-contract

Types of Contracts

Bilateral
"I promise to buy your house if you promise to sell your house."

Unilateral
"I promise to pay you $500 if you will drive my car from Los Angeles to New York."

Types of Contracts

- Executed vs. Executory contracts
- Valid contracts
- Void
- Voidable
- Unenforceable

FORMATION: OFFER AND ACCEPTANCE

CONTRACTING STEPS

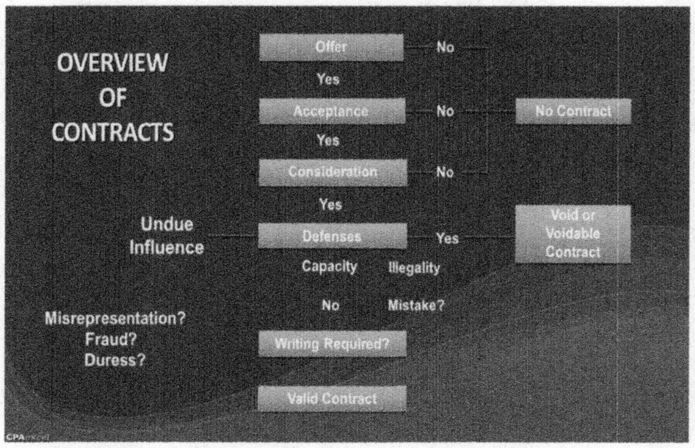

OFFER

	UCC	Common Law
1. Present Intent	Objective Basis	Objective Basis
2. Language	Subject Matter	All Details

Termination

Rejection*

Counteroffer* - Common law - mirror image rule

Revocation*

*Effective upon receipt

Termination of Offers

Death of offeror

Bankruptcy

Illegality

Types of Offers

Options

1. Paid-for offers
2. Consideration required
3. Irrevocable

Review Question

Dye sent Hill a written offer to sell a tract of land located in Newtown for $60,000. The parties were engaged in a separate dispute. The offer stated that it would be irrevocable for 60 days if Hill would promise to refrain from suing Dye during this time. Hill promptly delivered a promise not to sue during the term of the offer and to forego suit if Hill accepted the offer. Dye subsequently decided that the possible suit by Hill was groundless and therefore phoned Hill and revoked the offer 15 days after making it. Hill mailed an acceptance on the 20th day. Dye did not reply. Under the circumstances,

A. Dye's offer was supported by consideration and was not revocable when accepted.
B. Dye's written offer would be irrevocable even without consideration.
C. Dye's silence was an acceptance of Hill's promise.
D. Dye's revocation, not being in writing, was invalid.

Merchants' Firm Offers - UCC

1. Writing (Revised Article 2 – Record)
2. Signed - intent to authenticate (Revised Article 2 – authentication)
3. By a merchant - in the business of selling goods that are the subject matter of the contract
4. States that it will be kept open (max of three months)

Merchant's Firm Offer

UCC - Nonmerchants - need option

UCC - exceeds three months - need option

UCC Rules For Additional Terms in Acceptance*

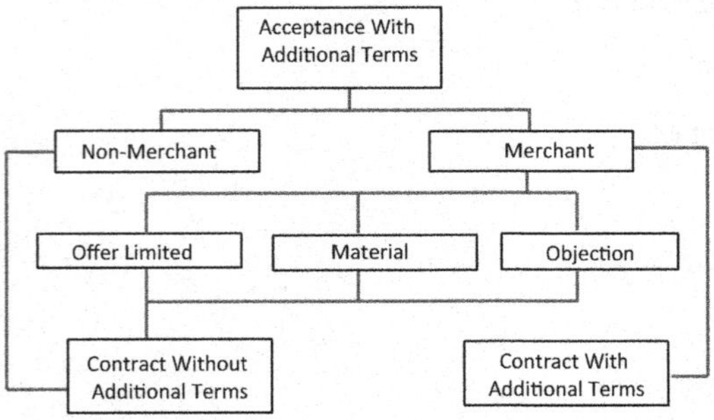

*Not conditional acceptance

Acceptance - Conditional

Misnomer

"I accept provided that"
"I accept on the condition that"
"I accept if"
"I accept if and only if"
"I accept but I must"

Counteroffer and rejection

Timing Rules for Acceptance

Type of Offer	UCC Method of Acceptance	Acceptance Effective?	Common Law Method of Acceptance
No means given	Same or faster method of comm.	When properly mailed (dispatched) Mailbox Rule applies	Same method of comm.
No means given	Slower method of comm.	When received if the offer is still open	Different method of comm.
Specified means (Stipulated)	Specified means used	Mailbox Rule	Specified means used
Specified means (Stipulated)	Specified means not used	Counteroffer and rejection	Specified means not used
Prompt shipment	Proper goods shipped	Upon shipment	N/A
Prompt shipment	Improper goods shipped	Breach and acceptance	N/A

Mary offers to buy Hal's desktop computer for $400. Hal sends Mary an e-mail of acceptance. The $400 is to be paid upon Hal's delivery of the computer. Which of the following properly classifies this contract?

- [ ] **A. This is a bilateral, valid, executory contract.**
- [ ] **B. This is a bilateral, valid, executed contract.**
- [ ] **C. This is a unilateral, express, executory contract.**
- [ ] **D. This is a unilateral, implied-in-fact, executed contract.**

On April 1, Fine Corp. faxed Moss an offer to purchase Moss' warehouse for $500,000. The offer stated that it would remain open only until April 4 and that acceptance must be received to be effective. Moss sent an acceptance on April 4 by overnight mail and Fine received it on April 5.

Which of the following statements is correct?

- [ ] A. **No contract was formed because Moss sent the acceptance by an unauthorized method.**
- [ ] B. **No contract was formed because Fine received Moss' acceptance after April 4.**
- [ ] C. **A contract was formed when Moss sent the acceptance.**
- [ ] D. **A contract was formed when Fine received Moss' acceptance.**

REG 2-2

CONTRACTS 2

Consideration

Selected Questions (1)

CONSIDERATION

Consideration

UCC & Common Law

1. Amount - irrelevant, but whatever it is, it must be paid

2. Bargained for exchange - promised induces the detriment and detriment induces the promise

Consideration

Benefit —— Detriment

Promisor —— Promisee

Detriment —— Benefit

Consideration

3. Definition

Doing what you're free not to do or not doing what you're free to do.

Consideration Issues

1. Charitable Subscriptions - enforceable despite lack of detriment on one side

2. Preexisting Obligation (Antecedent debt) not sufficient consideration

3. Output/Requirements (UCC)
   "I'll sell all my output."
   "I'll buy all I require."
   Enforceable in good faith

Consideration Issues

4. Modification
   - UCC - Good faith
   - Common law – additional consideration

Consideration Issues

5. Liquidated vs. Unliquidated
   Accord and Satisfaction
6. Statute of Limitations - promise to pay obligation discharged is enforceable if in writing
7. Discharge in Bankruptcy - promise to pay obligation discharged is enforceable if in writing

Consideration Issues

Which of the following requires consideration to be binding on the parties?

A. Material modification of a contract involving the sale of real estate.
B. Ratification of a contract by a person after reaching the age of majority.
C. A written promise signed by a merchant to keep an offer to sell goods open for 10 days.
D. Material modification of a sale of goods contract under the UCC.

Review Question

Which of the following will be legally binding despite the lack of consideration?

A. An employer's promise to make a cash payment to a deceased employee's family in recognition of the employee's many years of service.
B. A promise to donate money to a charity on which the charity relied in incurring large expenditures.
C. A modification of a signed contract to purchase a parcel of land.
D. A merchant's oral promise to keep an offer open for 60 days.

Grove is seeking to avoid performing a promise to pay Brook $1,500. Grove is relying on lack of consideration on Brook's part.

Grove will prevail if Grove can establish that

- ☐ A. Prior to Grove's promise, Brook had already performed the requested act.
- ☐ B. Brook's only claim of consideration was the relinquishment of a legal right.
- ☐ C. Brook's asserted consideration is only worth $400.
- ☐ D. The consideration to be performed by Brook will be performed by a third party.

REG 2-3

CONTRACTS 3

Contract Form - Statute of Frauds and Records

Selected Questions (1)

CONTRACT FORM: STATUTE OF FRAUDS AND RECORDS

Statute of Frauds

I. Land

- Options
- Contracts
- Leases
- Mortgages
- Exception: Partial performance
  Possession and/or improvements and payment

Statute of Frauds

II. Promises to pay debts of another

- Original vs. Collateral
- Surety
- Executor
- Bankruptcy discharge
- Statute of Limitations

Statute of Frauds

III. Contracts not to be performed within one year, measured from time of the agreement

October 2011 - Oral contract for audit to run from January 2012 until November 15, 2012

IV. Sales - Contracts for sale of goods $500 or more must be in writing

Contracts and Statute of Frauds

	REQUIRED TO BE IN WRITING?
Sale of golf cart for $750	Yes
Sale of 1/20 acre of land for $300	Yes
3-Year advertising services contract	Yes
Sale of a mobile home by manufacturer	DEPENDS
Sale of a horse for $350	No
Sale of a painting for $1000	Yes
Officer's guarantee of a corporate note	Yes
Sole proprietor's guarantee of a business note	No

What Satisfies the Statute of Frauds?

Record

Signature/authentication of party to be held liable

Sufficient terms (see contract formation requirements)

E-Sign Act

Federal law that requires that electronic signatures enjoy parity with written ones

Must show underlying intent to contract (screen pop-ups and "You are about to contract")

Must be able to reproduce the agreement

No means for verification of identity of parties – done by state laws

UCC - Exceptions

A. Merchant's confirmation memo - (two merchants required)
   - Writing (record)
   - Signed by one of the merchants
   - Underlying oral agreement
B. Part performance
   - Goods actually accepted - buyer
   - Payments actually received - seller
C. Specially manufactured
D. Admission - in any proceeding while under oath

Parol Evidence

If:

A. COMPLETE CONTRACT
B. NO AMBIGUITIES
C. FINAL WRITTEN FORM

Then:

No outside/extrinsic evidence to contradict the contract

Which of the following statements is true with regard to the Statute of Frauds?

- [ ] **A. All contracts involving consideration of more than $500 must be in writing.**
- [ ] **B. The written contract must be signed by all parties.**
- [ ] **C. The Statute of Frauds applies to contracts that can be fully performed within one year from the date they are made.**
- [ ] **D. The contract terms may be stated in more than one document.**

REG 2-4

CONTRACTS 4

Defenses to Formation

Performance and Remedies

Third Party Rights

Selected Questions (6)

DEFENSES TO FORMATION

Age

- Minors less than 18 – Voidable
- Effect of Misrepresentation of Age – Irrelevant
- Disaffirm - anytime during minority or for reasonable time after reaching majority (except necessaries (necessities)
- Returns only what consideration is left if any
- Ratify - upon reaching majority, by statement or conduct

Mental

- Declared Insane - Void; need not return consideration
- Insane - Voidable; must return consideration
  1. Did not understand nature of contracts
  2. Did not understand effect of this contract
- Drunk to extent of mental incapacity - voidable

Mistake

Unilateral mistake of fact - no defense

Unilateral mistake in computation- defense if within range or offeree knows

Mutual (bilateral) mistake of fact - defense

The Misrepresentation Defenses

Misrepresentation - Innocent or negligent

Fraudulent Misrepresentation - Intent to defraud; calculated deceit

Innocent Misrepresentation

Basis of the bargain

Fact or Promise

Rescission is only available remedy

Basis of the Bargain

Analyze the following statements:

Are they opinion could they be the basis for misrepresentation?

"This stock has never decreased in value."

"These suits are 100% wool."

"These bicycle locks are theft-proof."

"This toothpaste reduces cavities by 20%."

"This car gets twenty-two miles to the gallon."

"This car has not been in an accident."

"This fabric is the finest money can buy."

"This house has no easements running through the backyard."

Defenses - Fraud

If these are established:

1. Material misstatement/basis of bargain
2. Must prove knowledge
3. Must prove intent to defraud

Then: punitive damages awarded

Undue Influence

Confidential Relationship - need not be fiduciary relationship; relationship of dependence

Party deprived of meaningful choice

Duress

Subjective test

Deprived of meaningful choice

Defenses - Illegality

Interest rates
- Usury: charging of interest in excess of statutory maximum

Public policy
- Consumer contracts
- Exculpatory/hold-harmless clauses

Licensing
- Revenue
- Qualification - void

PERFORMANCE AND REMEDIES FOR BREACH

Timing: When Is Performance Due?

Conditions Precedent - event required to occur before performance is mandated

Conditions Concurrent - simultaneous conditions

Conditions Subsequent - statute of limitations

Timing: When Is Performance Discharged?

When conditions fail

When the parties agree: Release; waiver; and rescission (accord and satisfaction)

The NOVATION thing

Statute of limitations runs

Discharge of Performance

Impossibility - subjective test vs. objective test (Impracticability-UCC)

Illegality

Breach

Bankruptcy

Performance: What Is It? When Is It Complete?

Substantial Performance

1) Is it for practical purposes just as good?

2) Was it done in good faith?

3) Can party be compensated?

Performance

Anticipatory Repudiation - breach before performance is due

Options:

1. Sue
2. Seek substitute
3. Wait

Damages - Types

Rescission - used in misrepresentation; returns parties to original position

Nominal - technical breach

Compensatory - return parties to same positions as if there had been no breach

Damages - Types

Incidental - costs; lawyers' fees

Consequential - damages to third party

Liquidated - agreed-upon in advance damage; alternative to compensatory damages

Damages - Types

Punitive - available in cases of fraud

Specific Performance - requiring breaching party to perform; used against seller in land contract

THIRD PARTY RIGHTS

Assignment of Benefits

Allied construction owes Fred's Framing $7,000 for some subcontract work Fred did on Allied's townhouse project

Fred owes its supplier $8,000 and tells Allied to pay the supplier directly

Assignment of Benefits

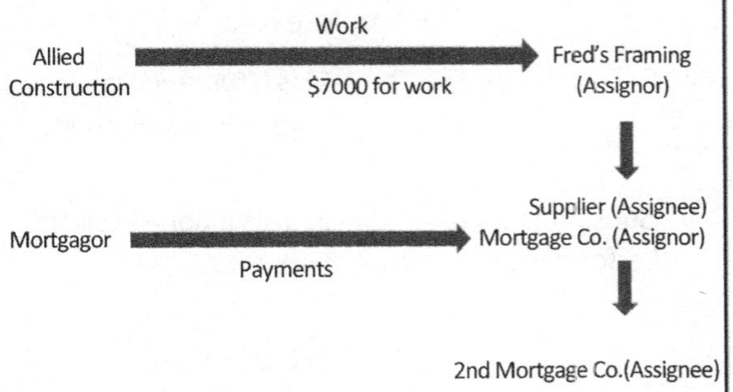

No assignment of personal rights - e.g. (credit rights)

Assignment Rights & Obligation

Fred Farmer has just purchased a new combine for $300,000

Fred will pay $2,000/month over 30 years to pay for the combine

Harvest sells the contract to Ace Finance Co.

NOTE: These are non-personal rights!

Assignment Rights & Obligation

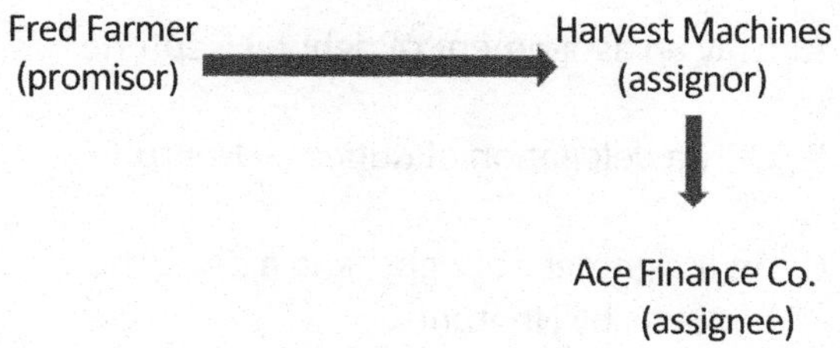

Payment:
Fred pays Ace when Ace notifies
Fred is not liable to Ace for payment made to Harvest before he was notified of the assignment

Assignment Rights & Obligation

Defenses:

Assignee has no greater rights than assignor. Ace is subject to Fred's contract defenses, e.g.: Breach of warranty, misrepresentation

Notification issues and payment

Delegation of Duties

Ida's Ice Cream Factory, Inc. has a contract with Mr. Ice for supplying ice

Mr. Ice has asked The Ice Man, Inc. to take over the supply contract

Delegation of Duties

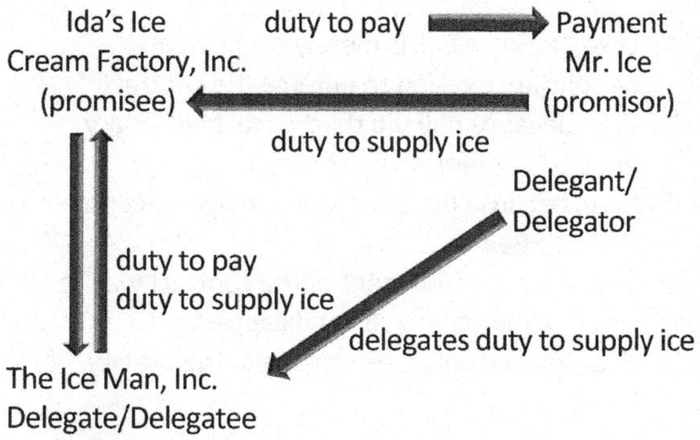

Review Question

On August 1, Neptune fisheries contracted in writing with West Markets to deliver to West 3,000 pounds of lobsters at $4.00 a pound. Delivery of the lobsters was due October 1 with payment due November 1. On August 4, Neptune entered into a contract with Deep Sea Lobster Farms which provided as follows: "Neptune Fisheries assigns all the rights under the contract with West Markets dated August 1 to Deep Sea Lobster Farms." The best interpretation of the August 4 contract would be that it was

Review Question

A. Only an assignment of right by Neptune

B. Only a delegation of duties by Neptune

C. An assignment of rights and a delegation of duties by Neptune

D. An unenforceable third-party beneficiary contract

Rights of Parties: Third Party Beneficiaries Donee Beneficiary

Insured (Promisee) | Life Insurance Company (Promisor) | Medical Care (Donee Beneficiary)

1.	Named beneficiary versus Life Insurance Donee beneficiary versus promisor	**Yes**
2.	Named beneficiary versus Insured Donee beneficiary versus promisee	**No**
3.	Insured (estate) versus Life Insurance Company Promisee versus Promisor	**Yes**

Rights of Parties: Third Party Beneficiaries Creditor Beneficiary

Insured (Promisee) | Medical Insurance Company (Promisor) | Medical Care (Creditor Beneficiaries)

1.	Medical care provider versus Medical insurance company Creditor beneficiaries versus promisor	**Yes**
2.	Medical care provider versus Insured Creditor beneficiaries versus promisee	**Yes**
3.	Insured versus Medical insurance company Promisee versus promisor	**Yes**

Rights of Parties:

Third Party Beneficiaries

Incidental Beneficiary

No Rights

Rights of Parties

Ace contracted with Big City to train and employ handicapped, unemployed veterans residing in Big City. Ace breached the contract and Bell, a resident of Big City, who is a handicapped, unemployed veteran, sues Ace for damages. Under the circumstances, Bell will...

Rights of Parties

A. Lose, because Bell is merely an incidental beneficiary entitled to enforce the contract

B. Win, because Bell is a third-party beneficiary entitled to enforce the contract

C. Lose, because Big City did not assign its contract rights to Bell

D. Win, because the intent of the contract was to confer a benefit on all handicapped, unemployed veterans residing in the big city

Egan, a minor, contracted with Baker to purchase Baker's used computer for $400. The computer was purchased for Egan's personal use. The agreement provided that Egan would pay $200 down on delivery and $200 thirty days later. Egan took delivery and paid the $200 down payment. Twenty days later, the computer was damaged through no fault of Egan. Five days after the damage occurred and one day after Egan reached the age of majority, Egan attempted to disaffirm the contract with Baker. Egan will

- [ ] **A. Be able to disaffirm despite the fact that Egan was not a minor at the time of disaffirmance.**
- [ ] **B. Be able to disaffirm only if Egan does so in writing.**
- [ ] **C. Not be able to disaffirm because Egan had failed to pay the balance of the purchase price.**
- [ ] **D. Not be able to disaffirm because the computer was damaged.**

Long purchased a life insurance policy with Tempo Life Insurance Co.

The policy named Long's daughter as beneficiary. Six months after the policy was issued, Long died of a heart attack.
Long had failed to disclose on the insurance application a known preexisting heart condition that caused the heart attack.
Tempo refused to pay the death benefit to Long's daughter.

If Long's daughter sues, Tempo will

- [ ] **A. Win, because Long's daughter is an incidental beneficiary.**
- [ ] **B. Win, because of Long's failure to disclose the preexisting heart condition.**
- [ ] **C. Lose, because Long's death was from natural causes.**
- [ ] **D. Lose, because Long's daughter is a third-party donee beneficiary.**

Paco Corp., a building contractor, offered to sell Preston several pieces of used construction equipment. Preston was engaged in the business of buying and selling equipment.
Paco's written offer had been prepared by a secretary who typed the total price as $10,900, rather than $109,000, which was the approximate fair market value of the equipment.
Preston, on receipt of the offer, immediately accepted it. Paco learned of the error in the offer and refused to deliver the equipment to Preston unless Preston agreed to pay $109,000.
Preston has sued Paco for breach of contract.

Which of the following statements is correct?

- [ ] **A. Paco will not be liable because there has been a mutual mistake of fact.**
- [ ] **B. Paco will be able to rescind the contract because Preston should have known that the price was erroneous.**
- [ ] **C. Preston will prevail because Paco is a merchant.**
- [ ] **D. The contract between Paco and Preston is void because the price set forth in the offer is substantially less than the equipment's fair market value.**

Teller brought a lawsuit against Kerr ten years after an oral contract was made and eight years after it was breached. Kerr raised the statute of limitations as a defense.

Which of the following allegations would be most important to Kerr's defense?

- ☐ **A. The contract was oral.**
- ☐ **B. The contract could not be performed within one year from the date made.**
- ☐ **C. The action was not timely brought because the contract was entered into ten years prior to the commencement of the lawsuit.**
- ☐ **D. The action was not timely brought because the contract was allegedly breached eight years prior to the commencement of the lawsuit.**

One of the criteria for a valid assignment of a sales contract to a third party is that the assignment must

- [ ] **A. Be supported by adequate consideration from the assignee.**
- [ ] **B. Be in writing and signed by the assignor.**
- [ ] **C. Not materially increase the other party's risk or duty.**
- [ ] **D. Not be revocable by the assignor.**

Which of the following would be unenforceable because the subject matter is illegal?

- ☐ A. **A contingent fee charged by an attorney to represent a plaintiff in a negligence action.**
- ☐ B. **An arbitration clause in a supply contract.**
- ☐ C. **A restrictive covenant in an employment contract prohibiting a former employee from using the employer's trade secrets.**
- ☐ D. **An employer's promise not to press embezzlement charges against an employee who agrees to make restitution.**

REG 3-1

UCC ARTICLE 2 - SALES 1

Application and Formation of Article 2 Contracts (AFTPDT formula)

Title and Risk of Loss

Selected Questions (2)

UCC ARTICLE 2 - SALES APPLICATION AND FORMATION

FORMULA FOR STUDYING UCC ARTICLE 2

AFTPDT

Application: Is this a contract for the sale of goods? Does the UCC apply?

Formation: Review the rules for formation of contracts (offer, acceptance, consideration and peculiar UCC sections)

Terms: The terms the UCC provides in absence of agreement of the parties

Performance requirements and rights in performance

Damages remedies and types of damages

Title and Third Party Rights

LAW OF CONTRACTS

	UCC	Common Law
Language	Uniform Commercial Code	Restatement of Contracts
	Goods - Tangible	Real estate
	Personal Property	Services

Application of UCC – Article 2

Contracts for sales of BOTH goods and services

Real property interests – who severs?

Merchants and non-merchant issues

Review Question

With regard to contracts governed by the UCC Sales Article, which one of the following statements is correct?

A. Merchants and non-merchants are treated alike.
B. The contract may involve the sale of any type of personal property.
C. The obligations of the parties to the contract must be performed in good faith.
D. The contract must involve the sale of goods for a price of $500 or more.

TOTAL UCC CONTENT

Article 2 Sales
Article 3 Negotiable Instruments/Commercial paper
Article 5 Letters of credit
Article 7 Documents of title
Article 9 Security interests

NOTE: **Don't cross the streams on coverage across articles!** For example, you can have an Article 9 security interest in items that are not goods! And a promissory note is covered under Article 3 even though the money was borrowed to buy real property.

FORMATION: TERMS

Need evidence of present intent to contract, not future promise
Open terms: UCC
Quantity issues - UCC (outputs/requirements)

	UCC	Common Law
Language	Need Subject Matter (quantity)	Need All Details

UCC OPEN TERMS

Price

Payment

Delivery

Review Question

Carson Corp., a retail chain, asked Alto Construction to fix a broken window at one of Carson's stores. Alto offered to make the repairs within 3 days at a price to be agreed on after the work was completed. A contract based on Alto's offer would fail because of indefiniteness as to the:

A. Price involved.
B. Nature of the subject matter.
C. Parties to the contract.
D. Time for performance.

Merchants' Firm Offers - UCC

1. Writing (Revised Article 2 – Record)
2. Signed - intent to authenticate (Revised Article 2 – authentication)
3. By a merchant - in the business of selling goods that are the subject matter of the contract
4. States that it will be kept open (max of 3 months)

Merchant's Firm Offer

UCC - Non - merchants - need option

UCC - exceeds 3 months - need option

Unilateral offer for shipment

Shipment is acceptance

If you ship the wrong thing (without advance notice) it is acceptance and breach at the same time

Acceptance - Conditional

Misnomer: It is **NEVER** acceptance under UCC or common law:

"I accept provided that…."
"I accept on the condition that…."
"I accept if…."
"I accept if and only if…."
"I accept but I must…."

Counter offer and rejection

UCC Rules For Additional Terms in Acceptance* or the Battle of the Forms

Differs from Common Law "Mirror Image" Rule

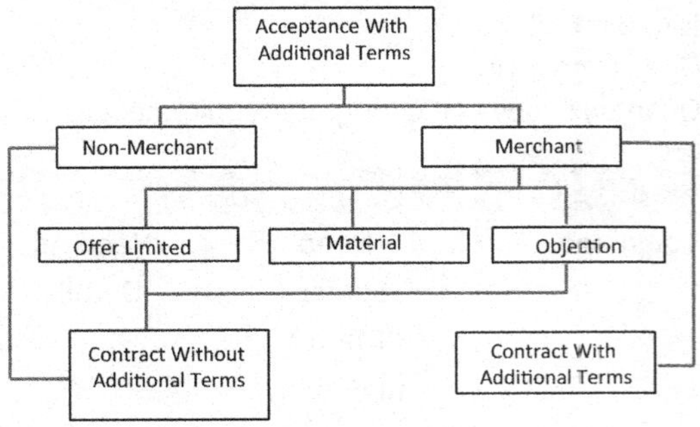

*Not conditional acceptance

Additional Terms - Acceptance

A. "I'll sell you my Peugeot bicycle for $100"

B. "I'll take it. Include your tire pump."

RESULTS

Contract Non-merchants
Contract Merchants

Additional Terms - Acceptance

A. "I'll sell you my 1974 white Ford Torino for $358. This offer is limited to these terms"

B. "I'll take it. Furnish a history of repairs"

RESULTS

Contract Non-merchants
Contract Merchants

Additional Terms - Acceptance

A. "I'll sell you my antique Coca Cola sign"

B. "I'll take it if you will deliver it"

RESULTS

Counter offer Non-merchants
Counter offer Merchants

UCC STATUTE OF FRAUDS

Sales - Contracts for sale of goods $500 or more must be in writing.

UCC - Exceptions

Merchant's confirmation memo - (two merchants required)
- Writing (record)
- Signed by one of the merchants
- Underlying oral agreement

Part performance
- Goods actually accepted - buyer
- Payments actually received – seller

Specially manufactured

Admission - in any proceeding while under oath

TITLE AND RISK OF LOSS

Identification

On existing goods, occurs at the time of contracting

On future and fungible goods, occurs when the goods are shipped, marked, or otherwise designated for the buyer

Passage of Title Under Article II

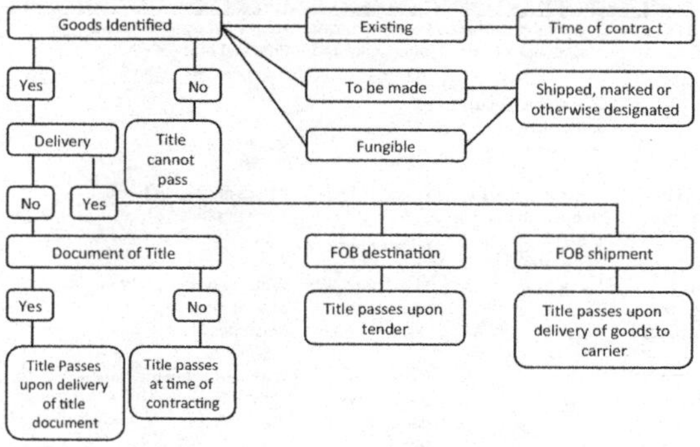

Shipping Terms

COD:
- Collect or cash on delivery (not shipment term, payment term)

CF:
- Lump sum; cost and freight
  - risk-buyer upon delivery to carrier
  - title-buyer upon delivery to carrier
  - expense-seller includes cost of freight in contract price

Common Carrier Liability
- Strict Liability except for natural disaster and improper packing

Risk of Loss

Identification must come first

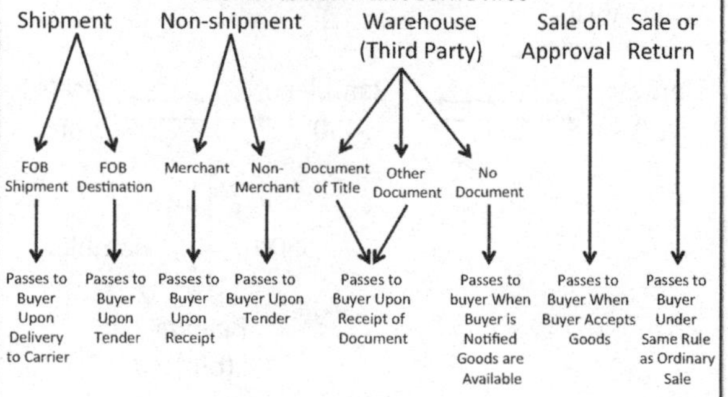

Review Question

Wexford Furniture, Inc. is in the retail furniture business and has stores located in principal cities in the United States. Its designers created a unique cocktail table. After obtaining prices and schedules, Wexford ordered 2,000 tables to be made to its design and specifications for sale as a part of its annual spring sales promotion campaign.

Which of the following represents the earliest time Wexford will have an insurable interest in the tables?

Review Question

A. At the time the goods are in Wexford's possession.
B. Upon shipment of conforming goods by the seller.
C. When the goods are marked or otherwise designated by the seller as the goods to which the contract refers.
D. At the time the contract is made.

Article II - Sales Shipment Contracts

	IDENTIFICATION	RISK OF LOSS	TITLE	SHIPPING COSTS
FOB Place of Shipment	1. Goods in existence at time of contract	Passes to buyer when delivered to carrier	Passes to buyer at time and place of shipment	Buyer
	2. Fungible goods-shipped, marked or otherwise designated			
FOB Place of Destination	3. Future goods shipped, marked or otherwise designated	Passes to buyer at time of tender (Effect of breach)	Passes at time and place of tender	Seller
Non-Shipment Contracts	Same	Merchant Seller- when buyer receives goods	With document of title- at time document is received	None
		Non-Merchant Seller - when goods are tendered	Without document of title -time of contracting	None

Article II - Sales Shipment Contracts

	IDENTIFICATION	RISK OF LOSS	TITLE	SHIPPING COSTS
Bailment/ Warehouse-man Contract	Same	Passes to Buyer: 1. With receipt of negotiable doc. of title; 2. On acknowledgement by Bailee; or 3. On receipt of non-negotiable document	Same as non-shipment	none
Sale on Approval	Same	Upon Buyer's Acceptance	Upon buyer's acceptance	Seller
Sale or Return	Same	Same as actual sale	Same as actual sale (consignment exception)	Buyer

Third Party Rights

VOIDABLE

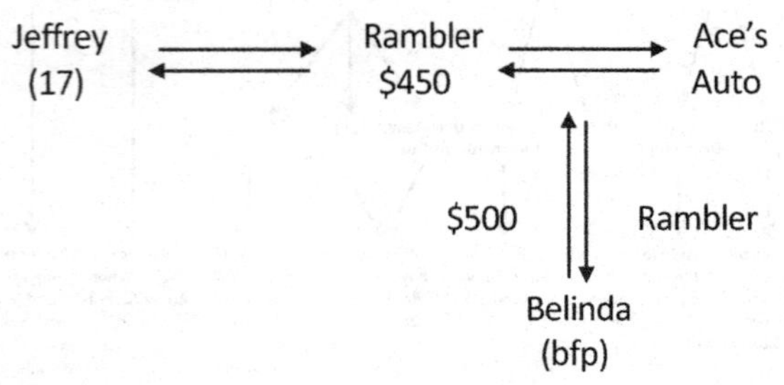

Third Party Rights

BAILMENT

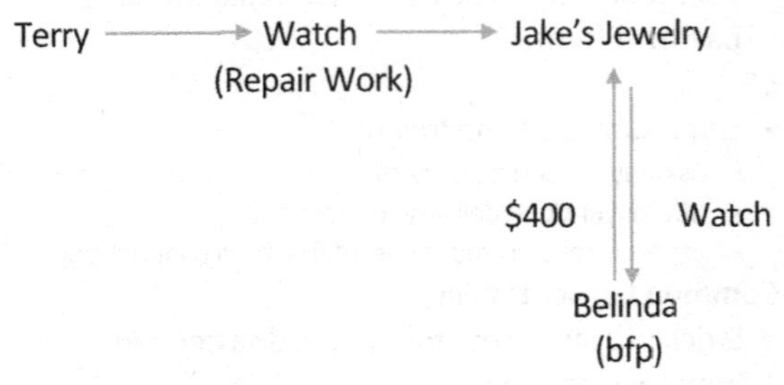

Third Party Rights

VOIDABLE

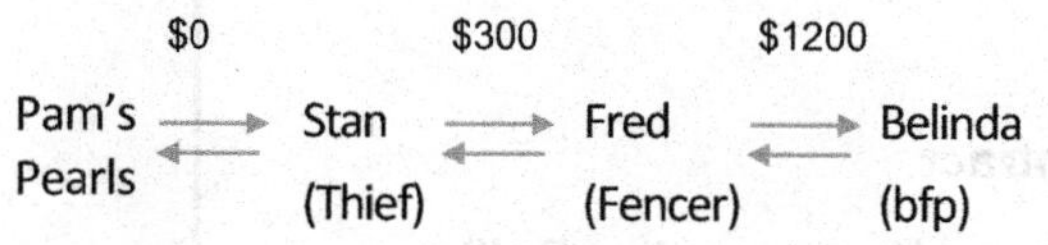

On September 10, Bell Corp. entered into a contract to purchase 50 lamps from Glow Manufacturing to be used in Bell Corp's executive company offices. Bell prepaid 40% of the purchase price. Glow became insolvent on September 19 before segregating, in its inventory, the lamps to be delivered to Bell. Bell will not be able to recover the lamps because

- [ ] A. Bell is regarded as a merchant.
- [ ] B. The lamps were not identified to the contract.
- [ ] C. Glow became insolvent fewer than 10 days after receipt of Bell's prepayment.
- [ ] D. Bell did not pay the full price at the time of purchase.

Under the UCC Sales Article, which of the following conditions will prevent the formation of an enforceable sale of goods contract?

- [ ] **A. Open price.**
- [ ] **B. Open delivery.**
- [ ] **C. Open quantity.**
- [ ] **D. Open acceptance.**

REG 3-2

UCC ARTICLE 2 - SALES 2

Terms: Warranties and Product Liability

Selected Questions (1)

TERMS: WARRANTIES AND PRODUCTS LIABILITY

Warranties

TYPE	CREATION	RESTRICTION	DISCLAIMER
Express	Affirmation of fact or promise of performance (samples, models, descriptions)	Must be part of the basis of the bargain	Cannot make a disclaimer inconsistent with an express warranty
Implied Warranty of Merchantability	Given in every sale of goods by a merchant ("fit for ordinary purposes")	Only given by merchants	(1) Must use disclaimer of quality or use "merchantability" or general disclaimer "as is" or "with all faults" (2) if written – (record) must be conspicuous
Implied Warranty of Fitness for a Particular Purpose	Seller knows of buyer's reliance for a particular use (buyer is ignorant)	Seller must have knowledge - Buyer must rely	(1) Must be in writing (record) (2) Must be conspicuous (3) Must be clear there are no warranties or (4) Also disclaimed with "as is" or "with all faults"
Title	Given in every sale	Does not apply in circumstances where apparent warranty is not given	Must state "There is no warranty of title"

Privity of Contract

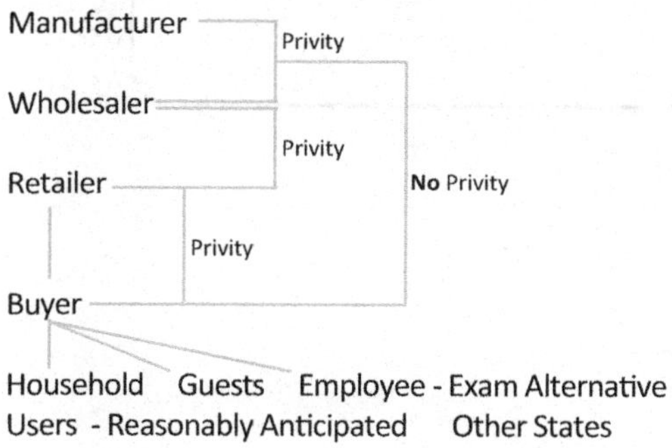

Product Liability

Contract	Tort
Express Warranty	Tort
Implied Warranty of Merchantability	402A – Strict Tort Liability
Implied Warranty of Fitness for Particular Purpose	Negligence

Product Liability: Strict Tort Liability

1. Defective condition unreasonably dangerous

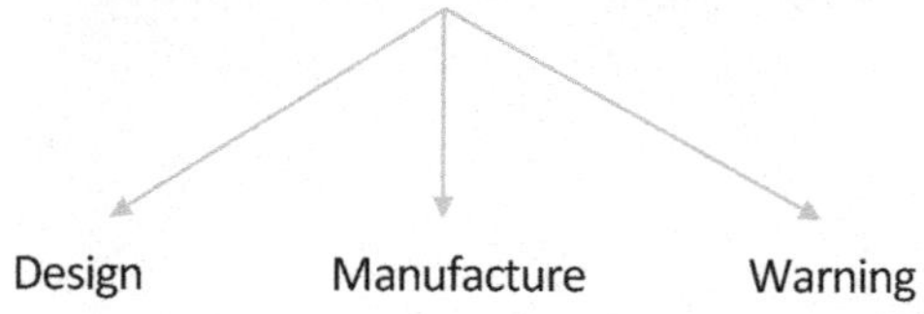

2. Defendant in business of using, selling, or manufacturing product
3. Condition of product is the same
4. Knowledge of defect

Which of the following statements is correct?

- ☐ **A. Acceptance of nonconforming goods precludes the buyer from pursuing any remedy against the seller.**
- ☐ **B. Unless agreed to the contrary, a buyer has a right to inspect the goods before payment at any reasonable time, place, or manner.**
- ☐ **C. Rejection notice by the buyer is effective when mailed and not when it is received by the seller.**
- ☐ **D. A buyer has a right to pay the seller by check, credit card, or other customary means of payment even if the seller demands cash.**

Under the Sales Article of the UCC, the warranty of title

- [ ] **A. Provides that the seller cannot disclaim the warranty if the sale is made to a bona fide purchaser for value.**
- [ ] **B. Provides that the seller deliver the goods free from any lien of which the buyer lacked knowledge when the contract was made.**
- [ ] **C. Applies only if it is in writing and signed by the seller.**
- [ ] **D. Applies only if the seller is a merchant.**

REG 3-3

UCC ARTICLE 2 - SALES 3

Performance

Remedies Under Article 2

Selected Questions (3)

PERFORMANCE

Right to Demand Assurances - Both
Right to Cure - Seller
Anticipatory Repudiation
Retraction of Anticipatory Repudiation

July 15	Aug 1	Sept 1	Oct 15	Dec 10
K signed	Angst and assurance	Anticipatory repudiation (breach)*	Retraction of repudiation	K due

*1) breach: sue
2) breach: substitute seller
3) breach: wait

BUYER'S RIGHTS IN GOODS

BUYER'S RIGHTS	WHEN	HOW
Inspection	When goods arrive; before payment (unless COD; CF; CIF)	Examination Lab test; Samples
Rejection	Single delivery - fail to conform in any respect Installment - substantially impairs value of installment or contract (if rejection in full) Must reject within reasonable time	Notification Non-use
Acceptance	After Inspection	Notification; Use; Failure to reject in reasonable time
Revocation of Acceptance	After acceptance; Must materially impair value AND EITHER a defect non-discoverable or a promise of cure	Notification; reshipment or non-use

Review Question

Bibbeon Manufacturing shipped 300 designer navy blue blazers to Custom Clothing Emporium. The blazers arrived on Friday, earlier than Custom had anticipated and on an exceptionally busy day for its receiving department. They were perfunctorily examined and sent to a nearby warehouse for storage until needed.
On Monday of the following week, upon closer examination, it was discovered that the quality of the blazer linings was inferior to that specified in the sales contract. Which of the following is correct insofar as Custom's rights are concerned?

Review Question

A. Custom can reject the blazers upon subsequent discovery of the defects.
B. Custom must retain the blazers since it accepted them and had an opportunity to inspect them upon delivery.
C. Custom's only course of action is rescission.
D. Custom had no rights if the linings were merchantable quality.

Right to Cure

Upon notification by buyer, prior to performance date, Seller has the right to get conforming goods to the buyer.

Right of Rejection

Parker ordered 50 cartons of soap from Riddle Wholesale Company. Each carton contains 12 packages of soap. The terms were: Eight dollars per carton 2/10, net/30, FOB buyer's delivery platform, delivery June 1.

During transit approximately one half the packages were damaged by the carrier. The delivery was made on May 28.

Review Question

1. Riddle had the risk of loss during transit.
2. If Parker elects to accept the undamaged part of the shipment, he will be deemed to have accepted the entire shipment.
3. To validly reject the goods, Parker must give timely notice of rejection to Riddle within a reasonable time after delivery.
4. If Riddle were notified of the rejection on May 28, Riddle could cure the defect by promptly notifying Parker of intention to do so and making a second delivery to Parker of conforming goods by June 1.
5. The Statute of Frauds is inapplicable to the transaction in the facts given above.

REMEDIES UNDER ARTICLE 2

Sellers' Remedies Under Article II

Name of Remedy	Stop Delivery	Resale Price	Market Price	Action for Price	Lost Profit
Section Number	2-702	2-706 2-710	2-708 2-710	2-709 2-708	2-708(2)
When Available	Insolvency* Advance breach by buyer	Buyer fails to take goods	Buyer fails to take goods	Specially manufactured goods	Anticip. Repud.
Nature of Remedy	Stop delivery of any size shipment or recover goods if insolvent; Stop delivery of large shipments for other reasons Reclaim*	K price - Resale price + Inciden. damages - Expenses saved	K price - Market price + Inciden. damages - Expenses saved	K price + Inciden. damages - Expenses saved	Profits + Inciden. damages - salvage value

*Misrepresentation of Insolvency (3 mos./10 day rules) (Revised UCC – any shipment. Any time

Buyer's Remedies Under Article II

Name of Remedy	Specific Performance (Replevin) (Identification)	Cover	Market
Section Number	2-711	2-712 2-715	2-713 2-715
When Available	Rare, unique goods	Seller fails to deliver	Seller fails to deliver
Nature of Remedy	Buyer gets goods (Incidentals)	Cover price - K price + Incidentals + Consequential damages - Expenses saved	Market price - K price + Incidentals + Consequential damages - Expenses saved

Under the Sales Article of the UCC, and unless otherwise agreed to, the seller's obligation to the buyer is to

- [ ] **A. Deliver the goods to the buyer's place of business.**
- [ ] **B. Hold conforming goods and give the buyer whatever notification is reasonably necessary to enable the buyer to take delivery.**
- [ ] **C. Deliver all goods called for in the contract to a common carrier.**
- [ ] **D. Set aside conforming goods for inspection by the buyer before delivery.**

Under the Sales Article of the UCC, which of the following events will release the buyer from all its obligations under a sales contract?

- [ ] A. **Destruction of the goods after risk of loss passed to the buyer.**
- [ ] B. **Impracticability of delivery under the terms of the contract.**
- [ ] C. **Anticipatory repudiation by the buyer that is retracted before the seller cancels the contract.**
- [ ] D. **Refusal of the seller to give written assurance of performance when reasonably demanded by the buyer.**

REG 3-4

UCC ARTICLE 3 - NEGOTIABLE INSTRUMENTS 1

Introduction to Negotiable Instruments and Negotiability

Selected Questions (2)

INTRODUCTION TO NEGOTIABLE INSTRUMENTS AND NEGOTIABILITY

Negotiable Instruments

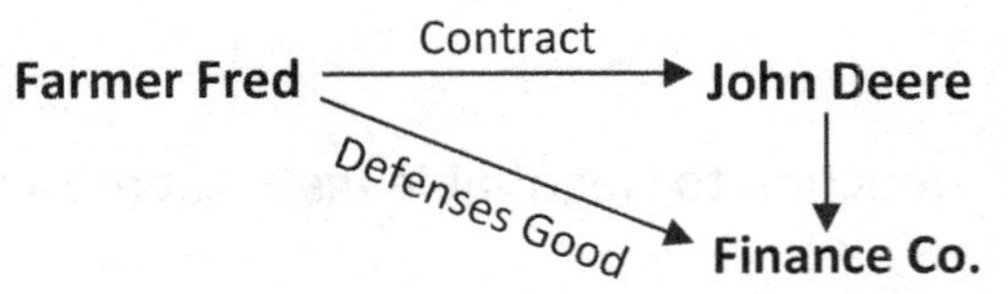

Negotiable Instruments

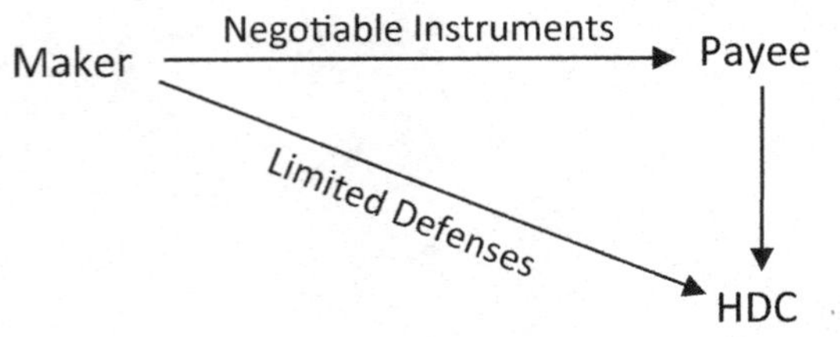

Negotiable Instruments

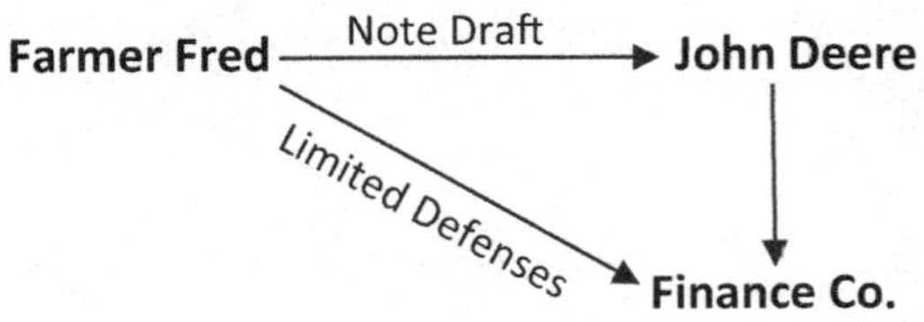

Negotiable Instruments

Contracts/Consumer (FTC Rule)

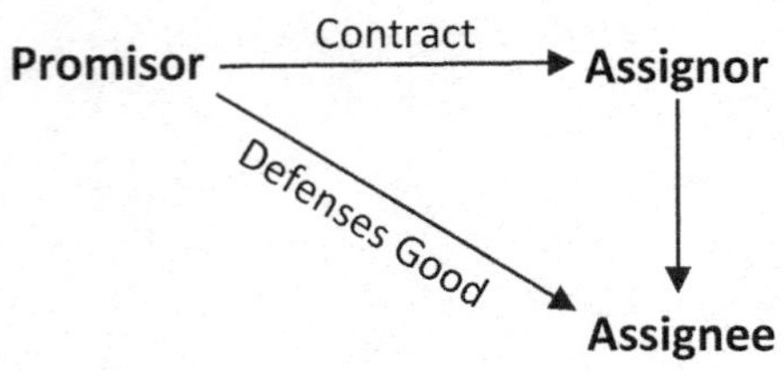

Types of Commercial Paper

I. Promises to Pay

A. Types/Parties

1. Notes
   Maker
   Payee

2. CDs
   Maker
   Payee

Types of Commercial Paper

II. Orders to Pay

A. Types/Parties

1. Checks
   Drawer
   Drawee
   Payee

Types of Commercial Paper

II. Orders to Pay

A. Types/Parties

2. Drafts
   Drawer
   Drawee
   Payee
   Sight Drafts
   Time Drafts
   Trade Acceptances (Seller must be drawer and payee) (must be time draft)

Review Question

Which of the following instruments is subject to the provisions of the Negotiable Instruments Article of the UCC?

A. A bill of lading
B. A warehouse receipt
C. A certificate of deposit
D. As investment security

Requirements for Negotiability

- Written
- Signed by Maker or Drawer - Anything placed with the intent to authenticate

Requirements for Negotiability

- Unconditional Promise or Order to Pay

e.g. - Account Reference - OK
Proceeds - NO
Government Accounts - OK
Partnership Assets - OK
Estates - OK (if not individual inheritance)
Trusts - OK
Sole Proprietorship – OK
Underlying Contract Reference - OK

Requirements for Negotiability

- Payable on Demand or at a Definite Time

e.g. - Acceleration Clauses - OK
Indefinite Event - No
Prepayment - OK

Requirements for Negotiability

- Sum certain in Money (Fixed Amount of Money)

e.g. - Payable in Stocks, Property - NO
Attorneys' Fees - OK
Market Rates - OK if readily ascertainable
Prime + 2% - NO - YES (1990 Code)
Pre - payment Reduction - OK

MONEY: Anything recognized as currency

Requirements for Negotiability

- Words of Negotiability

e.g. - "TO ORDER OF"	Order Paper
"TO CASH"	Bearer Paper
"TO BEARER"	Bearer Paper

"PAY TO" is non-negotiable unless it's a check

Words of Negotiability

"Pay to bearer"

"Pay to order of cash"

"Pay to John Jones"

"Pay to the order of John Jones and bearer"

"Pay to the order of John Jones or bearer"

"Pay to John Jones or bearer"

"Pay to cash"

"Pay to order of bearer"

"Pay to John Jones and bearer"

Interpretation

Handwritten over preprinted and typewritten

Typewritten over preprinted

Words over numbers

Under the Negotiable Instruments Article of the UCC, which of the following documents would be considered an order to pay?

I. Draft

II. Certificate of deposit

- [ ] **A. I only.**
- [ ] **B. II only.**
- [ ] **C. Both I and II.**
- [ ] **D. Neither I nor II.**

Below is a copy of a note Prestige Properties obtained from Tim Hart in connection with Hart's purchase of land located in Hunter, MT.
The note was given for the balance due on the purchase and was secured by a first mortgage on the land.

> **$200,000.00 Hunter, MT**
> **November 30, 2005**
>
> **For value received, six years after date, I promise to pay to the order of Prestige Properties TWO HUNDRED THOUSAND and 00/100 DOLLARS with interest at 11% compounded annually until fully paid. This instrument arises out of the sale of land located in MT, and the law of MT is to be applied to any question that may arise. It is secured by a first mortgage on the land conveyed. It is further agreed that:**
>
> **1. Maker will pay the costs of collection including attorney's fees upon default.**
> **2. Maker may repay the amount outstanding on any anniversary date of this note.**
>
> **/s/ Tim Hart**
> **-------**
> **Tim Hart**

This note is a

- [ ] **A. Nonnegotiable promissory note because it is secured by a first mortgage.**
- [ ] **B. Negotiable promissory note.**
- [ ] **C. Nonnegotiable promissory note because it permits prepayment and requires the maker's payment of the costs of collection and attorney's fees.**
- [ ] **D. Negotiable investment security under the UCC.**

REG 3-5

UCC ARTICLE 3 - NEGOTIABLE INSTRUMENTS 2

Transfer of Negotiable Instruments and Holders in Due Course

Presentment, Payment, and Dishonor of Negotiable Instruments

Liabilities and Discharge of Parties

Selected Questions (3)

TRANSFER OF INSTRUMENTS AND HOLDER IN DUE COURSE (HDC)

Negotiation

1. Transfer so that transferee becomes holder
2. Holder: in possession of an instrument that runs to him
3. Runs to: payable to/indorsed to/bearer

Negotiation

Requirements
- Bearer Paper - Delivery
- Order Paper - Delivery + Indorsement
  - Blank
  - Special - "Pay to"
  - Restrictive - for deposit only
  - Qualified - without recourse
  - 3-417(2)(d) (old) 3-416 (2)(d)(new)
    - waives warranty

Holders in Due Course

Holder

Value (antecedent debt - OK) (FIFO for Banks--allowing withdrawals on the check)

Good Faith

Holders in Due Course

No Notice of Defenses, Dishonor or Overdue

- e.g. Different Signature and writing in the Body
- Incomplete Instrument
- Postdated Checks
- Stale Checks (90 days)
- Circumstances

Notice of Problem

Payment has already been denied

Instrument is overdue

Knowledge of issues

Value - HDC

In order to be a holder in due course, the holder, among other requirements, must give value. Which of the following will satisfy the value requirement?

I. An antecedent debt
II. A promise to perform services at a future date

A. I only
B. II only
C. Both I and II
D. Neither I or II

Holders in Due Course - Exceptions

Exceptions

1. Shelter Provision - Attaining the status of a holder in due course

HDC —transfers→ gift → H (becomes HDC)

2. Shipping Through Exception – can't ship through to remove your knowledge

H_1 → HDC → back to H_1 (becomes HDC)

Holder in Due Course - Exceptions

Acquiring from a holder in due course gains you HDC standing even with knowledge of a problem

HDC ⇨ HOLDER (knows of problem)

Review Question

Can't ship through and improve position

Port → Johnson (H) → Kenner (HDC) → back to Johnson (H)

Answer: B

PRESENTMENT, PAYMENT, AND DISHONOR OF NEGOTIABLE INSTRUMENTS

Proper Presentment

1. Presentment - primary party

PRIMARY	SECONDARY
Maker	Payee; indorsers
Drawee	Drawer Payee Indorser

Proper Presentment

2. Time for Presentment

Due date – notes and trade acceptances

Demand – on demand

Presentment for Checks

Checks:

30 days -- to attach liability of indorsers
30 days – to attach liability of drawer (this limitation is a problem only if drawee bank fails)

Six-month presumption of good faith for banks cashing checks

The bank failure proposition

Check not presented within 30 days

Bank fails in the mean time

Drawer is excused from any amount above FDIC insurance: Janice owes Jake $270,000. Jake cashes the check 45 days after receiving it. Janice's bank fails. FDIC will cover (fluctuates) $250,000. Janice is off the hook for the $20,000

Dishonor – Notice Time Requirements

30 days for regular folks on checks

Exception: Banks under Article 4 – midnight of the next banking day is their deadline for notification of dishonor

Dishonor Process

3. Notice of Dishonor - Time midnight deadlines - bank*/person*

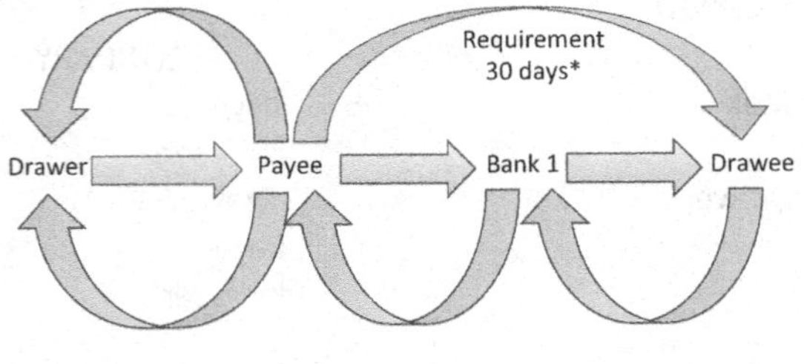

* Midnight of next banking day **30 days for persons and on other instruments

LIABILITIES AND DISCHARGE OF THE PARTIES

Contract Liability: Primary parties and secondary parties

Primary: Makes of notes and drawees of drafts
- Watch your banks as drawees

Secondary: Drawers
Indorsers

Accommodation: Steps into the liability status of the party he/she is accommodating

Warranty Liability

Warranty (3-416 old 3-417) (4-207)

1. Presenter's Warranties - last party before primary party
- Good title
- No knowledge signatures are unauthorized
- No material alteration

Warranty Liability

(3-416) (4-207)

2. Transferor's Warranties
- Good title
- Signatures are genuine and authorized
- No material alteration
- No defenses (without recourse indorsement waives)
- No knowledge of insolvency

HDC Defenses

Real/Universal	**Personal**	**Mixed**
Incapacity	Fraud in the Inducement	Duress
Illegality	Misrepresentation	
Fraud in Factum	Lack of consideration	
Bankruptcy	Original defense	
Lack of Payment	Warranty breach	
Forgery*	Breach of contract	
		Material alteration

*Watch exceptions

Liability - Alteration

Material Alteration: terms changed such as amount, interest, or days; removal from instrument; adding to instrument; completion without authorization; no correction

- HDC still collects according to original terms
- Non HDC collects nothing
- Negligence Issues

Signature Liability
Principal/Agent Liability

Signature	Liability?	Parol?
A. Agent	Agent	No
A. Agent, VP	Agent	Yes
P. Prince, A. Agent	Principal	Yes
P. Prince by A. Agent, VP	Principal	No
P. Prince	Principal	No

Liability - Forgery

Forgery Rules

Forgery of Drawer's Name

Forgery of Payee's Name

Payee/Indorser Forgery - Actions

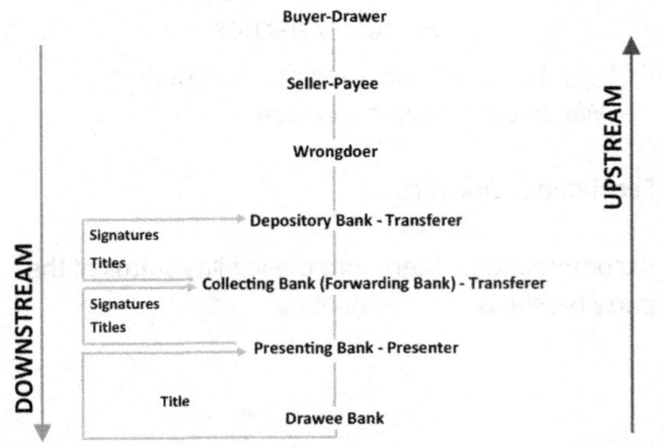

Exceptions to Forgery Liability Rules

1. Fictitious Payee
2. Negligence
3. Impostors

Bond fraudulently induced Teal to make a note payable to Wilk, to whom Bond was indebted. Bond delivered the note to Wilk. Wilk negotiated the instrument to Monk, who purchased it with knowledge of the fraud and after it was overdue.

If Wilk qualifies as a holder in due course, which of the following statements is correct?

- [ ] **A. Monk has the standing of a holder in due course through Wilk.**
- [ ] **B. Teal can successfully assert the defense of fraud in the inducement against Monk.**
- [ ] **C. Monk personally qualifies as a holder in due course.**
- [ ] **D. Teal can successfully assert the defense of fraud in the inducement against Wilk.**

Under the Negotiable Instruments Article of the UCC, which of the endorser's liabilities are disclaimed by a "without recourse" endorsement?

- [ ] **A. Contract liability only.**
- [ ] **B. Warranty liability only.**
- [ ] **C. Both contract and warranty liability.**
- [ ] **D. Neither contract nor warranty liability.**

One of the requirements to qualify as a holder of a negotiable bearer check is that the transferee must

- [ ] **A. Receive the check that was originally made payable to bearer.**
- [ ] **B. Take the check in good faith.**
- [ ] **C. Give value for the check.**
- [ ] **D. Have possession of the check.**

REG 3-6

UCC ARTICLE 5 & 7

Purposes, Requirements and Payment

Definitions, Forms, Negotiation, and Rights

Selected Questions (2)

ARTICLE 5 – PURPOSES, REQUIREMENTS AND PAYMENT

Key concept is separation of issues between parties and letter of credit

- Tool used by buyers to provide additional assurance of payment; buyer's bank agrees to pay when specified requirements met
- Must pay according to terms
- Cannot vary terms
- Must verify all requirements and documents for payment

ARTICLE 7 – DEFINITIONS, FORMS, NEGOTIATION, AND RIGHTS

Negotiable Documents of Title

1. Types of documents of title
   - Bill of Lading: issued by a carrier
   - Given to seller to evidence receipt of goods for storage
   - Warehouse Receipt
2. Negotiability
   - Words of negotiability: order or bearer

Negotiable Documents of Title

3. Due Negotiation
   - Holder
   - Takes in good faith
   - In ordinary course of business
   - Pays value (no pre-existing (antecedent) debt)
   - No notice of defense

Negotiable Documents of Title

4. Rights of holder by due negotiation
   - Title to document
   - Title to goods
   - Issuer obligated to hold or deliver goods according to document terms
   - Not subject to personal defenses
   - Subject to claims of stolen goods

Negotiable Documents of Title

5. Warranties of transfer of document of title for value
   - Document is genuine
   - Has no knowledge of any fact that would impair its validity or worth
   - Negotiation is rightful
   - Negotiation is effective to transfer title to document and goods

Liability of Carrier in Transit

Common carriers have absolute or strict liability EXCEPT:

- Acts of God
- Acts of public enemy (military forces)
- Defective packaging by shipper
- Inherent delicacy of goods – easily spoiled food

Review Question

Which of the following is not a warranty made by the seller of a negotiable warehouse receipt to the purchaser of the document?

A. The document transfer is fully effective with respect to the goods it represents
B. The warehouseman will honor the document
C. The seller has no knowledge of any facts that would impair the document's validity
D. The document is genuine

Review Question

Under the Documents of Title Article of the UCC, which of the following acts may limit a common carrier's liability for damages to the goods in transit?

A. Vandalism
B. Power outage
C. Willful acts of third person
D. Providing for a contractual dollar liability limitation

Review Question

Under the UCC, a warehouse receipt

A. Will not be negotiable if it contains a contractual limitation on the warehouseman's liability
B. Will qualify as both a negotiable warehouse receipt and negotiable commercial paper if the instrument is payable either in cash or by delivery of goods
C. May be issued only by a bonded and licensed warehouseman
D. Is negotiable if by its terms the goods are to be delivered to bearer or the order of a named person

Review Question

Thieves broke into the warehouse of Monogram Airways and stole a shipment of computer parts belonging to Valley Instruments. Valley had in its possession a negotiable bill of lading covering the shipment. The thieves transported the stolen parts to another state and placed the parts in a bonded warehouse. The thieves received a negotiable warehouse receipt which they used to secure a loan of $20,000 from Reliable Finance. These facts were revealed upon apprehension of the thieves. Regarding the rights of the parties:

Documents of Title

A. Reliable is entitled to a $20,000 payment before relinquishment of the parts

B. Monogram will be the ultimate loser of the $20,000

C. Valley is entitled to recover the parts free of Reliable's $20,000 claim

D. Valley is not entitled to the parts but may obtain damages from Monogram

Under the Documents of Title Article of the UCC, a negotiable document of title is "duly negotiated" when it is negotiated to

- [ ] **A. Any holder by indorsement.**
- [ ] **B. Any holder by delivery.**
- [ ] **C. A holder who takes the document in payment of a money obligation.**
- [ ] **D. A holder who takes the document for value, in good faith, and without notice of any defense or claim to it.**

Which of the following statements concerning a letter of credit is correct?

- [ ] **A.** **A letter of credit is a form of a negotiable instrument issued by a bank.**
- [ ] **B.** **Unless stated in the letter of credit, generally letters of credit are not transferable to third parties.**
- [ ] **C.** **In an international sales transaction, the seller is the applicant for the issue of a letter of credit.**
- [ ] **D.** **Since warranties under a sale of goods is governed by other laws such as the Uniform Commercial Code or the Convention on International Sales of Goods, the seller of goods under a letter of credit makes no additional warranties to the issue of the letter.**

REG 4-1

UCC ARTICLE 9 - SECURED TRANSACTIONS

Introduction and Creation of Security Interests

Perfection of Security Interests

Priorities in Security Interests

Rights of Secured Parties and Debtors

Selected Questions (6)

ARTICLE 9 - INTRODUCTION AND CREATION OF SECURITY INTERESTS

Parties, Terms, and Purpose

Secured Party/Creditor
Debtor
Collateral
Security Agreement
Security Interest
Financing Statement
Security for repayment, priority position

Attachment of Security Interest

A. SECURITY AGREEMENT
   1. Writing (exception is possession) (electronic record is sufficient)
   2. Signed (*authenticated) by debtor
   3. Description of collateral -* "reasonably identify"

   OR POSSESSION OR CONTROL

B. INTEREST IN THE COLLATERAL

C. UNDERLYING DEBT

Review Question

Under the Secured Transactions Article of the UCC, which of the following requirements is necessary to have a security interest attach?

	Debtor has rights in the collateral	Proper filing of a security agreement	Value given by the creditor
A.	Yes	Yes	Yes
B.	Yes	Yes	No
C.	Yes	No	Yes
D.	No	Yes	Yes

ARTICLE 9 - PERFECTION OF SECURITY INTERESTS

Methods of Perfection

1. Filing
2. Possession
3. Automatic
4. Temporary

Types of Collateral

*ALL FILINGS CENTRAL WITH THE EXCEPTION OF REAL PROPERTY (local) (moving to electronic system)

- Tangible Property
- Consumer Goods
- Equipment
- Inventory
- Farm products
- Fixtures

Types of Collateral

Intangible Property

- Patents
- Copyrights
- Trademarks

Types of Collateral

Miscellaneous

- Proceeds
- Negotiable Instruments
- Commercial tort claims
- Judicial liens in tort claims

Period of Perfection

5 years for filing

Can renew any time within last six months

For perfection by possession – as long as possession continues

Must use care with collateral

Perfection

Possession

- Negotiable Instruments
- Field Warehousing
- Control of accounts*

Review Question

Under the UCC Secured Transactions Article, which of the following actions will best perfect a security interest in negotiable instrument against any other party?

A. Filing a security agreement
B. Taking possession of the instrument
C. Perfecting by attachment
D. Obtaining a duly executed financing statement

Perfection

Temporary

- 4 - Month Rule - collateral moved to another state
- 21 - Day Rule - negotiable instruments
- 20 - Day Rule - See priorities *(old 10 days)

Automatic

- PMSI (Purchase Money Security Interest) - Consumer; not PMSI in inventory or equipment
- Proceeds (identify)

*Control -- accounts

ARTICLE 9 - PRIORITIES IN SECURITY INTERESTS

Priority of Security Interests Under Article IX

CONFLICT	PRIORITY
Secured party v. secured party	Pro rata share in collateral proceeds; First to attach
Unsecured party v. secured party	Secured party
Perfected secured party v. secured party	Perfected secured party
Perfected secured party v. perfected secured party	Party who is first to perfect
Perfected secured party v. lienor	Party who filed (financing statement or lien) first

Priority of Secured Interests Under Article IX

1. SECURED PARTY vs. UNSECURED PARTY
2. SECURED PARTY vs. SECURED PARTY-first to attach
3. UNSECURED PARTY vs. UNSECURED PARTY
4. PERFECTED SECURED PARTY vs. UNPERFECTED SECURED PARTY
5. PERFECTED SECURED PARTY vs. PERFECTED SECURED PARTY-first in time - first in right

Exceptions to the Priority of Secured Interests Under Article IX

CONFLICT	PRIORITY
PMSI in fixtures v. perfected secured party	PMSI creditor if perfected before annexation or within 20 days after annexation (PMSI will have priority even over prior perfected secured party)
PMSI in equipment v. Perfected Secured party	PMSI if perfected within 20 days after delivery
PMSI in Inventory v. Perfected Secured Party	PMSI if perfected before delivery and if perfected secured party given notice before delivery
PMSI in consumer goods v. buyer	Buyer unless perfection is by filing before purchase
Perfected secured party v. buyer	Buyers in ordinary course win even with knowledge

Buyers vs. Article IX Secured Creditor

Buyer in Ordinary Course		Buyer not in Ordinary Course	
Perfected Secured Creditor	Unperfected Secured Creditor	Perfected Secured Creditor	Unperfected Secured Creditor
Buyer	Buyer	Creditor (Except PMSI in Consumer Goods - unless filed)	Buyer (Assuming no knowledge)

Article IX - PMSI Buyer

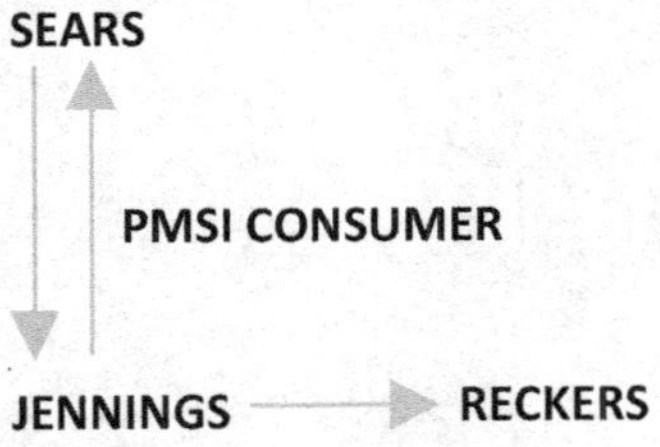

ARTICLE 9 – RIGHTS OF SECURED PARTIES AND DEBTORS

Right of release/termination

On consumer goods, termination statement must be filed within 30 days after the final payment is made or within 20 days of demand by consumer

Article IX

REMEDIES

CREDITOR: Suit or repossession

SELF-HELP - No Court Proceeding Required Before Repossession

BREACH OF PEACE ISSUES - No violation of civil or criminal laws

Article IX - Sale

1. 60% RULE - Creditor must sell collateral if debtor has paid 60% of cash price of collateral
   - Consumer goods - can demand sale (90 days)
2. REQUIREMENTS
   - Notice to debtor
   - Notice to other secured parties
   - Public or private
   - Reasonable: price/practices
   - All security interests are terminated

Article IX

3. DISTRIBUTION
   - Expenses
   - First priority
   - Second etc.
   - Debtor

AFTER SALE:
ALL SECURITY INTERESTS IN THE PROPERTY ARE TERMINATED

Review Question

Under the Secured Transactions Article of the UCC, which of the following remedies is available to a secured creditor when a debtor fails to make a payment when due?

	Proceed against the collateral	Obtain a general judgment against the debtor
A.	Yes	Yes
B.	Yes	No
C.	No	Yes
D.	No	No

Drew bought a computer for personal use from Hale Corp. for $3,000. Drew paid $2,000 in cash and signed a security agreement for the balance. Hale properly filed the security agreement. Drew defaulted in paying the balance of the purchase price. Hale asked Drew to pay the balance. When Drew refused, Hale peacefully repossessed the computer.

Under the UCC Secured Transactions Article, which of the following remedies will Hale have?

- ☐ A. **Obtain a deficiency judgment against Drew for the amount owed.**
- ☐ B. **Sell the computer and retain any surplus over the amount owed.**
- ☐ C. **Retain the computer over Drew's objection.**
- ☐ D. **Sell the computer without notifying Drew.**

You are auditing the records of a company and reviewing the secured debt held by the company. In your review you come upon a number of perfections by filing. Which of the following is correct?

- [ ] **A. Since the debtor has not signed uniform national filing forms, the company is not perfected and, thus, an unsecured creditor.**
- [ ] **B. In two of the filings, the description of the debtor's collateral is listed as "all assets," thus rendering the filings as being invalid.**
- [ ] **C. In one case, the security agreement was filed for perfection, rather than the uniform national form, thus, rendering the perfection invalid.**
- [ ] **D. One perfection is four years old. This perfection is valid for five years and can be extended another five years, if a continuation statement is filed during the six month period prior to the expiration of the original five year period.**

Under the UCC Secured Transaction Article, what is the effect of perfecting a security interest by filing a financing statement?

- [ ] A. **The secured party can enforce its security interest against the debtor.**
- [ ] B. **The secured party has permanent priority in the collateral even if the collateral is removed to another state.**
- [ ] C. **The debtor is protected against all other parties who acquire an interest in the collateral after the filing.**
- [ ] D. **The secured party has priority in the collateral over most creditors who acquire a security interest in the same collateral after the filing.**

Which of the following statements is correct concerning perfection of a security interest?

- [ ] **A. The proper place to file a financing statement for an individual debtor is the state where the collateral is located.**
- [ ] **B. The proper place to file a financing statement for a corporation is the state where the corporate headquarter is located.**
- [ ] **C. For perfection, the financing statement need not describe the collateral, thus a description such as "all assets" would be sufficient.**
- [ ] **D. A properly filed financing statement is effective for five years and can be extended for another five years if a continuation statement is filed within six months of the expiration of the five-year period.**

Pix Co., which is engaged in the business of selling appliances, borrowed $18,000 from Lux Bank.
Pix executed a promissory note for that amount and pledged all of its customer installment receivables as collateral for the loan. Pix executed a security agreement that described the collateral, but Lux did not file a financing statement.

With respect to this transaction

- [ ] **A. Attachment of the security interest did not occur because Pix failed to file a financing statement.**
- [ ] **B. Perfection of the security interest occurred despite Lux's failure to file a financing statement.**
- [ ] **C. Attachment of the security interest took place when the loan was made and Pix executed the security agreement.**
- [ ] **D. Perfection of the security interest did not occur because accounts receivable are intangibles.**

Under the UCC Secured Transactions Article, which of the following events will always prevent a security interest from attaching?

- [ ] **A. Failure to have a written security agreement.**
- [ ] **B. Failure of the creditor to have possession of the collateral.**
- [ ] **C. Failure of the debtor to have rights in the collateral.**
- [ ] **D. Failure of the creditor to give present consideration for the security interest.**

REG 4-2

DEBTOR-CREDITOR RELATIONSHIPS

Suretyship: Introduction, Creation, and Types

Suretyship: Rights of Parties

Selected Questions (4)

SURETYSHIP: INTRODUCTION, CREATION, AND TYPES

SURETYSHIP

CREDITOR
↑
PRINCIPAL DEBTOR
↑
SURETY (GUARANTOR) (Not guarantor of collection)

SUB-SURETY

CREDITOR
↑
PRINCIPAL DEBTOR
↑
SURETY A
↑
SURETY B

CO-SURETY

CREDITOR
↑
PRINCIPAL DEBTOR
↑
SURETY 1 SURETY 2

Suretyship - Co-Sureties

CO-SURETIES

A. $72,000
B. $108,000
C. $180,000

360,000 LOAN
240,000 BALANCE UPON DEFAULT
60,000 - DEBTOR PAYS
180,000 - C PAYS

Suretyship - Co-Sureties

$$\frac{\text{AMOUNT CO-SURETY GUARANTEED}}{\text{TOTAL SURETY AMOUNT}}$$

$$A \quad \frac{72}{360} X 180{,}000 = 36{,}000$$

$$B \quad \frac{108}{360} X 180{,}000 = 54{,}000$$

$90,000 DEBT

↑ ALDER $20,000 | FIELD $30,000 | HALL $40,000

Suretyship - Co-Sureties

MAXIMUM LIABILITY IF SOLVENT
IF BANKRUPT

$$A = \frac{20}{90} F = \frac{30}{90} H = \frac{40}{90}$$

$$\frac{\text{AMOUNT CO-SURETY GUARANTEED}}{\text{TOTAL SURETY AMOUNT LESS BANKRUPT SURETY'S AMOUNT}}$$

MAXIMUM LIABILITY IF 'A' IS BANKRUPT $F = \frac{30}{90-20} H = \frac{40}{90-20}$

MAXIMUM LIABILITY IF 'F' IS BANKRUPT $A = \frac{20}{90-30} H = \frac{40}{90-30}$

Review Question

West promised to make Noll a loan of $180,000 if Noll obtained sureties to secure the loan. Noll entered into an agreement with Carr, Gray, and Pine to act as co-sureties on his loan from West.

The agreement between Noll and the co-sureties provided for compensation to be paid to each of the co--sureties. It further indicated that the maximum liability of each co-surety would be as follows:

Review Question

Carr $180,000, Gray $60,000, and Pine $120,000.

West accepted the commitment of the sureties and made the loan to Noll. After paying nine installments totaling $90,000, Noll defaulted. Gray's debts (including his surety obligation) are discharged in bankruptcy.

Subsequently, Carr properly paid the entire debt outstanding of $90,000.

Review Question

What amounts may Carr recover from the co-sureties?

	Gray	Pine
A.	$0	$30,000
B.	$0	$36,000
C.	$15,000	$30,000
D.	$30,000	$30,000

SURETYSHIP: RIGHTS OF THE PARTIES

Rights of the Creditor

Proceed directly against surety (unless guarantor of collection)

Proceed against debtor

Proceed against collateral

Proceed against one surety or all sureties

Suretyship - Terminology

1. **SUBROGATION** - rights of surety after they pay -- steps into shoes of debtor and creditor; has same rights
2. **EXONERATION** - rights of surety to force principal debtor to pay
3. **CONTRIBUTION** - rights from co-sureties
4. **REIMBURSEMENT** - right of surety to collect from principal debtor

Suretyship - Terminology

1. Indemnity contract
2. Suretyship contract
3. Surety
4. Third-party beneficiary
5. Cosurety
6. Statute of Frauds
7. Right of contribution
8. Reimbursement
9. Subrogation
10. Exoneration

Suretyship - Terminology

A. Relationship whereby one person agrees to answer for the debt or default of another.
B. Requires certain contracts to be in writing to be enforceable.
C. Jointly and severally liable to creditor.
D. Promises to pay debt on default of principal debtor.
E. One party promises to reimburse debtor for payment of debt or loss if it arises.
F. Receives intended benefits of a contract.
G. Right of surety to require the debtor to pay before surety pays.
H. Upon payment of more than his/her proportionate share, each cosurety may compel other cosureties to pay their shares.
I. Upon payment of debt, surety may recover payment from debtor
J. Upon payment, surety obtains same rights against debtor that creditor had.

Suretyship - No Release

1. Fraud by debtor
2. Misrepresentation by debtor
3. Changes in loan terms (e.g., extension of payment) (compensated surety)
4. Release of principal debtor
5. Bankruptcy of principal debtor
6. Insolvency of principal debtor
7. Death of principal debtor
8. Incapacity of principal debtor
9. Lack of enforcement by creditor
10. Creditor's failure to give notice of default
11. Failure of creditor to resort to collateral

Suretyship - Release

Release of Surety

1. Proper performance by debtor
2. Release, surrender or destruction of collateral (to extent of value of collateral)
3. Substitution of debtor
4. Fraud/misrepresentation by creditor
5. Refusal by creditor to accept payment from debtor
6. Change in loan terms (uncompensated surety only and must be material)
7. Statute of frauds
8. Statute of limitations

Review Question

Which of the following defenses would a surety be able to assert successfully to limit the surety's liability to a creditor?

A. A discharge in bankruptcy of the principal debtor
B. A personal defense the principal debtor has against the creditor
C. The incapacity of the surety
D. The incapacity of the principal debtor

Wright cosigned King's loan from Ace Bank. Which of the following events would release Wright from the obligation to pay the loan?

- [ ] **A. Ace seeking payment of the loan only from Wright.**
- [ ] **B. King is granted a discharge in bankruptcy.**
- [ ] **C. Ace is paid in full by King's spouse.**
- [ ] **D. King is adjudicated mentally incompetent.**

Which of the following rights does one cosurety generally have against another cosurety?

- [ ] A. **Exoneration.**
- [ ] B. **Subrogation.**
- [ ] C. **Reimbursement.**
- [ ] D. **Contribution.**

Nash, Owen, and Polk are co-sureties with maximum liabilities of $40,000, $60,000, and $80,000, respectively. The amount of the loan on which they have agreed to act as co-sureties is $180,000.
The debtor defaulted at a time when the loan balance was $180,000. Nash paid the lender $36,000 in full settlement of all claims against Nash, Owen, and Polk.

The total amount that Nash may recover from Owen and Polk is

- [ ] A. **$0**
- [ ] B. **$24,000**
- [ ] C. **$28,000**
- [ ] D. **$140,000**

Smith takes his grandfather clock to A.S. Clockwise, a seller of clocks, for cleaning and repairs. Clockwise has a clearly stated policy that all repairs must be paid for in cash unless prior credit arrangements have been approved. The estimated cost of the cleaning and repairs is stated as $100-$125. Clockwise makes the repairs and, with cleaning, the bill is $120. Smith owns a number of non-exempt assets. When Smith comes to pick up his grandfather clock, he refuses to pay cash, and Clockwise refuses to turn over the grandfather clock to Smith. Which of the following is the best lien remedy available for Clockwise?

- [ ] **A. Mechanic's lien.**
- [ ] **B. Writ of execution.**
- [ ] **C. Attachment of non-exempt assets.**
- [ ] **D. Artisan's lien.**

REG 4-3

REAL PROPERTY

Real Property

Selected Questions (2)

REAL PROPERTY

Types of Ownership

A. Fee Simple (Absolute) -

B. Fee Simple (Defeasible) –

	Present	Future
1.	Determinable -	Possibility of Reverter

"To A so long as it is used for school purposes"

Grantor (heirs) have title at moment clause is violated

2. Subject to condition subsequent - Right of Entry

Types of Ownership

"To A provided that liquor is never sold on the premises"

Grantor (heirs) have right to claim title when clause is violated

C. **Life Estate** — **Reversion**

to my husband for life,

then to my children — **Remainder**

Leases

Tenancies - temporary possession/leases

1. For Years - lease for a specific period
2. Periodic - month-to-month
3. At Will - by agreement - either side can terminate – no damages.
4. At Sufferance - lease has ended; tenant remains
5. Sublease vs. Assignment portion full
6. Warranty of habitability

Leases

Which of the following provisions must be included in a residential lease agreement?

A. A description of the leased premises
B. The due date for payment of rent
C. A requirement that the tenant have public liability insurance
D. A requirement that the landlord will perform all structural repairs to the property

Easement Appurtenant

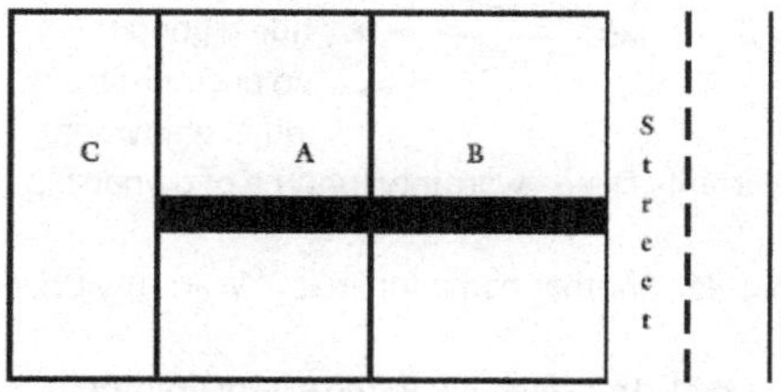

C needs to get to her property from the street, passing through A's and B's property

Types of Easements

Easements appurtenant

Negative easement

Easements by express reservation

Easements by implication

Scenic easements

Conservation easements

Easements in gross

Easements by Necessity

Easements in gross

Affirmative easement

Easements by express grant

Easements by necessity

Fixtures

Fixtures - personal property turned to real property:

Factors that determine:

1. Degree of attachment
2. Degree of ownership
3. Damage upon removal
4. Relationship to property
5. Agreement of parties

Liens Terminology

Mechanic's Liens

- Statutory right
- Strict filing and time requirements
- Used when creditor has furnished materials, labor, or services related to repair or improvement of real estate

Artisans' Liens

- Statutory right
- Improvement of property (jeweler who repairs; artist who paints mural in lobby of office building)

Transfer of Real Property

Adverse possession

- Hostile
- Open
- Notorious
- Exclusive
- For statutory period

Will/Inheritance

Gift

Sale

Transfer of Real Property: Deeds

Transfer → Writing, Delivery

Warranty Deed → transfer is proper, title is good, no encumbrances, quiet enjoyment

Special Warranty Deed - warranty for time of ownership

Bargain & Sale: Another name for Special Warranty Deed

Quitclaim Deed - transfers title to the extent grantor has title

Transfer: Delivery and Recording

Delivery of deed is needed

Recording recommended but failure to record does not mean title does not pass[1]

RECORDING

Race - first to record (first in time, first in right)

Notice - last bfp to take title (failure of others to record)

Race/Notice - first bfp to record

[1]Not required to transfer: required for future protection

Real Property Financing

Financing Real Property Purchases

A. MORTGAGE

1. Creation → Writing; → Underlying debt
2. Parties → Mortgagor – buyer/borrower; → Mortgagee-creditor

Real Property Financing

Transferability

Assumption - original mortgagor, and transferee personally liable, property subject to foreclosure

Jones ($80,000 mgt) Buyer Blain buys for $100,000; Blain pays $20,000; Assumes $80,000

Subject to: Original mortgagor is personally liable; property subject to foreclosure

Jones carries Blain for $100,000 at higher rate; pays original mortgage

Real Property Financing

Foreclosure - certificate of sale/judicial procedure

Right of redemption - 6 months after sale; sheriff's deed

Deficiency judgment - residential exemption in some states

Co-Ownership of Real Property

A. Tenancy in Common
   1. Creation - any time, any interest
   2. Transferability - inter vivos or testamentary
   3. Death of Tenant

B. B. Joint Tenancy (ROS)
   1. Creation - Time - Title - Interest - Possession
   2. Transferability
   3. Death of Tenant

A B C → D — D is tenant in common (1/3)

A B D

A **B** D — A (2/3) and D (1/3) are tenants in common

Types of Ownership

C. Tenancy by the Entirety
   1. Creation - TTIP & Marriage
   2. Transferability
   3. Death of Tenant

D. Community Property - 50/50 marital property ownership

E. Tenancy in Partnership

Partnership A B C

A and B hold property

Which of the following factors help determine whether an item of personal property has become a fixture?

	Manner of affixation	Value of the item	Intent of the annexor
☐	Yes	Yes	Yes
☐	Yes	Yes	No
☐	Yes	No	Yes
☐	No	Yes	Yes

On August 15, 1994, Tower, Nolan, and Oak were deeded a piece of land as tenants in common. The deed provided that Tower owned 1/2 the property and Nolan and Oak owned 1/4 each. If Oak dies, the property will be owned as follows:

- [ ] **A.** **Tower 1/2, Nolan 1/4, Oak's heirs 1/4.**
- [ ] **B.** **Tower 1/3, Nolan 1/3, Oak's heirs 1/3.**
- [ ] **C.** **Tower 5/8, Nolan 3/8.**
- [ ] **D.** **Tower 1/2, Nolan 1/2.**

REG 4-4

BANKRUPTCY

Prebankruptcy Options, Introduction to and Declaration of Bankruptcy

Bankruptcy Process

Distribution of Debtor's Estate

Discharge and Reaffirmation Agreements

Selected Questions (8)

PRE-BANKRUPTCY OPTIONS, INTRODUCTION TO AND DECLARATION OF BANKRUPTCY

Creditors' Remedies

1. Composition - Discharges debts if debtor performs as to all creditors who agreed
2. Assignment - Creditors may petition debtor into bankruptcy and set aside assignment
3. Judgment/Judgment Lien
4. Judgment Execution
   a. Attachment
   b. Garnishment
      - SS is exempt
      - Cannot garnish more than 25% of take-home pay
      - Employees cannot be terminated because of garnishment order against employee
   c. Homestead Exemption - protection for equity in home but still subject to mortgage and IRS

Bankruptcy - Chapter 7

Chapter 7 – Liquidation

Voluntary/Involuntary
No involuntary for farmers and nonprofits

Eligibility: Individuals, partnerships, corps.

Requirements
Exemptions - *S&Ls; Credit unions; SBA; RRs; Municipalities; insurers*

Trustee

Bankruptcy - Chapter 11

Chapter 11 – Reorganization

Voluntary/Involuntary

Automatic Stay
No involuntary for farmers; non-profits

Bankruptcy - Chapter 11

Eligibility: individuals, partnerships, corps

Requirements

Exemptions - same as Chap 7 *plus stockbrokers* (RR's OK)

Need not have trustee

Approval of Reorganization Plan: ½ the creditors with 2/3 claims

Chapter 12

The family farmer chapter

Only voluntary petitions

50/50 requirement: 50% of income from farm and 50% of debts due to farm

Total maximum debt: $3,792,650

Bankruptcy - Chapter 13

Chapter 13 - Consumer Debt Adjustment Plan
Voluntary
Eligibility
- Income
- < $360,475 unsecured debts
- < $1,081,400 secured debts

Requirements
Exemptions - only individuals permitted to file
Trustee

Bankruptcy - Declaration

VOLUNTARY PETITIONS
REQUIREMENTS - Petitioner has debts (consumer exceptions under 2005 reforms)
AUTOMATIC RELIEF

INVOLUNTARY PETITIONS
LIABILITY FOR WRONGFUL FILING
REQUIREMENTS
- < 12 creditors = 1/$14,425
- > 12 creditors = 3/$14,425

ENTRY OF STAY

Bankruptcy - Wrongful Filing

Damages for Wrongful Involuntary Filing
- Court Costs
- Attorney Fees
- Compensatory Damages
- Punitive Damages

Review Question

Strong Corp. filed a voluntary petition in bankruptcy under the reorganization provisions of Chapter 11 of the Federal Bankruptcy Code. A reorganization plan was filed and agreed to by all necessary parties. The court confirmed the plan and a final decree was entered.
Which of the following parties ordinarily must confirm the plan?

	1/2 of the secured creditors	2/3 of the shareholders
A.	Yes	Yes
B.	Yes	No
C.	No	Yes
D.	No	No

Bankruptcy - Chapter 13

Chapter 13 - Consumer Debt Adjustment Plan
- Hearing for approval of plan

After 3 or 5-year period, if debt plan met, court grants discharge, with exceptions

Declaration of Bankruptcy (New)

	Chapter 7	Chapter 11	Chapter 13
Trustee	Yes	No	Yes
Eligible persons:			
Individuals	Yes	Yes	Yes
Partnerships	Yes	Yes	No
Corporations	Yes	Yes	No
Voluntary	Yes	Yes	Yes
Involuntary	Yes, except for farmers and non profits	Yes, except for farmers and non profits	No
Exemptions	S&L's, Credit Unions, SBA, RRs, municipalities	Same as Chapter 7 plus stockbrokers*	Only individuals allowed
Requirements - voluntary	debts	debts	income < $360,475 unsecured < $1,081,400 secured
Requirements - involuntary	< 12 = 1/$14,725 12 = 3/$14,725	< 12 = 1/$14,725 12 = 3/$14,725	N/A

*RR's are eligible

Review Question

A voluntary petition filed under the liquidation provisions of Chapter 7 of the Federal Bankruptcy Code:

A. Is not available to a corporation unless it has previously filed a petition under the reorganization provisions of Chapter 11 of the Federal Bankruptcy Code
B. Automatically stays collection actions against the debtor except by secured creditors
C. Will be dismissed unless the debtor has 12 or more unsecured creditors whose claims total at least $10,000
D. Does not require the debtor to show that the debtor's liabilities exceed the fair market value of assets

Effect of Bankruptcy Petition

Order for relief upon filing of petition
- Liens, foreclosures, etc. are stayed
- Payments handled through the bankruptcy court

Bankruptcy process begins

BANKRUPTCY PROCESS

Anatomy of Bankruptcy Case

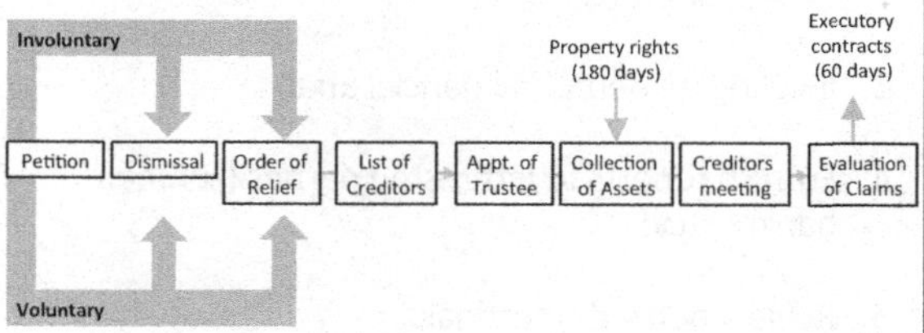

Anatomy of Bankruptcy Case

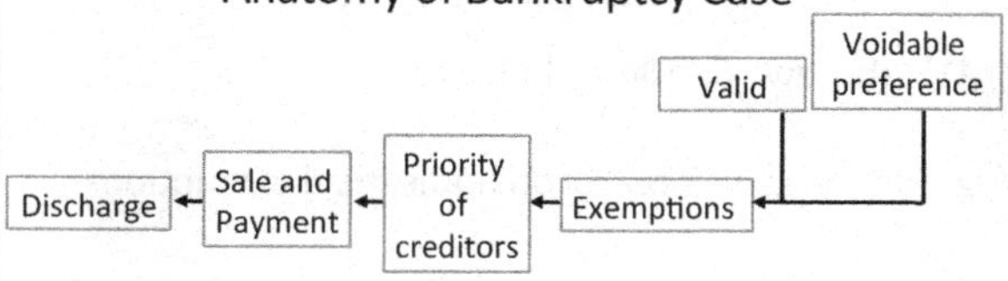

*insolvent = "bankruptcy" sense (liabilities > assets)

SS
Disability
Alimony

1. 1yr. fraud
2. 1yr. insolvent* and unfair
3. 1yr. insider
4. 90 days - insolvent* - not ordinary course of business (presumed)
5. Security for antecedent debt

OK (not voidable)
Limits on consumer debt/cash contemporaneous exchange; regular payments

Bankruptcy – Test for Dismissal

The Means Test
- Determines whether bankruptcy can proceed or whether debtor is involved in "substantial abuse" of the bankruptcy system
- Means Test: Calculation of debtor's monthly income averaged over the last six months less allowed expenses
- Monthly income X 12: If this figure exceeds state's median income by more than $6,000, then substantial abuse is presumed
- Debtor can rebut by showing "special circumstances" or "adjustments" with no alternatives

Duties of debtor

1. Schedule of all assets
2. List of all creditors
3. Schedule of current income and expenses
4. Certificate from approved credit counseling agency
5. Copy of most recent federal income tax return

Effect of bankruptcy

Automatic stay when petition is granted

Judgments stop

Liens stop

Enforcement actions stop

Duties of trustee

1. Appointed by government
2. Collect debtor's assets
3. Investigate debtor's financial affairs
4. Furnish reports to interested parties (Lehman bankruptcy)
5. Review debtor's materials
6. Is the representative for the debtor's estate

What is included in debtor's estate

Tangible and intangible property

All property acquired within 180 days following bankruptcy

- Inheritances and gifts
- Property from divorce, separation, or property settlement
- Life insurance proceeds

Review Question

Under the liquidation provisions of Chapter 7 of the federal Bankruptcy Code, certain property acquired by the debtor after the filing of the petition becomes part of the bankruptcy estate. An example of such property is:

A. Inheritances received by the debtor within 180 days after the filing of the petition
B. Child support payments received by the debtor within one year after filing the petition
C. Social Security payments received by the debtor within 180 days after the filing of the petition
D. Wages earned by the debtor within one year after the filing of the petition

Exemptions - Bankruptcy

1. State Law: Can limit choice to state
2. Federal Law: Control on homestead exemptions
3. Debtor's Choice

Homestead Exemptions

If homestead is acquired within 3.5 years of bankruptcy filing, homestead equity exempted is limited to $146,450

Must have lived in the state for two years

Exemptions

Numbers changed as of April 10, 2010

Motor vehicle	$ 3,450
Household furnishings	$11,525
Other property (wildcard)	$ 1,150
Tools of profession	$ 2,175
Life insurance	$ 11,525
Jewelry	$ 1,450

Anatomy of Bankruptcy Case

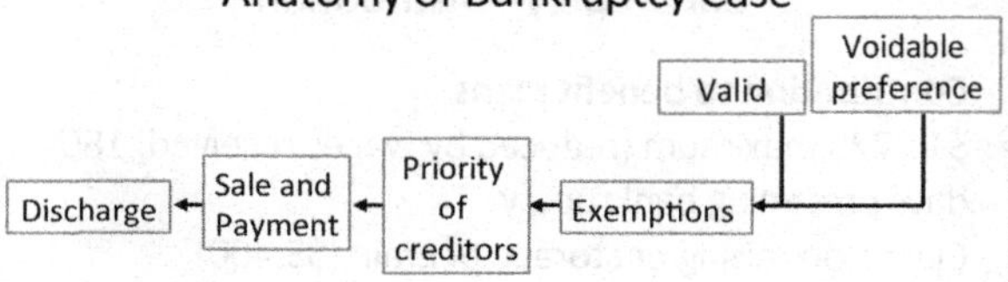

*insolvent = "bankruptcy" sense (liabilities > assets)

SS
Disability
Alimony

1. 1yr. fraud
2. 1yr. insolvent* and unfair
3. 1yr. insider
4. 90 days - insolvent*- not ordinary course of business (presumed)
5. Security for antecedent debt

<u>OK</u> (not voidable)

Limits on consumer debt/cash contemporaneous exchange; regular payments

Review Question

On May 1, 1998, 2 months after becoming insolvent, Quick Corp., an appliance wholesaler, filed a voluntary petition for bankruptcy under the provisions of Chapter 7 of the Federal Bankruptcy Code. On October 15, 1997, Quick's board of directors had authorized and paid Erly $50,000 to repay Erly's April 1, 1997, loan to the corporation. Erly is a sibling of Quick's president. On March 15, 1998, Quick paid Kray $100,000 for inventory delivered that day.

Which of the following is not relevant in determining whether the repayment of Erly's loan is a voidable preferential transfer?

Review Question

A. Erly is an insider

B. Quick's payment to Erly was made on account of an antecedent debt

C. Quick's solvency when the loan was made by Erly

D. Quick's payment to Erly was made within 1 year of the filing of the bankruptcy petition

Bankruptcy - Voidable Transfers

A debtor may attempt to conceal or transfer property to prevent a creditor from satisfying a judgment. Which of the following actions will be considered an indication of fraudulent conveyance?

	Debtor remaining in possession after transfer	Secret conveyance	Debtor retains an equitable benefit in the property conveyed
A.	Yes	No	Yes
B.	No	Yes	Yes
C.	Yes	Yes	No
D.	Yes	Yes	Yes

DISTRIBUTION OF DEBTOR' S ESTATE

Bankruptcy - Distribution

DISTRIBUTION PRIORITIES

Secured Creditors (to the extent of repossession)

Claims for child support and alimony

Bankruptcy - Distribution

Administration Costs

Attorneys, Accountants, Trustees, Appraisers
Claims arising in ordinary course of business after bankruptcy petition is filed but before order of relief (involuntary)

Employee Wages (not officers)
$11,725 maximum
3 months preceding petition (90 days)

Bankruptcy - Distribution

Contribution to benefit plans
$11,725 maximum (reduced by wages received) 180 days preceding bankruptcy
Claims on raising or storage of grain ($5,400)

Consumer deposits
- $2,600 maximum

Taxes (federal, state and local)

Unsecured creditors

Review Question

On July 1, 1986, Mix was petitioned by Able into bankruptcy under the liquidation provisions of the Bankruptcy Code. Able and Baker are unsecured creditors of Mix, owed $20,000 and $40,000 respectively. Mix also owed Carr $80,000, secured by a valid perfected security interest in bankruptcy on Mix's machinery, valued at $20,000. Mix has no other debts, except for 1986 federal income taxes.
Shortly after the filing of the petition, Lang was appointed trustee in Mix's bankruptcy. In Lang's capacity as trustee,
Lang:
Engaged Ring & Co., CPAs, as the accountants for the bankruptcy estate.
Included as part of the bankruptcy estate, an inheritance that Mix became entitled to receive on December 15,1986 and that Mix actually received on January 15,1987.

Review Question

Lang has sold the property in the estate (including the sale of Mix's machinery for $20,000, which Carr consented to) and now the sole asset of the estate is $60,000 cash. Lang wishes to distribute the $60,000 so as to satisfy the following claims and expenses of the estate:

Unsecured claim for 1986 federal income taxes	$ 6,000
Carr's claim	$80,000
Able's and Baker's claims	$60,000
Expenses necessary to maintain and sell the unsecured property of the estate.	$ 1,000
Ring's fee for services rendered	$ 3,000

There are no other claims

Review Question

1. Carr	20,000
2. Expenses	1,000 + 3,000
3. Taxes	6,000
4. Able	20,000
Baker	40,000
Carr	60,000

Review Question

$20,000 to Carr; $4,000 exp.

$6,000 taxes

$30,000 remaining is divided pro rata among Able, Baker and Carr

Review Question

Total Owed

$60,000 Carr
$20,000 Able
$40,000 Baker

$120,000

Review Question

Carr 60,000/120,000 X 30,000 = $15,000

Able 20,000/120,000 X 30,000 = $ 5,000

Baker 40,000/120,000 X 30,000 = $10,000

Review Question

Knox operates an electronics store as a sole proprietor. On April 5, 1988, Knox was involuntarily petitioned into bankruptcy under the liquidation provisions of the Bankruptcy Code. On April 20, a trustee in bankruptcy was appointed and an order for relief was entered. Knox's non-exempt property has been converted to cash, which is available to satisfy the following claims and expenses as may be appropriate:

Review Question

Claims and Expenses	$20,000
Claims by Dart Corp. (one of Knox's suppliers) for computers ordered on April 6, 1988 and delivered on credit to Knox on April 10, 1988.	
Fee earned by the bankruptcy trustee	$15,000
Claim by Boyd for a deposit given to Knox on April 1, 1988, for a computer Boyd purchased for personal use but that had not yet been received by Boyd.	$ 1,500

Review Question

Claim by Noll Co. for the delivery of stereos to Knox on credit. The stereos were delivered on March 4, 1988, and a financing statement was properly filed on March 5, 1988. These stereos were sold by the trustee with Noll's consent for $7,500 for their fair market value — $ 5,000

Fees earned by the attorneys for the bankruptcy estate — $10,000

Claims by unsecured general creditors
The cash available for distribution includes the proceeds from the sale of the stereos — $ 1,000

Review Question

What amount will be distributed to the trustee as a fee if the cash available for distribution is $15,000?

A. $6,000
B. $9,000
C. $10,000
D. $15,000

Review Question

What amount will be distributed to Boyd if the cash available for distribution is $50,800?

A. $480
B. $800
C. $900
D. $1,500

Review Question

What amount will be distributed to Dart if the cash available for distribution is $41,000?

A. $10,100
B. $11,000
C. $16,000
D. $20,000

Review Question

On July 15, 1988, White a sole proprietor, was involuntarily petitioned into bankruptcy under the liquidation provisions of the Bankruptcy Code. White's non-exempt property has been converted to $13,000 cash, which is available to satisfy the following claims:

Unsecured Claim for 1986 state income tax — $10,000

Fee owed to Best & Co., CPAs, for services rendered from April 1, 1988, through June 30, 1988 — $ 6,000

Unsecured claim by Stieb for wages earned as an employee of White during March, 1988 — $ 3,000

There are no other claims

Review Question

What is the maximum amount that will be distributed for the payment of the 1986 state income tax?

A. $ 4,000
B. $ 5,000
C. $ 7,000
D. $10,000

Review Question

In a voluntary bankruptcy proceeding under Chapter 7 of the Federal Bankruptcy Code, which of the following claims incurred within 180 days prior to filing will be paid first?

A. Unsecured federal taxes
B. Utility bills up to $1,000
C. Voluntary contributions to employee benefit plans
D. Employee vacation and sick pay up to $2,000 per employee

DISCHARGE AND REAFFIRMATION AGREEMENTS

Bankruptcy – Non-Discharge

NON-DISCHARGEABLE DEBTS

1. Taxes within 2 years of filing bankruptcy petition
2. Liability for obtaining money or property by false pretenses
3. Willful and malicious injuries
4. Debts incurred by driving DWI
5. Alimony, maintenance or child support
6. Unscheduled debts (unless actual notice)
7. Debts resulting from fraud as a fiduciary (embezzlement)

Bankruptcy – Non-Discharge

NON-DISCHARGEABLE DEBTS

8. Government fines or penalties imposed within 3 years prior
9. Educational loans due within 5 prior years (unless hardship)
10. Prior bankruptcy debts in which debtor waived discharge
11. Mortgage Issues
12. Sarbanes-Oxley – bonuses; fraud
13. Consumer debt incurred within 90 days of filing -- $550 permitted – Cash withdrawals on credit cards within 70 days ($875).

Bankruptcy – Non-Discharge

14. Reaffirmation agreements

- writing
- filed with court
- not rescinded prior to discharge

Bankruptcy - Discharge

Larson, an unemployed carpenter, filed for voluntary bankruptcy on August 14, 1990. Larson's liabilities are listed below.

Credit Card Charge due May 2, 1989	$3,000
Bank loan incurred June 1990	$5,000
Medical expenses incurred June 1983	$7,000
Alimony due during 1988	$1,000

Bankruptcy - Discharge

Under the provisions of Chapter 7 of the Federal Bankruptcy Code, Larson's discharge will not apply to the unpaid

A. Credit card charges
B. Bank loan
C. Medical expenses
D. Alimony

A subsequent holder of a negotiable instrument may cause the discharge of a prior holder of the instrument by any of the following actions except

- [ ] **A. Unexcused delay in presentment of a time draft.**
- [ ] **B. Procuring certification of a check.**
- [ ] **C. Giving notice of dishonor the day after dishonor.**
- [ ] **D. Material alteration of a note.**

Peters Co. repairs computers. On February 9, 2003, Stark Electronics Corp. sells Peters a circuit tester on credit.
Peters executes an installment note for the purchase price, a security agreement covering the tester, and a financing statement that Stark files on February 11, 2003. On April 13, 2003, creditors other than Stark file an involuntary petition in bankruptcy against Peters.

What is Stark's status in Peters' bankruptcy?

- [ ] A. **Stark will be treated as an unsecured creditor, because Stark did not join in the filing against Peters.**
- [ ] B. **Stark's security interest constitutes a voidable preference, because the financing statement was not filed until February 11.**
- [ ] C. **Stark's security interest constitutes a voidable preference, because the financing statement was not filed 90 days or fewer before the bankruptcy proceeding was filed.**
- [ ] D. **Stark is a secured creditor and can assert a claim to the circuit tester that will be superior to the claims of Peters' other creditors.**

In a voluntary bankruptcy proceeding under Chapter 7 of the Federal Bankruptcy Code, which of the following claims, filed within 90 days of the filing for bankruptcy, will be paid first?

- [ ] **A. Unsecured federal taxes.**
- [ ] **B. Utility bills up to $1,000.**
- [ ] **C. Voluntary contributions to employee benefit plans.**
- [ ] **D. Employee vacation and sick pay up to $2,000 per employee.**

Under the federal Bankruptcy Code, which of the following rights or powers does a trustee in bankruptcy not have?

- ☐ A. **The power to prevail against a creditor with an unperfected security interest.**
- ☐ B. **The power to require persons holding the debtor's property at the time the bankruptcy petition is filed to deliver the property to the trustee.**
- ☐ C. **The right to use any grounds available to the debtor to obtain the return of the debtor's property.**
- ☐ D. **The right to avoid any statutory liens against the debtor's property that were effective before the bankruptcy petition was filed.**

Under the liquidation provisions of Chapter 7 of the federal Bankruptcy Code, certain property acquired by the debtor after the filing of the petition becomes part of the bankruptcy estate.

An example of such property is

- [ ] **A. Municipal-bond interest received by the debtor within 180 days of the filing of the petition.**
- [ ] **B. Alimony received by the debtor within one year of the filing of the petition.**
- [ ] **C. Social Security payments received by the debtor within 180 days of the filing of the petition.**
- [ ] **D. Gifts received by the debtor within one year of the filing of the petition.**

Which of the following statements is correct?

- [ ] **A. Failure of the debtor to attend (unless excused) the creditor's meeting is a failure to co-operate and grounds for denial of the debtor's discharge in a Chapter 7 bankruptcy.**
- [ ] **B. A written statement signed by the debtor that s/he has attended sessions with an approved credit-counseling agency is required as a duty of the debtor.**
- [ ] **C. If the court finds that a debtor meets the median-family-income test, the court cannot dismiss a Chapter 7 petition based on abuse.**
- [ ] **D. A copy of the debtor's federal tax return for the most recent year prior to filing is not required, owing to the privacy right of the debtor.**

On February 28, 2005, Master, Inc., had total assets with a fair market value of $1,200,000 and total liabilities of $990,000. On January 15, 2005, Master made a monthly installment note payment to Acme Distributors Corp., a creditor holding a properly perfected security interest in equipment having a fair market value greater than the balance due on the note.

On March 15, 2005, Master voluntarily filed a petition in bankruptcy under the liquidation provisions of Chapter 7 of the Federal Bankruptcy Code. One year later, the equipment was sold for less than the balance due on the note to Acme.

If a creditor challenged Master's right to file, the petition would be dismissed

- [ ] A. If Master had fewer than 12 creditors at the time of filing.
- [ ] B. Unless Master can show that a reorganization under Chapter 11 of the Federal Bankruptcy Code would have been unsuccessful.
- [ ] C. Unless Master can show that it is unable to pay its debts in the ordinary course of business or as they come due.
- [ ] D. If Master is an insurance company.

To file for bankruptcy under Chapter 7 of the Federal Bankruptcy Code, an individual must

- [ ] **A. Have debts of any amount.**
- [ ] **B. Be insolvent.**
- [ ] **C. Be indebted to more than three creditors.**
- [ ] **D. Have debts in excess of $5,000.**

REG 4-5

AGENCY

Types of Agency Relationships and Creation

Duties of Agents and Principals

Contract Liability of Agents and Principals

Tort Liability of Agents and Principals

Selected Questions (8)

TYPES OF AGENCY RELATIONSHIPS AND CREATION

Agency Types

General

Special

Universal agent

Power of Attorney

Independent contractors

Examples of agency relationships

- Employees
- Real estate agents

Formation of Agency: Express Agency

General Requirements

1. Writing, but only if agent's contracts must be in writing
2. Capacity of the principal

Not required:

1. Capacity of the agent
2. Consideration – can be a gratuitous agency

Express agency relationship includes implied agency authority – whatever is customary

Formation of Various Types of Agency Relationships

Apparent Authority (Ostensible)

- Position
- Lingering Apparent Authority
  - Actual
  - Constructive (Public)

Estoppel

Ratification

- Retroactive
- Full Knowledge
- Accepts or Fails to reject

DUTIES OF AGENT AND PRINCIPAL

Agency - Duties

Duties of Agent

Follow instructions

Fiduciary

Duties of Principal

Liability

Disclosed

Partially disclosed

Undisclosed

→ See Contract Liabilities

Agency - Duties

Principal's Duties to Agent

Compensation - gratuitous

Reimbursement - expenses

Indemnification - see charts

Termination of Agency

Agreement

- Automatic termination date
- Accomplishment of task

Unilateral Act

- You're fired
- I quit

Operation of Law

- Death
- Insanity/Lack of capacity
- Bankruptcy
- Breach of Fiduciary Duty

Review Question

Harris is a purchasing agent for Elkin, a sole proprietor. Harris has the express authority to place purchase orders with Elkin's suppliers. Harris typically conducts business through the mail and has very little contact with Elkin. Elkin was incapacitated by a stroke and was declared incompetent in a judicial proceeding. Subsequently, Harris placed an order with Ajax, Inc. on behalf of Elkin. Neither Ajax nor Harris were aware of Elkin's incapacity. With regard to the contract with Ajax, Elkin (or Elkin's legal representative) will...

Review Question

A. Not be liable because Harris was without authority to enter into the contract.
B. Not be liable provided that Harris had placed orders with Ajax in the past.
C. Be liable because Harris was acting within the scope of Harris' authority.
D. Be liable because Ajax was unaware of Elkin's incapacity.

CONTRACT LIABILITY OF PRINCIPALS AND AGENTS

Agency

Agent

Liability

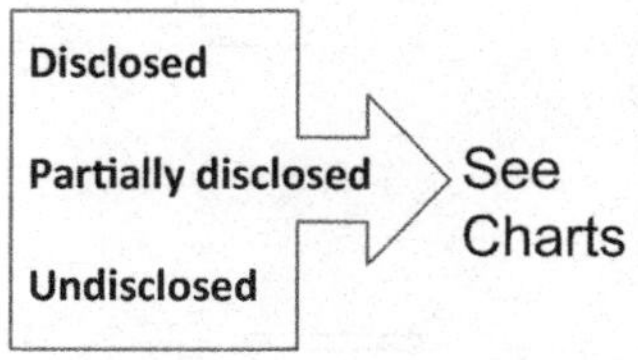

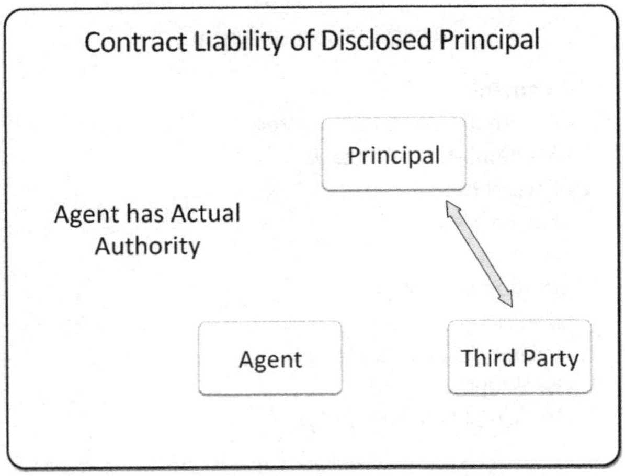

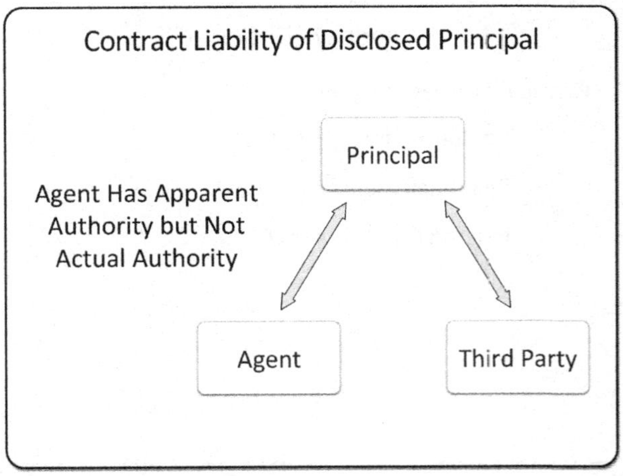

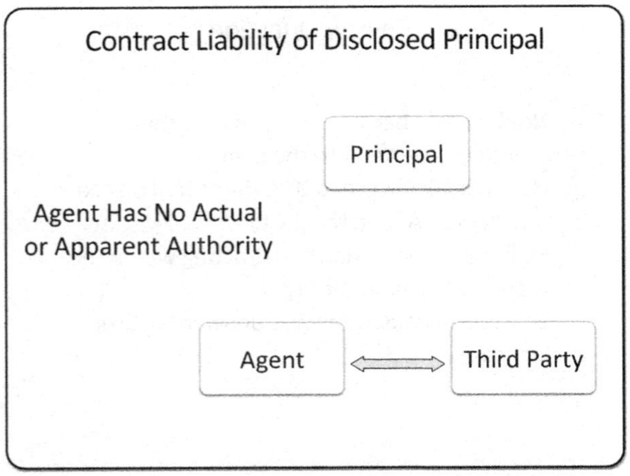

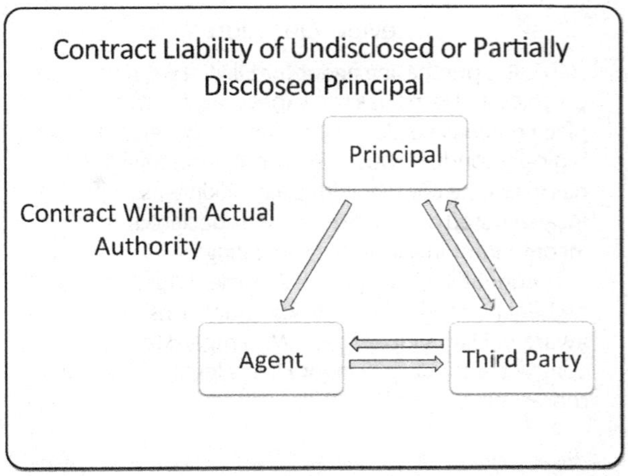

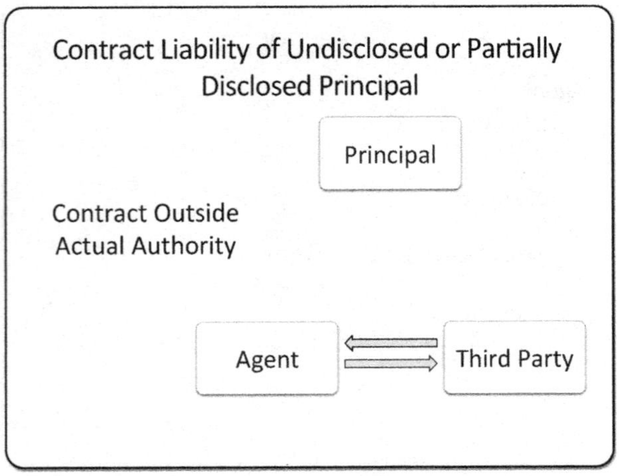

Review Question

Parc contracted with Furn Brothers Corp. to buy hotel furniture and fixtures on behalf of Global Motor House, a motel chain. Global instructed Parc to use Parc's own name and not to disclose to Furn that Parc was acting on Global's behalf.
Who is liable to Furn on this contract?

	Parc	Global
A.	Yes	No
B.	No	Yes
C.	Yes	Yes
D.	No	No

Review Question

During your examination of the financial statements of Bonanza Development Corporation, you reviewed certain land transactions involving John Walters as agent for Bonanza. Bonanza feared the price of land would skyrocket if it became known that is was trying to purchase a large number of tracts of land to develop a shopping center. It therefore instructed Walters not to disclose to prospective sellers that he was acting as an agent on its behalf. The agreement between Walters and Bonanza was in writing and signed by both parties.

Questions:

1. Bonanza is an undisclosed principal
2. Unless Bonanza ratifies the contracts made by Walters, it has no liability thereon
3. Walters has committed a fraud in failing to notify prospective buyers of the fact he is acting as Bonanza's agent
4. Bonanza cannot enforce the contracts made by Walters secretly on its behalf
5. Walters will not be entitled to the commissions agreed to by Bonanza in that he has entered into an illegal bargain
6. If Walters gave the usual warranties in connection with the purchase of the land, Bonanza would be liable on them even though Walters was not authorized to make them

Review Question

Which of the following statements is (are) correct regarding the relationship between an agent and a nondisclosed principal?

I. The principal is required to indemnify the agent for any contract entered into by the agent within the scope of the agency agreement
II. The agent has the same actual authority as if the principal has been disclosed

A. I only
B. II only
C. Both I and II
D. Neither I nor II

TORT LIABILITY OF AGENTS AND PRINCIPALS

Tort Liability - Agents

Servant vs. Independent Contractor
Degree of control

Doctrine of Respondeat Superior (Vicarious liability)

"Let the master answer"
Principal
↓
Servant

Scope of Employment vs. frolic and detour

Agent Tort Authorized

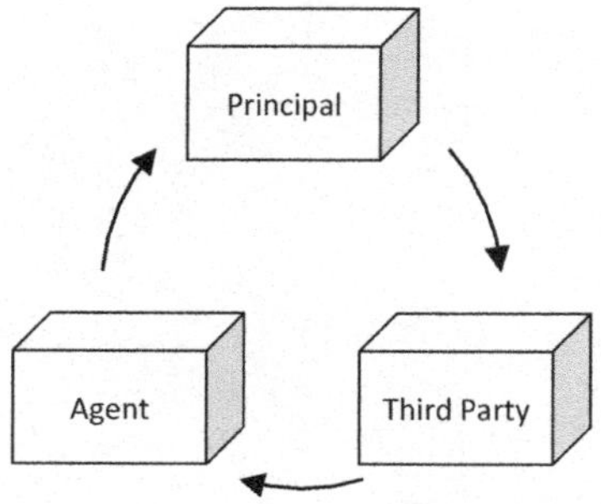

Agent Tort Not Authorized

No liability for principal EXCEPT:

1. Negligent hiring
2. Negligent supervision
3. Implicit approval

Review Question

Your client, Sanitary Dairies, Inc., had employed Harold Stone as a milk-truck driver. Stone negligently ran the truck into the car of Ronald Green, injuring Green, his wife, and damaging Green's car. Stone was also injured in the collision.

A. If Stone had never had a previous accident, Sanitary Dairies would not be liable.
B. Stone can avoid liability in that he was engaged in the performance of his principal's business.
C. If Green is shown to have been contributorily negligent, he cannot recover for his injuries or for the damage to the car.
D. Stone is entitled to receive worker's compensation.

Orr gives North power of attorney. In general, the power of attorney

- [ ] A. **Will be valid only if North is a licensed attorney at law.**
- [ ] B. **May continue in existence after Orr's death.**
- [ ] C. **May limit North's authority to specific transactions.**
- [ ] D. **Must be signed by both Orr and North.**

Forming an agency relationship requires that

- [ ] **A. The agreement between the principal and agent be supported by consideration.**
- [ ] **B. The principal and agent not be minors.**
- [ ] **C. Both the principal and agent consent to the agency.**
- [ ] **D. The agent's authority be limited to the express grant of authority in the agency agreement.**

Ogden Corp. hires Thorp as a sales representative for nine months at a salary of $3,000 per month, plus 4% of sales.

Which of the following statements is correct?

- [ ] **A. Thorp is obligated to act solely in Ogden's interest in matters concerning Ogden's business.**
- [ ] **B. The agreement between Ogden and Thorp formed an agency coupled with an interest.**
- [ ] **C. Ogden does not have the power to dismiss Thorp during the nine-month period without cause.**
- [ ] **D. The agreement between Ogden and Thorp is not enforceable, unless it is in writing and signed by Thorp.**

Maco Corp. develops shopping centers and regularly engages real estate brokers to act on its behalf in acquiring parcels of land.
The brokers are authorized to enter into such contracts, but are instructed to do so in their own names, without disclosing Maco's identity or Maco's relationship to the transaction.

If a broker enters into a contract with a seller on Maco's behalf,

- [ ] A. Maco will be bound by the contract because of the broker's apparent authority.
- [ ] B. The broker will not be personally bound by the contract, because the broker has express authority to act.
- [ ] C. Maco will not be liable for any negligent acts of the broker committed while acting on Maco's behalf.
- [ ] D. The broker will have the same authority as he would have had if Maco's identity had been disclosed.

Frost's accountant and business manager has the authority to

- [ ] **A. Mortgage Frost's business property.**
- [ ] **B. Obtain bank loans for Frost.**
- [ ] **C. Insure Frost's property against fire loss.**
- [ ] **D. Sell Frost's business.**

Easy Corp. is a real estate developer and regularly engages real estate brokers to act on its behalf in acquiring parcels of land. The brokers are authorized to enter into such contracts, but are instructed to do so in their own names without disclosing Easy's identity or its relationship to the transaction. If a broker enters into a contract with a seller on Easy's behalf:

- [ ] A. The broker will have the same actual authority as if Easy's identity had been disclosed.
- [ ] B. Easy will be bound by the contract because of the broker's apparent authority.
- [ ] C. Easy will not be liable for any negligent acts committed by the broker while acting on Easy's behalf.
- [ ] D. The broker will not be personally bound by the contract, because the broker has express authority to act.

REG 5-1

FEDERAL SECURITIES REGULATION

Defining a "Security"

The Registration Process

Exempt Transactions and Securities

Liability Provisions: 1933 Act

Purposes, Requirements and Provisions of the 1934 Act

Criminal Liability

Selected Questions (3)

DEFINING A "SECURITY"

Defining a "Security"

The federal securities laws define "security" by example

Common examples are: corporate stock, bonds, debentures, collateral trust certificates, puts, calls, straddles, options

Catch-all categories include: investment contracts and "**any interest or instrumentality commonly known as a security**"

Defining a "Security"

Elements of investment contract:

- Investment of money
- In a common enterprise
- With an expectation of profit
- To be earned primarily by the actions of others

THE REGISTRATION PROCESS

Procedures

Issuer files a registration statement with the SEC and then waits 20 business days for the SEC to declare the registration statement effective

- During the 20-day waiting period, the SEC theoretically reviews the registration statements

Three periods allow different activities; roughly:

1. Pre-filing: no offers and no sales
2. Waiting: oral offers and a few written offers, but no sales
3. Post-effective: offers and sales now okay

Procedures

The primary written document allowed during the waiting period is the "red herring" prospectus, which is replaced by the final prospectus after the effective date

Securities Offering Reform Package (SORP)

Shelf registration was enacted to allow the largest companies to file one registration statement to cover all shares it intended to issue during the next two years

In 2005, in the SORP, the SEC enacted "company registration" for very large firms. Two primary things to remember are...

Securities Offering Reform Package (SORP)

WKSIs. The biggest companies are designated Well-Known Seasoned Issuers (WKSIs) and they can essentially offer their shares without regard to the rules mentioned before because the market is always well informed about them

FWPs. WKSIs can freely use supplemental written literature called "free writing prospectuses" (FWPs) if they file them with the SEC

- Other issuers can also use FWPs under proper circumstances and at proper times

EXEMPT TRANSACTIONS AND SECURITIES

Exempt Securities

A number of securities are exempt from the registration process, primarily because they are subject to alternative forms of regulation, including:

- Bank and government securities
- Federally-regulated common carriers
- Bankruptcy receivers/trustees
- Insurance and annuity policies

There are three primary types of exemptions:

1. Small Offering Exemptions
2. Private Placement Exemptions
3. Intrastate Offering Exemptions

Exempt Transactions

Regulation D clarifies the key small offering and private placement exemptions mentioned earlier

- **Rule 504**: allows qualified issuer to raise up to $1m in a 12-month period without registering
- **Rule 505**: allows qualified issuer to raise up to $5m in a 12-month period without registering
- **Rule 506**: allows qualified issuers to raise unlimited amounts without registering, if sell only to sophisticated investors or others represented by "purchaser representatives"

Blue Sky Laws

Much state securities regulation has been preempted by federal law, but remember:

States can:

- Enforce antifraud rules
- Require "notice" filing

States cannot:

- Engage in "merit regulation"
- Register "covered" securities

1933 ACT LIABILITY PROVISIONS

Introduction

There are three key liability provisions under the 1933 Act.

1. Sec. 11
2. Sec. 12(a)(1)
3. Sec. 12(a)(2)

Section 11

Essence: Section 11 remedies false statements or omissions in a registration statement as of the effective date

What a plaintiff must prove to win:

1. A false statement or omission in the RS on the effective date
2. Materiality
3. Tracing
4. Damages

Section 11

Potential defendants:

1. The issuer
2. Officers & Directors
3. Underwriters
4. "Experts"

Defenses include:

1. Due diligence
2. Alternate causation
3. Statute of limitations

Section 12(a)(1)

Essence: remedies violation of Section 5' s registration provisions:

1. Sale of unregistered securities
2. Failure to deliver prospectus
3. Use of inadequate prospectus;
4. Offer before RS is filed

Section 12(a)(1)

What plaintiffs must show to win:

1. D violated Section 5
2. D was a "seller"
3. P lost money

Defenses:

1. Statute of limitations

Section 12(a)(2)

Essence: remedies false statements and omissions in oral statements and in "free writing"

What a plaintiff must prove to win:

1. False statements or omissions;
2. Materiality
3. D is a "seller"
4. Tracing
5. Damages

Defenses:

1. Due diligence
2. Alternative loss causation
3. Statute of limitations

PURPOSES, REQUIREMENTS AND PROVISIONS OF THE 1934 ACT

Purposes of the 1934 Act

The '34 Act, among other things:

- Punishes fraud in the secondary markets
- Regulates the securities industry
- Created the SEC
- Created the periodic disclosure system

Disclosure Requirements

In the '34 Act's Periodic Disclosure System:

- "Reporting companies" include firms that are:
  - Exchange-listed, and
  - Have 500 shareholders and $10m in assets

Must file:

- Form 10 (when they become reporting companies)
- Form 10-K (annually)
- Form 10-Q (quarterly)
- Form 8-K (between quarters if important developments occur)

Key Provisions

There are two key provisions:

1. Section 10(b)
2. Section 18(a)

Section 10(b)

Section 10(b) is the most significant securities law provision in the world

It punishes fraudulent statements and omissions in the purchase or sale of securities in virtually every setting:

- Public company or private company
- Primary market or secondary market
- Broad range of defendants, including accountants

Section 10(b)

What a plaintiff must prove to win a 10(b) case:

- False statement or omission
- Materiality
- Reliance
- Causation
- Purchase or Sale
- Damages

Defenses.

1. Statute of Limitations

Section 18(a) Provides:

"Any person who shall make or cause to be made any statement in any application, report, or **document filed** pursuant to [this Act], which statement was at the time and in light of the circumstances under which it was made false or misleading with respect to any material fact, shall be liable to any person (not knowing that such statement was false or misleading) who, **in reliance upon such statement**, shall have purchased or sold a security at a price which was affected by such statement, for damages caused by such reliance, **unless the person sued shall prove that he acted in good faith and had no knowledge that such statement was false or misleading.**"

Section 18(a)

Courts hold that plaintiffs establish a prima facie case for recovery by showing:

- Defendant made or caused to be made a false or misleading statement or omission
- In a filed document
- Materiality
- Plaintiff's purchase or sale of securities
- Plaintiff's "eyeball" reliance
- Causation
- Damages

Section 18(a)

Defenses:

- D acted in good faith and without knowledge that the statement was false or misleading; and
- Statute of limitations (1-year/3-year)

CRIMINAL LIABILITY

Criminal Liability

The intentional violation of **any** provision of the 1933 or 1934 Acts is a crime

Criminal charges are brought by the Department of Justice

Burden of proof = beyond a reasonable doubt

For a CPA to be liable for damages under the anti-fraud provisions of Section 10(b) and rule 10b-5 of the Securities Exchange Act of 1934, a plaintiff must prove all of the following, except that

- **A. The plaintiff relied on the financial statements audited by the CPA.**
- **B. The CPA violated generally accepted auditing standards.**
- **C. There was a material misrepresentation of fact in the financial statements audited by the CPA.**
- **D. The CPA acted with scienter.**

Petty Corp. made a public offering subject to the Securities Act of 1933. In connection with the offering, Ward & Co., CPAs rendered an unqualified opinion on Petty's financial statements included in the SEC registration statement.
Huff purchased 500 of the offered shares. Huff has brought an action against Ward under Section 11 of the Securities Act of 1933 for losses resulting from misstatements of facts in the financial statements included in the registration statement.

To succeed, Huff must prove that

- [ ] **A. Ward performed the audit negligently.**
- [ ] **B. The misstatements were material.**
- [ ] **C. Ward rendered its opinion with knowledge of material misstatements.**
- [ ] **D. Huff relied on the financial statements included in the registration statement.**

Non-WKSI issuer World Corp. wanted to make a public offering of its common stock. On May 10, World prepares and files a registration statement with the SEC.
On May 20, World places a "tombstone ad," announcing that it was making a public offering. On May 25, World issues a preliminary prospectus and the registration statement became effective on May 30.

On what date may World first sell the shares?

- [ ] **A. May 10.**
- [ ] **B. May 20.**
- [ ] **C. May 25.**
- [ ] **D. May 30.**

REG 5-2

OTHER FEDERAL LAWS AND REGULATION 1

Anti-Discrimination

Employee Welfare

Federal Unemployment Tax Act (FUTA)

Fair Labor Standards Act (FLSA)

Employee Benefits

Selected Questions (2)

ANTI-DISCRIMINATION

Title VII of the Civil Rights Act of 1964

Punishes employment discrimination based on:

- Race
- Color
- Religion
- Sex (Covers sexual harassment - including same-sex harassment)
- National Origin

Defenses:

- **B**ona **F**ide **O**ccupational **Q**ualification (BFOQ)
- Legitimate seniority or merit system

Age Discrimination in Employment Act (ADEA)

The ADEA protects (workers over 40) against age discrimination:

- No mandatory retirement
- No discrimination in terms & conditions of employment

Americans with Disabilities Act (ADA)

The ADA:

- Aims to encourage companies to make use of the talents of the disabled
- Protects: qualified individuals with a disability that substantially limits a major life activity
- Requires: reasonable accommodations

EMPLOYEE WELFARE

Social Security Act

Purpose: to provide partial replacement of earnings when worker retires

"Fully insured" workers contributed for at least 40 quarters (10 years)

- "Currently insured" workers may still receive some benefits

Also funds Medicare, covering:

- Portion of medical costs of those 65 or older, and
- Some benefits for younger disabled workers

Does not fund Medicaid

Federal Insurance Contributions Act (FICA)

Social Security and Medicare (but not Medicaid) are financed through payroll taxes imposed upon:

- Employers
  - Pay half and withhold other half from employee's salary
- Employees

Tax applies only to "wages," such as:

- Salary
- Commissions
- Bonuses
- Fringe Benefits

Federal Insurance Contributions Act (FICA)

Doesn't apply to "passive" income, such as:

- Reimbursed employee expenses
- Interest income

Payroll Tax Liability

If corporations do not withhold payroll taxes, 26 USC 6672 may impose them upon "responsible persons," who:

Were required to "collect, truthfully account for, and pay over" the tax

- Key question: Did the person have the discretion to decide which, when and in what order debts or taxes would be paid?

Willfully failed to do so

- Doesn't require desire to defraud the government, only that he spent money in other ways while aware of the tax liability

Self-Employment Contributions Act

The self-employed pay social security tax on their own self-employed taxable earnings:

- Pay as employer and employee
- Only on active income

FEDERAL UNEMPLOYMENT TAX ACT (FUTA)

Federal Unemployment Tax Act (FUTA)

Purpose: provide benefits to workers who lose their jobs and can't find new ones

FUTA taxes: paid by employer only

Benefits are paid by states which also collect taxes that are offset by federal contribution

Coverage: mandatory for qualified employees

To be eligible for unemployment compensation, must be:

- Involuntarily terminated
- Available and looking for work, and
- Not receiving disqualifying income, such as:
  - Retirement Benefits
  - Disability Benefits

FAIR LABOR STANDARDS ACT (FLSA)

Fair Labor Standards Act (FLSA)

Four major sections:

1. Minimum Wages
2. Overtime Standard
3. Child Labor Restrictions
4. Equal Pay (for women) Provision

Fair Labor Standards Act (FLSA)

Minimum Wage:

- Year-end bonuses not considered
- Independent Contractors not covered

Overtime

- Employees working > 40 hours/wk. must be paid 1-1/2 times their hourly wage for extra hours
- No offset for weeks when work less than 40 hours

Neither Min. Wage nor Overtime provisions apply to:

- Executives
- Professional Employees, like CPAs

EMPLOYEE BENEFITS

Employee Retirement Income Security Act (ERISA)

Does not require employers to provide employee pension or welfare benefit plans, but does:

- Encourage them to do so via tax benefits
- Prohibit discrimination in such plan

Employee Retirement Income Security Act (ERISA)

Types of Pension Plans:

- Defined-Benefit Plans: employees are guaranteed a specified monthly income for life
- Defined-Contribution Plans: employers promise to contribute to a retirement account that hopefully will be wisely invested
  - Pension Benefit Guaranty Corp. insures defined benefit plans only

"Fiduciaries" who manage ERISA retirement plans may be sued for violations of the act

Pension and Retirement Plan Liability

Fiduciaries include anyone who:

- Exercises discretionary management or control over the plan
- Renders investment advice for a fee, or
- Has discretionary authority in administering plan

Accountants who merely audit plans will not be "fiduciaries"

COBRA

Purpose: Provide health insurance in some circumstances after a job loss
COBRA applies if employee lose health benefits due to:

- Termination (includes firings, layoffs, and quits)
- Reduced hours

Coverage: An extra 18 months, or 29 if insured was disabled

Note: employee pays for this continued coverage

Family Medical Leave Act

Purpose: balance employees' workplace demands with family needs

Entitled to 12 weeks unpaid leave w/o losing job, if eligible:

- Worked for employer at least 12 months, and
- At least 1,250 hours during previous 12 months

Family Medical Leave Act

Leave provided for:

- Birth of a child
- Employee's serious health condition
- Caring for family member with serious health condition

Under the Fair Labor Standards Act, if a covered, non-exempt employee works consecutive weeks of 45, 42, 38, and 33 hours, how many hours of overtime must be paid to the employee?

- A. 0
- B. 7
- C. 18
- D. 20

Which of the following types of income is subject to taxation under the provisions of the Federal Insurance Contributions Act (FICA)?

- [ ] A. **Interest earned on municipal bonds.**
- [ ] B. **Capital gains of $3,000.**
- [ ] C. **A vehicle received as a productivity award.**
- [ ] D. **Dividends of $2,500.**

REG 5-3

OTHER FEDERAL LAWS AND REGULATION 2

Health and Safety

Union and Employee Relations

Antitrust

Copyright

Patents

Money Laundering

Selected Questions (3)

HEALTH AND SAFETY

Workers' Compensation Act

Purpose: provide nearly-automatic compensation for employees who suffer work-related injuries or disease

- Doesn't cover independent contractors

Mechanism: employers carry WC insurance

Workers' Compensation Act

Benefits: given automatically for on-the-job injuries.
Quid pro quo: employees cannot sue boss, except for:

- Intentional torts, or
- Gross negligence

Can sue third-parties

Employees' carelessness usually doesn't bar recovery of WC benefits

Occupational Safety & Health Act (OSHA)

Purpose: Promote job safety

Enforced by: Occupational Safety & Health Administration (OSHA)

Employers must:

- Provide a workplace free from "recognized hazards" likely to cause death or serious physical harm (injury or disease)
- Comply with OSHA standards
- Keep records of job-related injuries and report them to OSHA

Occupational Safety & Health Act (OSHA)

Employee rights if a violation threatens physical harm or injury:

- File a request for inspection
- Refuse in good faith to work
- Not be retaliated against for exercising rights

UNION AND EMPLOYEE RELATIONS

The National Labor Relations Act

NLRA protects employees':

- Right to form, join, or assist unions
- Right to bargain collectively through their chosen union; and
- Right to engage in concerted activities (such as strikes) for the purpose of collective bargaining

Process: Once 30% of eligible employees sign authorization cards, an employee group may petition for an election to certify a union

Unfair Labor Practices

Employers may not:

- Interfere with union organizing efforts
- Should not bribe workers to vote against a union
- Threaten workers
- Dominate or interfere with the union
- Discriminate against a union member, or
- Refuse to bargain collectively

Unfair Labor Practices

Unions may not:

- Coerce employees
- Require employers to agree not to do business with nonunion companies
- Refuse to bargain collectively, or
- Engage in an illegal strike or secondary boycott

Strikes

- To be legal, strikes must be supported by a majority of members
- Must give employer 60 days notice before striking for modification of a collective bargaining agreement
- "Wildcat" strikes by a minority of workers are illegal
- Secondary strikes against third-parties to coerce them to oppose management are illegal
- Workers generally have no right to picket on the employer's private property

ANTITRUST

Primary Statutes

Sherman Act

- Section 1 prohibits conspiracies in restraint of trade
- Section 2 prohibits monopolies and attempts to monopolize

Clayton Act

- Section 2 prohibits price discrimination
- Section 3 prohibits tying and exclusive dealing arrangements
- Section 7 forbids anticompetitive mergers

Primary Statutes

FTC Act

- Section 5 prohibits "unfair methods of competition"

Robinson-Patman Act

- Section 2 further addresses price discrimination

Conspiracies in Restraint of Trade

Key to violation: **collusion**

Rule of reason: collusion is illegal only if it "unreasonably" restricts competition

If primary purpose of collusion is to restrain trade, then it is likely illegal even if the effect on competition is slight

Conspiracies in Restraint of Trade

If primary purpose of collusion is not to restrain trade, then it is probably okay unless competition is substantially diminished

Per se illegal:

- Price fixing
- Market division
- Boycotts

Monopolization

Key: having an overwhelming degree of market power enabling firm to control prices or exclude competition

Market Power is the ability to raise prices without losing most customers

Markets may be:

- Product markets (e.g., fasteners such as buttons, zippers, etc.), or
- Geographic markets

Intent to Monopolize

Intent is typically inferred from:

- Predatory (below cost) pricing with intent to drive out competitors, or
- Nonprice predation via such means as:
  - Tying up customers with long-term contracts unjustified by cost savings
  - Taking key employees from a small competitor
  - Falsely disparaging competitors' products
  - Sabotage

Mergers

Horizontal mergers between competitors are especially likely to diminish competition and be illegal if the combined market share exceeds 30%

Vertical mergers between firms in a distribution chain are unlikely to be illegal unless the vertical market is already concentrated and both firms have large market shares

Conglomerate mergers that are neither horizontal nor vertical (e.g., a steel company buys an ice cream company), are probably okay

COPYRIGHT

Overview

There are four primary types of intellectual property:

1. Trademarks are any distinctive words, phrases, symbols, or designs adopted for the purpose of identifying the origin of goods being offered for sale. The Nike "swoosh" is an example.

Overview

There are four primary types of intellectual property:

2. Trade secrets e.g. Coca-Cola formula. A trade secret is any type of knowledge that is not generally known and is not readily available through legal means, if the knowledge gives its owner a competitive advantage over rivals who lack the knowledge.

Overview

There are four primary types of intellectual property:

3. Copyrights

4. Patents

Introduction to Copyrights

Copyrights are designed to protect "original works of authorship"

Purpose: encourage creative expressions such as:

- books
- music
- drama
- graphics
- choreography

Elements of Copyrightability

An expressive work is protectable under copyright law if it is:

A. Fixed in some tangible medium of expression

B. Creative; and

C. Original

Copyright Procedure

Copyright procedure is self-executing. Once an expression is reduced to a tangible medium, e.g., words are written on paper or sounds are recorded, the author is entitled to copyright protection. No filing is needed.

However, registering a copyright with the U.S. Copyright Office may be a good idea because it protects authors in countries that have not signed the Berne Convention and wards off "innocent infringement" claims.

Length of Protection

Currently, copyright law in the U.S. protects a work for the life of the author, plus 70 years

A work-for-hire: shorter of: 95 years from the date of publication or 120 years from the date of creation

- Example: A work for hire occurs when ABC Co. hires musician Jan to write a jingle to advertise its new product, intending to own the copyright itself

Elements of a Copyright Infringement Claim

An author of a book, for example, may sue the author of a similar book by showing:

A. Ownership of a valid copyright; and

B. Unauthorized copying of original elements of P's work by D
   - Intent to copy is not an element of the tort of copyright infringement

Fair Use Defense

There are several defenses to a copyright infringement claim, including the "fair use" defense, which may protect uses for purposes such as criticism, comment, news reporting, teaching, scholarship, or research.

Example:

- A teacher makes multiple copies of an article in today's newspaper for purposes of facilitating classroom discussion, or
- A literary critic quotes some lines from a novel for purposes of illustrating his point about how good or bad the author's writing is.

PATENTS

Introduction

A patent is a government-granted exclusive right to make, use or sell an invention

Purpose: to encourage inventive activity

Patentable Subject Matter

The law recognizes patents for:

1. Processes
2. Machines
3. Products
4. Compositions of matter
5. Any improvements upon these
6. New plant varieties

Patentable Subject Matter

The law does not patent:

1. Printed matter (which is the subject of copyright law)
2. Naturally occurring substances
3. Ideas, or
4. Scientific principles

Patentable Subject Matter

In recent years, methods of doing business (such as Amazon's "one-click" purchasing system) have been protected

These are all "utility" patents, although the law also recognizes "design patents" for non-functional ornamental design elements in a functional product

Elements of Patentability

An invention may be patented if:

1. It involves patentable subject matter
2. It is useful
   - A product is not useful if it:
     1. Doesn't work
     2. Is a hoax, or
     3. Is merely an abstract idea
3. It is novel; and
4. It is nonobvious (to a person with ordinary skill in that area)

Patent Filing

Unlike a copyright, which is self-executing, a patent requires filing with the U.S. Patent and Trademark Office (PTO)

With some exceptions, the application must be filed within one year after the invention was created

Length of Protection

Utility patent: 20 years from the date of filing

Design patent: 14 years from the date of filing

MONEY LAUNDERING

Introduction

Definition: **Money laundering** is the process by which one conceals the existence, illegal source, or illegal application of income, and disguises that income to make it appear legitimate

Is relevant to such activities as:

1. Drug dealing
2. Terrorism, and
3. Income tax evasion

Key Statutes

Bank Secrecy Act of 1970 requires record keeping and reporting by banks and other financial institutions to trace the movement of currency into and out of the U.S. or deposited into banks

Bank Secrecy Act of 1970 requires banks to

1. Report cash transactions over $10,000
2. Identify persons conducting all transactions, and
3. Maintain a traceable paper trail

Key Statutes

31 U.S.C. §5324. This statute helps prevent evasion of the BSA by making it illegal to break large transactions down into pieces smaller than $10,000 each in order to evade these reporting requirements

Money Laundering Control Act of 1986. In the criminal area, the key statute is the Money Laundering Control Act of 1986, which has been amended repeatedly over the years, but remains composed primarily of two provisions:

1. 18 U.S.C. 1956
2. 18 U.S.C. 1957

Money Laundering

Prohibited Transactions and Transportation. Section 1956 contains two primary prohibitions:

1. It prohibits **transaction money laundering** where the prohibited act is the financial transaction itself. Four primary examples are financial transactions conducted with intent to
   - Promote unlawful activity
   - Engage in violations of Sections 7201 or 7206 of the Tax Code
   - Attempt to conceal the nature, location, source, ownership or control of proceeds from specified unlawful activity; and
   - Attempt to avoid state or federal reporting requirements

Money Laundering

2. It prohibits **transportation money laundering**, the transportation of criminally derived funds into or out of the United States with the intent to
   - Promote illegal activity
   - Transport illegal proceeds in an attempt to hide them; or
   - Transport illegal proceeds to avoid reporting requirements

Money Laundering: Property Transactions

Section 1957 addresses monetary transactions in criminally derived property over $10,000

The property might be derived from unlawful activities such as drug dealing, gambling, mail fraud, wire fraud, or any of an exceedingly long list of offenses

Role of Accountants

As feds have gotten better at tracking cash, bad guys are increasingly relying on attorneys and accountants to help them evade detection

Sam patents a "rat zapper," a shoe-box-sized device that uses bait to lure in a rat and then kills it with an electrical charge. Lon files a patent application for a "gopher zapper," a slightly bigger device that uses bait to lure in a gopher and then kills it with an electrical charge. What is true regarding Lon's application?

- [ ] **A. It will probably be denied, as not being useful.**
- [ ] **B. It will probably be denied as not involving patentable subject matter.**
- [ ] **C. It will probably be denied for failing the non-obviousness requirement.**
- [ ] **D. All of the above are correct.**

A small computer software firm wishes to sue Microsoft for monopolizing its market. What must the firm establish in order to win the case?

- [ ] **A. Microsoft enjoys overwhelming market power.**
- [ ] **B. Microsoft intends to monopolize the market.**
- [ ] **C. A and B.**
- [ ] **D. None of the above.**

Which one of the following statements concerning worker's compensation laws is generally correct?

- [ ] **A. Employers are strictly liable, without regard to whether or not they are at fault.**
- [ ] **B. Worker's compensation benefits are not available if the employee is negligent.**
- [ ] **C. Worker's compensation awards are not reviewable by the courts.**
- [ ] **D. The amount of damages recoverable is based on comparative negligence.**

REG 5-4

BUSINESS STRUCTURE 1

Selection of a Business Entity

Formation

Operations

Termination

Financial Structure

Selected Questions (3)

SELECTION OF A BUSINESS ENTITY

Introduction

There are numerous ways to organize a business enterprise

Forms are often chosen because they minimize taxation or liability of the owners, or both

Sole Proprietorship

A single-owner business. The firm's assets and liabilities belong solely to its owner

General partnership

An association of two or more persons to carry on as co-owners a business for profit

Profits are allocated and taxable directly to the partners

The partnership is a legal entity for most purposes

Joint venture

A one-shot general partnership-type relationship

Governed by general partnership law, so any distinction between the two is generally unimportant for legal purposes

Limited Partnership

A partnership with at least one general partner and at least one limited partner

Limited partners give up certain of the general management rights that partners in a general partnership have in exchange for limited liability

A limited partnership must have at least one general partner who will be generally liable for the firm's obligations

Limited Liability Partnership (LLP)

Carries greater protection from liability than either general or limited partnerships

Created primarily to protect professionals from undue malpractice liability arising from errors of their partners

Limited Liability Partnership (LLP)

Liable only for

1. Their own malpractice, and
2. The malpractice of those they directly supervise

Most states also protect partners from personal liability for LLP contractual obligations

Must carry minimum levels of malpractice insurance

Limited Liability Limited Partnership (LLLP):

- Allows the general partner(s) of a limited partnership to enjoy limited liability, just like limited partners
- Third-parties must protect themselves contractually
- LPs may become LLLPs merely by including a one-line statement to that effect in their certificate of limited partnership
- Both GPs and LPs will remain liable for the consequences of torts that they personally commit while carrying out partnership business
- Authorized in only 20 states or so

Corporation

- An artificial legal entity whose owners (shareholders) typically enjoy limited liability
- Creation of the notion of an artificial legal entity in order to encourage people to invest in others' business ideas is one of the great advances in Western legal thought
- On the other hand: Double taxation
- By intelligent tax planning one may minimize the impact of double taxation

Subchapter S corporation

Can eliminate the double taxation that most corporations (called Subchapter C corporations) face by meeting certain requirements of Subchapter S of the Internal Revenue Code, including:

- No more than 100 shareholders
- Unanimous election
- Only certain types of shareholders

Limited Liability Company (LLC)

- Allows owners of businesses to gain the liability-limiting advantages of the corporate form while enjoying the single, pass-through tax benefits of the partnership form of business
- Can operate like a general partnership (member-managed) or like a corporation (manager-managed)
- Virtually all states allow "single-member" LLCs
- Most popular form today

Limited Liability Company (LLC)

Generally, LLCs will be the best form for most small businesses, LLPs for professional firms such as accounting firms and law firms, and corporations for very large entities, such as IBM or General Motors

FORMATION

Formation

Two types of organizations do not require formal filing:

1. Sole Proprietorships

2. General Partnerships
   - May file: Statement of Partnership Authority

Formation

All the other forms require filing with the Secretary of State or some comparable state office:

- Corporations: Articles of Incorporation
- LLCs: Operating Agreement
- LPs: Partnership Agreement
- LLPs: Partnership Agreement
- LLLPs: Partnership Agreement

Formation

Articles of Incorporation must include:

- Name (indicating corp. status: "Corp.", "Inc.", etc.)
- Number of authorized shares
- Address of registered office
- Name of registered agent at that office
- Names and addresses of incorporators

Basic Steps in Organizing a Corporation

1. Execute articles of incorporation and file with Sec. of State

2. Hold organizational meeting
   - Elect board of directors
   - Adopt promoters' contracts

Promoters and Liability

Definition: A person who takes the initiative in founding and organizing a corporation

Owes fiduciary duties to:
- The proposed corporation
- Other promoters
- Contemplated investors

May profit in contracts with corporation, if:
- Approval from a fully informed board
- Approval from fully informed original shareholders

Promoters and Liability

Firm is liable on promoters' contracts if board adopts them (expressly or impliedly)

These corporate rules are being applied to LLCs and LLPs that face similar situations

OPERATIONS

Introduction

How firms operate necessarily varies with their particular structure

Example: Sole Proprietorship

The sole owner of a sole proprietorship makes all important decisions or delegates these decisions to someone of his or her choosing

Example: GP & LLP

Absent agreement to the contrary, all partners have equal rights in the management and conduct of business affairs

Absent agreement to the contrary, majority vote governs all ordinary course-of-business matters

Example: GP & LLP

However, unanimity is needed to take actions contrary to the partnership agreement or to take action regarding "**extraordinary matters,**" which might include such actions as:

1. Admitting a new partner to the partnership
2. Assigning partnership property
3. Disposing of goodwill; or
4. Doing any other act which would make it impossible to carry on the ordinary business of the partnership

Example: LLP

An LLP is essentially a general partnership carrying limited liability

LLPs are sometimes called limited liability general partnerships, and operate much as general partnerships

Example: LP & LLLP

In these two forms of limited partnerships, one or more general partners make management decisions while limited partners generally sit on the sidelines playing the role of passive investors

If limited partners in LPs (not LLLPs) leave the sidelines and become actively involved in control of the limited partnership, they may forfeit their limited liability as to creditors who rely upon their apparent role as general partners

Example: LLC

LLCs can operate in one of two ways:

1. **Owner-managed**: LLC members may choose to run the business themselves, as if they were general partners (enjoying limited liability)

2. **Manager-managed**: LLC members may choose, on the other hand, to delegate managerial powers to one or more members or non-members

Example: Corporation

General operations.

1. Shareholders elect directors
2. Directors select officers
3. Officers run things day-to-day

Piercing the Corporate Veil

Because corporations are distinct legal entities, their obligations are typically not visited upon their shareholders personally

- However, when small, closely-held corporations are involved, it is possible that courts might "pierce the corporate veil" and reach into shareholders' pockets to satisfy corporate obligations
- Courts will not pierce the corporate veil of public corporations
- Key reason to pierce: "to prevent the corporate form from being used to defeat public convenience, justify wrong, protect fraud, or defend crime"

Piercing the Corporate Veil

The following considerations (usually in combination) may induce a court to pierce the corporate veil:

- Commingling of funds and other assets of the corporation with those of individual shareholders
- Diversion of the corporation's funds or assets to the personal use of shareholders
- Failure to maintain the necessary corporate formalities
- Failure to adequately capitalize the corporation for the reasonably foreseeable risks of the enterprise

Piercing the Corporate Veil

Courts tend to apply comparable factors in deciding whether to pierce LLCs and LLPs

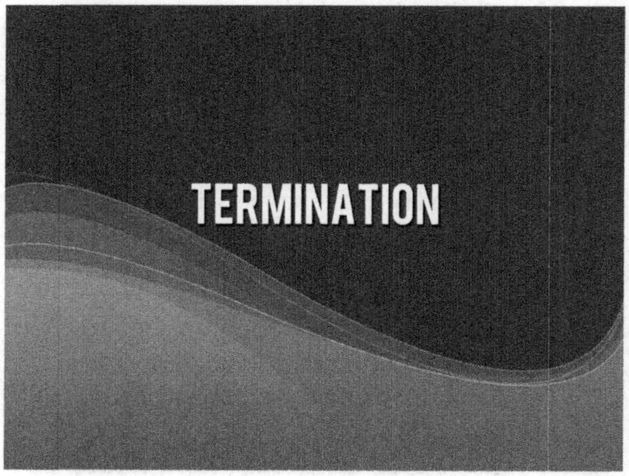

Introduction

As in other areas, termination rules for firms vary with their form of organization

Example: Sole Proprietorship

Sole Proprietorships terminate when their sole owner dies or otherwise departs the business

Example: Partnership

Detailed rules are set out in RUPA regarding termination of general partnerships. Practices regarding LPs, LLPs, LLLPs, and even LLCs are quite similar

Under RUPA, addition or subtraction of partners does not automatically lead to dissolution of the partnership (as was formerly the case)

Example: Partnership

Rather, causes of "dissociation" of a partner from the partnership include:

1. Notice of a partner's express will to dissolve the partnership
2. Death of a partner
3. Bankruptcy of a partner
4. Expulsion of a partner

Example: Partnership

After a partner dissociates, one of two things must happen. Either:

1. The partnership dissolves and is wound up, or
2. The departing partner is bought out

Example: Partnership

Buy-Out Formula:

Value of account on day of dissociation - Damages caused (if dissociation was wrongful)*

* Valued by greater of liquidation value or going-concern value

Example: Partnership

Waiting Period: 90-day "cooling off" period between dissociation and liquidation

Priorities in winding up the partnership business:

1. Creditors (including partners) are paid first.
2. If there's not enough money to pay creditors, partners will have to contribute
3. If funds are left over after paying creditors, then the partnership shall make a distribution to partners

Example: Corporation

Corporations may be voluntarily dissolved upon approval of their directors and shareholders.

1. Typically, a majority of directors vote to propose dissolution and a majority of shareholders vote to approve the proposal.

Example: Corporation

Corporations may be involuntarily dissolved administratively by the Secretary of State for such reasons as:

1. Failure to pay franchise taxes;
2. Failure to file annual reports; or
3. Failure to properly establish and maintain a registered agent or office.

Corporations may be involuntarily dissolved judicially in:

1. An action by the attorney general, where:
   - The corporation fraudulently obtained approval for its articles of incorporation, or
   - The corporation has abused its legal authority.

Example: Corporation

Corporations may be involuntarily dissolved judicially in:

2. An action by shareholders
   - If management is deadlocked
   - If those controlling the corporation are acting in an illegal or oppressive way, such as by looting the corporation or wasting its assets; or
   - If the shareholders are deadlocked and cannot elect directors

Example: Corporation

An action by creditors if a judgment creditor's claim is unsatisfied and the corporation is insolvent or if the corporation admits in writing that the creditor's claim is due and owing and that it is insolvent

Other major organic changes (in addition to dissolution) include:

1. Sale of all or substantially all of a corporation's assets (not in the ordinary course of business), and
2. Mergers or consolidations with other corporations

Example: Corporation

Shareholder interests are protected in such transactions that can so fundamentally alter their interests by:

1. **Procedures**: directors owing a fiduciary duty must propose and shareholders must approve in a vote; and
2. **Appraisal rights**: dissenting shareholders may request that their shares be purchased at a court-valued rate pursuant to their appraisal rights (also called dissenters' rights)

FINANCIAL STRUCTURE

Introduction

All the partnership forms (GPs, LPs, LLP, LLLPs) automatically allocate income to partners or members and can elect single (pass-through) taxation, so the more complicated financial issues tend to relate to corporations

Partnership Financial Matters

Capital Accounts: Under RUPA, each partner is deemed to have an account that is:

1. Credited with an amount equal to the money plus the value of any other property, net of the amount of any liabilities, the partner contributes to the partnership, and the partner's share of the partnership profits

Partnership Financial Matters

Contribution
+ Share of Profits
- Liabilities
= Account Balance

Partnership Financial Matters

2. Account is charged with an amount equal to the money plus the value of any other property, net of the amount of any liabilities, distributed by the partnership to the partner and the partner's share of partnership losses

Account balance reduced by distributions
+
share of losses

Partnership Financial Matters

Partners are to be reimbursed for:

1. Payments made and indemnified for liabilities incurred in the ordinary course of the partnership business; and
2. Advances to the partnership made beyond agreed capital contributions

As noted elsewhere, absent agreement to the contrary, partners share profits and losses equally

Corporate Financial Structure

Issuing Shares: Corporate shares should not be issued unless two tests are met:

1. **Quality tests**: shares can be issued in exchange for cash, promissory notes, or any other items of tangible or intangible value to the corporation
2. **Quantity tests**: must be issued for at least par (face value) or amount authorized by board

Corporate Financial Structure

If shares are issued for less than amount authorized, then the following may be liable to creditors and other shareholders:

1. Directors who allowed the sale
2. Buyers who paid too little
3. Transferees of original buyer who both know that he paid too little and who pay too little themselves

Corporate Financial Structure

Dividends and Other Distributions

1. Authorized by Board of Directors
2. Must:
   - Be consistent with shareholders' rights
   - Not render corp. unable to meet its bills as they come due ("bankruptcy insolvency")
   - Not leave corp. with fewer assets than liabilities ("equity insolvency")

LLC Financial Structure

The key LLC financial provisions tend to reflect comparable corporate (or, occasionally, partnership) provisions

Contributions to an LLC, as with a corporation or partnership, may be made in cash, property or services

Like corporations, LLCs may not make distributions to members if after doing so the firm would be insolvent

Lewis, Clark, and Beal enter into a written agreement to form a partnership. The agreement requires that the partners make the following capital contributions: Lewis, $40,000; Clark, $30,000; and Beal, $10,000.
It is also agreed that, in the event that the partnership experiences losses in excess of available capital, Beal will contribute additional capital to the extent of the losses. The partnership agreement is otherwise silent about division of profits and losses.

Which of the following statements is correct?

- [ ] **A. Profits are to be divided among the partners in proportion to their relative capital contributions.**
- [ ] **B. Profits are to be divided equally among the partners.**
- [ ] **C. Losses will be allocated in a manner different from the allocation of profits, because the partners contributed different amounts of capital.**
- [ ] **D. Beal's obligation to contribute additional capital would have an effect on the allocation of profit or loss to Beal.**

The partners of College Assoc., a general partnership, decide to dissolve the partnership and agree that none of the partners will continue to use the partnership name.

Under the Uniform Partnership Act, which of the following events will occur on dissolution of the partnership?

	Each partner's existing liability will be discharged.	Each partner's apparent authority will continue.
☐	Yes	Yes
☐	Yes	No
☐	No	Yes
☐	No	No

Which of the following statements is correct concerning the similarities between a limited partnership and a corporation?

- [ ] **A. Each is created under a statute and must file a copy of its certificate with the proper state authorities.**
- [ ] **B. All corporate stockholders and all partners in a limited partnership have limited liability.**
- [ ] **C. Both are recognized for federal income-tax purposes as taxable entities.**
- [ ] **D. Both are statutorily permitted to exist in perpetuity.**

REG 5-5

BUSINESS STRUCTURE 2

Rights & Duties

Authority of Owners & Managers

Selected Questions (1)

RIGHTS AND DUTIES

Introduction

In any firm, the rights and duties of owners, officers, employees, creditors, and other stakeholders are very important

The rules regarding LPs, LLPs, and LLLPs will be roughly the same as for general partnerships

General Partnerships

Absent agreement to the contrary partners are entitled to:

1. Equal management rights; and
2. Have their capital contribution repaid and share equally in profits

General Partnerships

Property Rights:

1. Partnership property belongs to the partnership
2. Partners are entitled to use or possess partnership property, but only on behalf of the partnership

General Partnerships

Charging Orders:

1. Creditors of individual partners may not seize partnership property to satisfy individual debts of partners
2. Rather, they may go to court to obtain a charging order in which the judge orders the other partners to pay any distribution due to the debtor partner to that partner's creditor instead

General Partnerships

Compensation: Partners are not entitled to compensation for work performed for the partnership, except for "reasonable compensation" rendered in winding up the business of the partnership

Delectus Personae: Partners may veto admission of potential new partners, because new partners may be added only upon unanimous consent of existing partners

General Partnerships

Information rights:

1. Partners and their agents are entitled to access to partnership books and records during ordinary business hours
2. Each partner and the partnership shall furnish to partners and their legal representatives:
   - Without demand: any information concerning the partnership's business and affairs reasonably required for proper exercise of partners' rights
   - Upon demand: any other partnership information reasonably requested

General Partnerships

Standards of Conduct: The only fiduciary duties a partner owes to the partnership and other partners are the:

Duty of Loyalty, which includes:

1. Accounting for any benefit derived
2. Avoiding conflicts of interest; and
3. Refraining from competing with the partnership business

General Partnerships

Duty of Care, which includes refraining from engaging in:

1. Grossly negligent or reckless conduct
2. Intentional misconduct, or
3. Knowing violation of the law

Corporations

Shareholders have few duties, but several important rights:

1. To vote for corporate directors
2. To inspect corporate records for proper purposes at proper times and in proper locations
3. To have their financial priorities respected; e.g., if they hold preferred shares
4. To exercise appraisal rights when they dissent from major organic changes
5. To file derivative lawsuits against officers, directors and others who have committed wrongful acts that have injured the corporation

Corporations

Directors (and officers) have several important duties, including:

1. **Duty of Attention**. "Directors must direct." They must not be mere figureheads; at a minimum they must:
   - Attend most board meetings
   - Gain a basic familiarity with the company's business; and
   - Study the company's F/S

Corporations

2. Duty of Care. Directors are not expected to be perfect, but must act:

1. In good faith
2. With the care of an ordinarily prudent person in a like position; and
3. In a manner reasonably believed to be in the best interests of the corporation

Corporations

3. Duty of Loyalty. Directors owe a fiduciary duty of loyalty to the corporation and its shareholders, meaning:

1. They should avoid conflicts of interest
2. Transactions between a director and the corporation are not automatically void, but will be scrutinized carefully. Such transactions are permitted if:
   - They are approved by an affirmative majority of disinterested directors
   - They are approved by a majority of knowledgeable shareholders **or**
   - They are "fair" to the corporation
3. Directors should respect the corporate opportunity doctrine by not appropriating for themselves business opportunities that rightfully belong to the corporation

Corporations

Directors' Rights:

1. **Right to Rely.** Directors have the right to rely upon the reports of officers and other directors unless they have some reason to be suspicious
2. **Business Judgment Rule.** Courts are not business experts, so they normally do not second-guess business decisions of directors or officers. Rather, they apply the "business judgment rule" which states:

Corporations

"In the absence of a showing of bad faith on the part of the directors or of a gross abuse of discretion, the business judgment of the directors will not be interfered with by the courts. The acts of directors are presumptively acts taken in good faith and inspired for the best interests of the corporation, and a minority stockholder who challenges their bona fides of purpose has the burden of proof."

Corporations

Officers:

1. Run the corporation day-to-day (under the supervision of the board of directors), and are very powerful and have the opportunity to abuse that power
2. Constrained by the same duties of care and loyalty that constrain directors

LLCs

Whether an LLC is member-managed or manager-managed, managers owe duties of care and loyalty to the (other) members

An operating agreement may limit, but not totally eliminate fiduciary duties

RULLCA also provides: members shall discharge their duties consistently with contractual obligations of "good faith and fair dealing"

LLCs

Additionally, courts protect members by:

1. Allowing them to escape an operating agreement by convincing a court that its provisions are "manifestly unreasonable"; and
2. Providing judicial dissolution if those managing the firm are guilty of "oppressive conduct"

AUTHORITY OF OWNERS AND MANAGERS

Introduction

Agency law provides the basic rules for the authority of owners and managers of various forms of business to bind their firms

As in other areas, the rules for general partnerships are nearly identical to those for LPs, LLPs, and LLLPs

General Partnerships

General Principles: As a general rule, agency law provides:

1. An act of a partner for apparently carrying on in the ordinary course the partnership business binds the partnership, unless:
   - The person with whom the partner was dealing knew or had received notification that the partner lacked authority
   - The partner had no authority to act for the partnership in the particular matter

General Partnerships

2. An act of a partner which is not apparently for carrying on in the ordinary course the partnership's business binds the partnership only if the act was authorized by the other partners

General Partnerships

A partner binds both the partnership and the other partners if he or she acts with:

1. Actual authority (expressed or implied); or
2. Apparent authority, which cannot exist where:
   - The third party knows of a partner's lack of authority, or
   - The partner's action is one that requires unanimity, such as an agreement to admit a new partner

General Partnerships

Ratification: An act lacking both actual and apparent authority may still bind a partnership that ratifies the action expressly or by knowingly accepting the benefits of the agreement

General Partnerships

Tort liability: Consistent with agency law, partnerships are generally liable for the torts committed by their partners or other agents within the scope of their employment

1. **Intentional torts**. A partnership is usually liable if a partner commits an intentional tort while trying to advance partnership interests, even if he or she does so in a wrongful way
2. **Misapplication of Funds**. RUPA imposes virtually strict liability on a partnership for the misapplication of money received by the partnership "in the course of its business"

General Partnerships

Joint and Several Liability: Under RUPA, contract and tort liability are typically joint and several, meaning that a creditor may sue any general partner and hold that partner completely liable without suing the others

However, RUPA provides that the assets of the partnership must be exhausted before the partnership creditor proceeds against the individual assets of the general partners

General Partnerships

Late Arrivers: If a general partner joins an existing partnership, he or she is personally liable for all subsequently-incurred debts, but is liable for preexisting debts only out of his or her partnership contribution

Corporation

The Corporate Pyramid: The corporation is typically viewed as a pyramid. Shareholders are passive investors whose input into corporate management is their vote for directors. Directors then set overall corporate policy and select officers. Officers are at the top of the pyramid, making the day-to-day decisions that bind the firm.

Corporation

Directors: Most state corporate codes provide that "the business and affairs of a corporation shall be managed under the supervision of a board of directors." Directors have broad authority to:

1. Borrow money
2. Sell corporate property
3. Hire and fire officers and other employees
4. Declare or refuse to declare dividends
5. Make or refuse to make other distributions to shareholders'
6. Set the salaries of employees, officers, and even themselves; and

Corporation

7. Propose for shareholder approval:
   - Sale of major corporate assets
   - Mergers or consolidations with other firms
   - Dissolution; and
   - Amendments to the articles of incorporation

Corporation

Officers: run the firm day-to-day and typically have various types of authority to bind the firm, including:

Express authority, derived from:
- Articles of incorporation
- By-laws
- Directors' resolutions
- Statutes

Corporation

Implied authority: derived by virtue of their offices. The general trend is to find broad authority inherent in the offices of CEO, CFO, etc., but in questionable situations the other party may always demand a board of directors resolution

Ratification: Even if an officer acts without either express or implied authority, the board of directors could always bind the corporation by ratifying the contracts

LLCs

The operating agreement should indicate whether the LLC will be member-managed or manager-managed

Absent provision to the contrary, it is assumed that an LLC will be member-managed

LLCs

If member-managed, an LLC will operate much like a general partnership:

1. Each member has equal rights in management
2. Ordinary business issues are decided by majority vote
3. Acts outside the ordinary course of business require unanimous approval; and
4. The operating agreement may be amended only with the consent of all members

LLCs

If manager-managed, an LLC will operate much like a limited partnership, with the managers assuming the role of the general partner:

1. Except as otherwise provided in RULLCA, matters related to the activities of the company will be decided exclusively by the managers
2. Managers have equal rights in management and conduct of the firm
3. Issues arising in the ordinary course of business are decided by majority vote of the managers
4. Consent of all managers is required to engage in extraordinary transactions, such as sale of all or substantially all firm property, approval of a merger, or amending the operating agreement;
5. Managers may be removed at any time, with or without cause, by a majority vote of the members

LLCs

Partnership law generally provides for "statutory apparent authority," indicating that a partnership will generally be bound whenever a general partner acts to carry on the business of the partnership in the usual way

The RULLCA provides to the contrary - that "a member is not an agent of the limited liability company solely by reason of being a member"

Under the Revised Model Business Corporation Act (RMBCA), a corporate director is authorized to

- [ ] **A. Rely on information provided by the appropriate corporate officer.**
- [ ] **B. Serve on the Board of Directors of a competing business.**
- [ ] **C. Self control of the corporation.**
- [ ] **D. Profit from insider information.**

REG 6-1

PROPERTY TRANSACTIONS 1

Introduction to Tax Review

Sales and Dispositions of Assets

Capital Gains and Losses

Selected Questions (4)

INTRODUCTION TO TAX REVIEW

Structure of Regulation

Format
- 3 Multiple-Choice Question (MCQ) testlets consisting of 72 questions
- 1 Testlet containing 6 short Task-Based Simulations (TBS)
- No written communication tasks

Grading
- Multiple Choice Questions: 60%
- Task Based Simulations: 40%

Regulation Content Specification

I. Ethics, Professional and Legal Responsibilities (15%-19%)
II. Business Law (17-21%)
III. Federal Tax Process, Procedures, Accounting, and Planning (11% - 15%)
IV. Federal Taxation of Property Transactions (12% - 16%)
V. Federal Taxation of Individuals (13% - 19%)
VI. Federal Taxation of Entities (18% - 24%)

Tax Law Coverage in Material

The CPA Exam is a closed exam; only a limited number of questions are released each year.

However, we can predict based on our expertise what is likely to be tested.

Preparing for multiple choice versus TBS.

Tax Law Coverage in Material

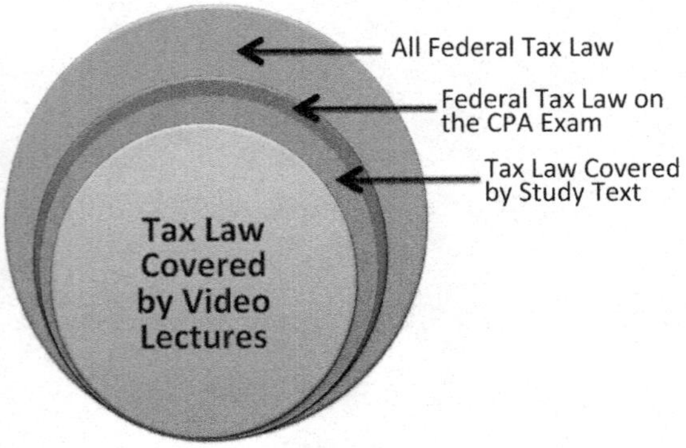

Tax Law Coverage in Material

Material does not focus on detailed exceptions that are not likely to be tested.

Do not focus on phase-outs or inflation adjusted items.

Two main types of tax law material to master:
- **Review** and **Recognize** (do not need to memorize long lists of specific tax items).
- **Learn** and **Apply** (problem solving and critical thinking skills).

Study Tips

Video, Study Text, Questions, TBS

Tax Forms

Multiple short study sessions are more productive than marathon sessions.

When you take the exam you will not be reading solutions - you will be creating them - so prepare by doing the same.

Perseverance - - - one lesson at a time.

Test Taking Tips

- Learn the basics very well. That will take care of 90% of the problems.
- If you are not sure of the correct answer, try to rule out alternatives you believe are incorrect.
- Answer all multiple choice questions.
- Use keyword searches for research question.
- Don't worry about the few questions you do not know; could be a pre-test question.
- If you have to guess, choose the answer that is **worse** for the taxpayer.

Summary

Review! Review! Review!

Work Problems

Focus on breadth, not depth

One Step (Lesson) at a time

SALES AND DISPOSITIONS OF ASSETS

Classification of Assets

Mutually Exclusive

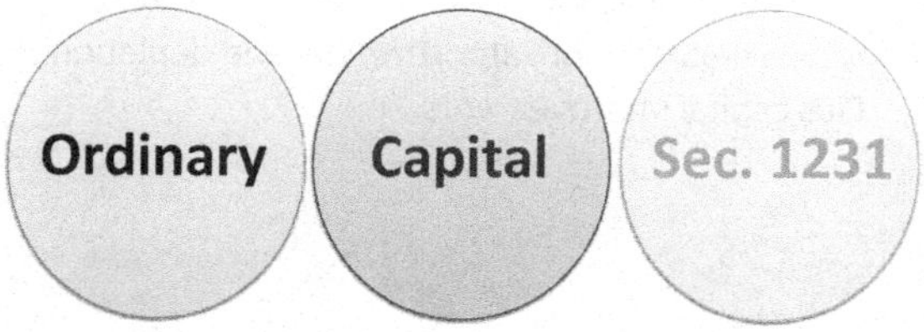

Classification of Assets

ORDINARY ASSETS

- Accounts and Notes Receivable
- Inventory
- Trade or Business Assets owned for a year or less

SECTION 1231 ASSETS

- Trade or Business Assets owned for more than a year

Classification of Assets

CAPITAL ASSETS

- All other assets are capital assets.
- The most common capital assets are those used in one's personal activities and in investment activities.

Classification of Assets Example

Platt owns land that is operated as a parking lot. A shed was erected on the lot for the related transactions with customers.

With regard to capital assets and Section 1231 assets, how would these assets be classified?

Property Transaction

Any time that a property transaction occurs, the taxpayer must compute a realized gain or loss. Property transactions include sales or disposition of assets.

The term "**sale or disposition**" includes sales, exchanges, trade-ins, casualties, condemnations, thefts, and retirements.

Realized Gains and Losses

Realized gain or loss is computed as follows:

Amount Realized
- Adjusted Basis

Realized Gain/Loss

Realized Gains and Losses

Amount realized includes:
- Cash received
- Fair market value of any property received
- Liabilities assumed by the buyer
- Less selling expenses

Realized Gains and Losses

Adjusted basis equals the cost or other acquisition basis of the property.
- Cost includes any liabilities or expenses connected with the acquisition
- Minus depreciation, amortization, and depletion
- Plus capital improvements

Basis Rules

Basis in an asset is usually determined by its cost, which includes all of the expenditures required to place an asset in service, including:

- Transportation
- Installation
- Testing
- Taxes

Review Question

Ralph Birch purchased land and a building which will be used in connection with Birch's business. The costs associated with this purchase are as follows:

Cash down payment	$ 40,000
Mortgage on property	350,000
Survey costs	2,000
Title and transfer taxes	2,500
Charges for hookup of gas, water, and sewer lines	3,000
Back property taxes owed by the seller that were paid by Birch	5,000
	$ 402,500

What is Birch's tax basis for the land and building?

Recognized Gains and Losses

You should assume that all realized gains and losses should be recognized unless you are aware of a tax rules that excludes or defers the gain or loss.

Note that in general, losses from the sale or disposition of all personal use assets are not recognized.

Gifts and Inheritances

Two major exceptions to the cost basis rules are for:

- Gifts
- Inheritances

Gifts – Basis Rules

If property is gifted to a taxpayer, the donee's basis is:

1) Gain basis = adjusted basis of the donor
2) Loss basis = lower of
   - FMV at date of gift, or
   - adjusted basis of the donor
3) Depreciable basis = gain basis
4) The basis is increased for the portion of any gift tax paid by the donor due to appreciation in the property:

$$\text{Adjustment paid} = \frac{\text{(Unrealized Appreciation)}}{\text{FMV at date of gift} - \text{annual exclusion}} \times \text{Gift tax}$$

Gifts – Basis Rules Example

Farr made a gift of stock to her child, Pat. At the date of gift, Farr's stock basis was $10,000 and the stock's fair market value was $15,000. No gift taxes were paid.

What is Pat's basis in the stock for computing gain?

GAIN $10,000 ✓

LOSS $10,000

Gifts – Basis Rules Solution

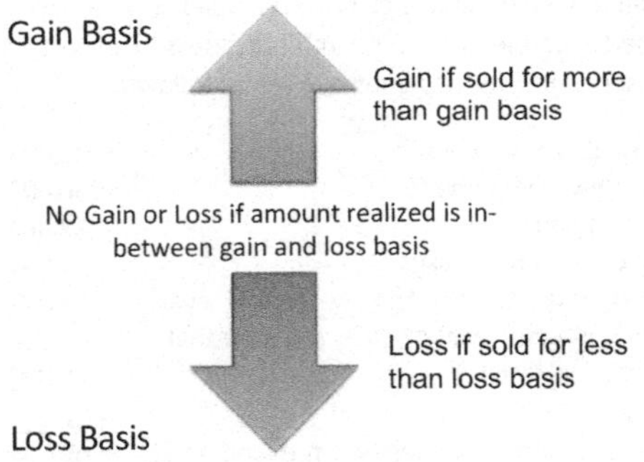

Inheritances – Basis Rules

Basis to the beneficiary is the fair market value of the asset on the **date of death** of the taxpayer, or the alternate valuate date (six months after the date of death) if that is elected by the estate's executor.

Holding Period – Gifts and Inheritances

Does the holding period of the donor/decedent carryover to the new owner?

Gifts: If the property is sold for a gain, the holding period carries over.

If the property is sold for a loss, the holding period does not carry over.

Inheritances: Holding period is always long-term.

Property Transactions Fundamentals

5 items to know for every property transaction:

1. Realized gain or loss
2. Recognized gain or loss
3. Character of the gain or loss
4. Holding period of the retained asset (could be zero)
5. Basis in the retained asset, if any (could be zero)

CAPITAL GAINS AND LOSSES

Capital Gains and Losses

The most common capital assets are those used in one's personal activities and in investment activities.

Long-term if held more than one year

Short-term if held one year or less

Four categories:
- Long-term capital gain – preferential rates (individuals only)
- Long-term capital loss
- Short-term capital gain – ordinary rates
- Short-term capital loss

Netting Capital Gains/Losses Example

Baker Corp., a calendar year C corporation, realized taxable income of $36,000 from its regular business operations for Year 1.

In addition, Baker had the following capital gains and losses this year:

Netting Capital Gains/Losses Example

Short-term capital gain	$8,500	
Short-term capital loss	(4,000)	4,500
Long-term capital gain	1,500	2,500
Long-term capital loss	(3,500)	

Baker did not realize any other capital gains or losses since it began operations. What is Baker's total taxable income this year?

$36,000 + $2,500 = $38,500

Capital Losses - Individuals

If the combination of net short-term and net long-term gains and losses is negative, then individuals can deduct this "net capital loss" up to $3,000 per year.

The deduction is "for" AGI and is limited to taxable income (any excess loss carries forward).

Capital Losses - Corporations

Corporations can only use a "**net capital loss**" to offset capital gain net income.

Unused net capital losses are short-term capital losses, and they can be carried back three years and forward five years.

Long-Term Capital Gains – Individuals

Net capital gain is taxed at a maximum rate of 15 percent. If the taxpayer's regular tax rate is 15 percent or lower, then the maximum tax rate is reduced to 0 percent.

Net capital gain attributable to **straight-line depreciation** claimed on real estate is taxed at a maximum rate of 25 percent.

Net capital gain from **collectibles** is taxed at a maximum rate of 28 percent.

Netting Capital Gains/Losses

A net short-term or long-term loss is applied against a net long-term gain.

The group of long-term gains taxed at the highest rate is offset first.

Netting Capital Gains/Losses

Example: TP has net short-term capital loss of $20,000. He has also realized a net long-term gain of $50,000 comprised of the following net gains and losses:

$10,000 gain on the sale of coins held 3 years

$25,000 gain on the sale of securities held 3 years

$15,000 gain on the sale of realty (attributable t o depreciation)

Solution

Capital Loss 20,000

28% - coins (10,000)

25% - recapture (10,000)

$10,000 gain on the sale of coins held 3 years 0

$25,000 gain on the sale of securities held 3 years $25,000

$15,000 gain on the sale of realty taxable gain $5,000

$30,000

Stocks and Bonds

The date of purchase/sale for stocks and bonds is the **trade date**, not the **settlement date.**

The **trade date** is the day that the purchase or sale actually occurs.

The **settlement date** is the day that the stock is delivered or that payment is actually made.

Section 1244 Losses

The first $50,000 of losses ($100,000 for married filing joint) from the sale of Section 1244 stock will be treated as an **ordinary loss.**

The individual selling the stock must be the **original holder** of the stock.

To qualify as Section 1244 stock, the total capitalization of the corporation cannot exceed $1,000,000 at the time the stock is issued.

Jackson, a single individual, inherits Bean Corp. common stock from his parents. Bean is a qualified small business corporation under Code Section 1244.
The stock costs Jackson's parents $20,000 and has a fair market value of $25,000 at the parents' date of death. During the year, Bean declares bankruptcy and Jackson is informed that the stock is worthless.

What amount may Jackson deduct as an ordinary loss in the current year?

- A. **$0**
- B. **$3,000**
- C. **$20,000**
- D. **$25,000**

Joe Hall owns a limousine for use in his personal service business of transporting passengers to airports. The limousine's adjusted basis is $40,000. In addition, Hall owns his personal residence and furnishings, that together cost him $280,000.

Hall's capital assets amount to

- [ ] A. **$320,000**
- [ ] B. **$280,000**
- [ ] C. **$40,000**
- [ ] D. **$0**

Hall, a divorced person and custodian of her 12-year-old child, files her 2012 federal income-tax return as head of a household. She submits the following information to the CPA, who prepares her 2012 return:

- The divorce agreement, executed in 1 provides for Hall to receive $3,000 per month, of which $600 is designated as child support. After the child reaches 18, the monthly payments are to be reduced to $2,400 and are to be continued until remarriage or death. However, for the year 2012, Hall receives a total of only $5,000 from her former husband. Hall pays an attorney $2,000 in 2012 in a suit to collect the alimony owed.
- In June 2012, Hall's mother gifts her 100 shares of a listed stock. The donor's basis for this stock, which she bought in 1985, was $4,000, and market value on the date of the gift was $3,000. Hall sells her stock in July 2012 for $3,500. The donor pays no gift tax.
- During 2012, Hall spends a total of $1,000 on state lottery tickets. Her lottery winnings in 2012 totaled $200.
- Hall earns a salary of $25,000 in 2012. Hall is not covered by any type of retirement plan, but contributes $2,000 to an IRA in 2012.
- In 2012, Hall sells an antique that she bought in 1995 to display in her home. Hall pays $800 for the antique and sells it for $1,400, using the proceeds to pay a court-ordered judgment.
- Hall pays the following expenses in 2012 pertaining to the home that she owns: realty taxes, $3,400; mortgage interest, $7,000; casualty insurance, $490; assessment by city for construction of a sewer system, $910; and interest of $1,000 on a personal, unsecured bank loan, the proceeds of which were used for home improvements. Hall does not rent out any portion of the home.

The $600 gain that Hall realizes on the sale of the antique should be treated as

- [ ] A. **Ordinary income.**
- [ ] B. **Long-term capital gain.**
- [ ] C. **An involuntary conversion.**
- [ ] D. **A non-taxable antiquities transaction.**

Fred Berk buys a plot of land with a cash payment of $40,000 and a purchase-money mortgage of $50,000. In addition, Berk pays $200 for a title insurance policy.

Berk's basis in this land is

- [ ] **A. $40,000**
- [ ] **B. $40,200**
- [ ] **C. $90,000**
- [ ] **D. $90,200**

REG 6-2

PROPERTY TRANSACTIONS 2

Section 1231 Assets

Sections 1231 Assets - Cost Recovery

Selected Questions (3)

SECTION 1231 ASSETS

Definition

Section 1231 Assets are assets that are used in a trade or business and have been owned for more than one year.

Segment asset sales for the year into Section 1231 Gains and Section 1231 Losses.

Section 1231 Netting

To the extent section 1231 gains exceed section 1231 losses, the net gain is treated as **a long-term capital gain** (subject to a lookback limit for losses during the previous 5 years).

If section 1231 losses exceed section 1231 gains, the loss is deductible as an **ordinary loss**.

Section 1231 Netting

The lookback provision states that the net Section 1231 gains must be offset by net Section 1231 losses from the **five preceding tax years** that have not previously been recaptured.

To the extent of these losses, the net Section 1231 gain is treated as **ordinary income**.

Lookback Rule Example

The results of Digimatic Corporation's first 3 years of operations are presented below

Year	Results of Operations
1	Sec. 1231 losses of $10,000
2	Sec. 1231 losses of $15,000
3	Sec. 1231 gain of $75,000

Digimatic Corporation's Year 3 Sec. 1231 gain can best be characterized as . . .

Lookback Rule Solution

Year 3 Gain	75000
Year 1 Loss	(10,000) OI
Year 2 Loss	(15000) OI
Taxed as LTCG	50,000

Taxed as Ordinary Income

25,000

Recapture Rules

Recapture applies only to Section 1231 assets because only assets used in a business are depreciable.

Section 1250 Recapture – **Realty** (land and assets permanently attached to land).

Section 1245 Recapture – **Personalty** (assets other than realty).

Assets Subject to Recapture

Section 1231 Assets

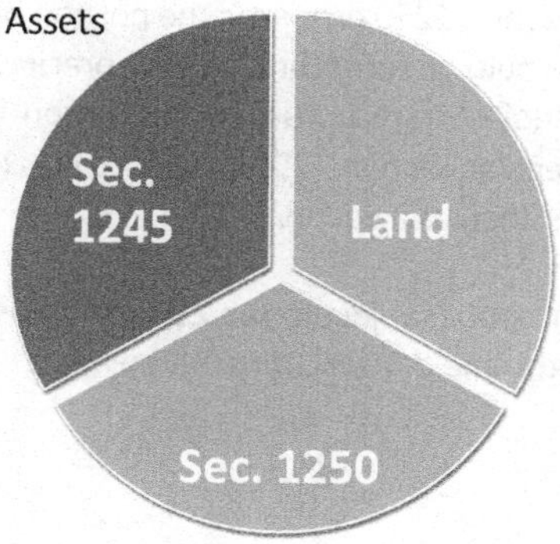

Section 1245 Recapture

If the Section 1231 property was depreciable, the gain from the sale is subject to recapture as ordinary income.

The amount not recaptured is categorized as Section 1231 gains.

Depreciable personalty is Section 1245 property. All depreciation taken on Section 1245 property is subject to being recaptured as ordinary income.

Recapture Example

Mr. Monopoly sold equipment used in his business for $11,000. The equipment cost $10,000 and Monopoly had properly claimed MACRS deductions totaling $4,000

Straight-line depreciation, if it had been used, would have been $2,500. What is the amount of gain that should be reported under Sec. 1231 and 1245?

Recapture Solution

Amount Realized 11,000

Adjusted Basis 10,000 − 4,000 (6,000)

Realized/Recognized Gain 5,000

Section 1245 Ordinary Income 4,000

Section 1231 Gain 1,000

Section 1250 Recapture

Depreciable realty is Section 1250 property.

Only the excess of actual depreciation over straight-line depreciation is subject to recapture as ordinary income.

25% Recapture Rate

For Section 1250 property, the portion of the gain that would be recaptured if all depreciation taken was subject to recapture under Section 1245 over the regular Section 1250 recapture is taxed at 25%, rather than as a Section 1231 gain.

The amount subject to the **25% rate** is usually the **straight-line depreciation** on the asset.

Recapture Solution

Gain

5,000

SOLD 11,000
COST 10,000

Sec. 1250	25% Gain	Sec. 1231
4,000 (2,500) 1,500 EXCESS	2,500	1,000

Section 1250 Recapture - Corporations

Rules are the same as for individuals, except:

1. Straight-line depreciation is not taxed at a 25% rate.
2. Rather, additional depreciation is recaptured to the extent of 20% multiplied by:
   - Recapture if the property was Sec. 1245 property
   - Less: Section 1250 depreciation recapture

This additional amount is Sec. 291 recapture.

Recapture Solution - Corporations

Gain

5,000

Sec. 1250	Sec. 291	Sec. 1231
EXCESS 1,500	S,1245 4,000 S,1250 (1,500) 2,500 x20% OI 500	$3,000

SECTION 1231 ASSETS: COST RECOVERY

MACRS - Personalty

200% declining-balance method with a **half-year convention**; taxpayer gets one-half year depreciation in the year of acquisition and one-half year in the year of disposal.

5-year property includes trucks, automobiles, computers, machinery and equipment

7-year property includes office furniture and fixtures

Half-Year Convention Computation

Assume that business furniture of $10,000 is purchased on March 10 of Year 1.

Compute the depreciation allowed on the furniture for Year 1:

10,000 X 14.29% = 1,429

Compute the depreciation allowed on the furniture if it sold in Year 3:

10,000 x 17.49% x 1/2 = 875

MACRS - Personalty

Taxpayers can elect to use the straight line method.

A mid-quarter convention is used if **more than 40%** of all personalty is placed in service during the last quarter of the taxable year.

Review Question

Data Corp., a calendar year corporation, purchased and placed into service office equipment during November Year 1 costing $100,000. No other equipment was placed into service during Year 1. Under the general MACRS depreciation system, what convention must Data use?

A. Full-year
B. Half-year
C. Mid-quarter
D. Mid-month

Mid-Quarter Computation

Compute the depreciation allowed on the office equipment for Year 1:

100,000 X 5% = $5,000

Compute the depreciation allowed on the office equipment if it sold on January 27, Year 3:

100,000 X 22.80% X 1.5/12 = $2,850

MACRS - Realty

Straight line depreciation with mid-month convention; taxpayer gets one-half month depreciation in the month of acquisition and one-half month in the month of disposal.

Residential realty is depreciated over **27.5 years**.

Nonresidential realty is depreciated over **39 years**.

Review Question

On August 2 Graham purchased and placed into service an office building costing $264,000 including $30,000 for the land. What was Graham's MACRS deduction for the office building this year?

Total Cost	264,000
Land	(30,000)
Depreciable Basis	234,000 X 1/39 X 4.5/12 = 2,250

Residential Realty Depreciation

Assume that an apartment building is purchased on April 30 for $500,000.
Compute the depreciation allowed on the apartment building for Year 1:

500,000 x 2.576% = 12,880

Compute the depreciation allowed on the apartment building if it sold on Feb. 12 of Year 3:

$500,000 \times 3.636\% \times \frac{1.5}{12} = 2,273$

Section 179

Taxpayers can elect to expense a certain amount of **tangible personalty** used in a trade or business.

Investment property is not eligible.

New or used property is eligible.

Section 179

There are two limitations on this deduction:

1. The annual limit is reduced dollar-for-dollar for personalty placed in service during the year that exceeds a threshold. This reduction **does not create a carryforward** to future tax years.
2. The Sec. 179 expense cannot exceed the taxable income from the business. Any excess is carried forward to future taxable years.

Section 179

The basis of the property for cost recovery purposes is reduced by the Sec. 179 amount, even if the deduction is limited by the taxable income rule.

Bonus Depreciation

For 2012, taxpayers can elect to immediately depreciate **50%** of many types of personalty (100% in 2011).

The remaining basis is depreciated under the regular MACRS rules. Section 179 expensing is taken into account before bonus depreciation.

Bonus Depreciation

Bonus depreciation applies only to **new** property.

AMT adjustments are not required for property for which bonus depreciation has been elected.

Luxury Auto Limits

Special rules limit the amount of depreciation that can be claimed on a passenger automobile (GVW of 6,000 pounds or less).

These **assume 100% business/investment** use. For mixed-use autos, the limit is multiplied by the percentage of business/investment use.

Luxury Auto Limits

For autos purchased in 2012, the limit is $3,160. If business/investment use was 70%, the limit is:

3,160 x 70% = 2,212

Listed Property

Listed Property includes assets such as **computers and vehicles** that can be used for both business and personal purposes. Note that cell phones are not defined as listed property.

To use accelerated cost recovery the **business use** of listed assets must exceed 50% of total use. Investment use is not considered.

Both business and investment use are depreciated.

Listed Property

Failure to meet the business use test means:

- Cost recovery is limited to straight-line (ADS).
- ADS depreciation must be used for the entire depreciable life of the asset, even if the 50% test is met in future years.
- Excess depreciation from prior years must be recaptured.

Intangible Assets

Intangible assets that are **acquired**, not created, can be amortized on a **straight-line** basis over **15-years**.

Examples include goodwill, franchises, trademarks, etc.

Other assets (**covenants not to compete**, computer software, film, sound recordings, video tapes, **patents**, copyrights) qualify if acquired in connection with the acquisition of a trade or business.

Kaitlin owns a computer that she uses for business, investment, and personal use, as follows:

Personal use.	**25%**
Investment use.	**30%**
Business use.	**45%**

Will Kaitlin's use qualify her to use accelerated or straight-line depreciation, and what percentage of the asset's basis qualifies to be depreciated?

- [ ] **A. Straight-line, 45%.**
- [ ] **B. Accelerated, 45%.**
- [ ] **C. Straight-line, 75%.**
- [ ] **D. Accelerated, 75%.**

ACE Landscaping purchased equipment for $3,000 in the current year that it plans to use 100% for business purposes. The equipment qualifies as 5-year property. The deprecation percentages provided in the MACRS tables are as follows:

Year 1	**20.00%**
Year 2	**32.00%**
Year 3	**19.20%**
Year 4	**11.52%**
Year 5	**11.52%**
Year 6	**5.76%**

On August 20 of Year 3 ACE sells the equipment for $1,800. The depreciation allowed for the equipment for Year 3 is (rounded to the nearest dollar):

- A. $ 0
- B. $173
- C. $288
- D. $575

On January 2, 2008, Bates Corp. purchases and places into service seven-year MACRS tangible property costing $100,000. On December 31, 2012, Bates sells the property for $102,000, after having taken $47,525 in MACRS depreciation deductions.

What amount of the gain should Bates recapture as ordinary income?

- [ ] A. **$0**
- [ ] B. **$2,000**
- [ ] C. **$47,525**
- [ ] D. **$49,525**

REG 6-3

PROPERTY TRANSACTIONS 3

Like-Kind Exchanges and Involuntary Conversions

Other Nonrecognition Transactions

Selected Questions (2)

LIKE-KIND EXCHANGES AND INVOLUNTARY CONVERSIONS

Like-Kind Exchanges

Losses are never recognized from a like-kind exchange.

Recognized gain is the lesser of
- Realized gain, or
- Boot received.

Boot is any **non-like kind property** received as part of the exchange. Liabilities assumed by the other party to the exchange are considered boot.

Like-Kind Exchanges

Realty for realty is like-kind. (Realty is land and buildings).

Personalty is divided into broad asset classes, and assets must be within the same class to be like-kind.

Examples of asset classes are office furniture, fixtures, and equipment; computer equipment; automobiles; and light-duty trucks.

Like-Kind Exchanges

The like-kind exchange rules:

- do not apply to personal-use property;
- apply **only to business and investment** property.

Business property can be exchanged for investment property.

Review Question

Leker exchanged a van that was used exclusively for business and had an adjusted tax basis of $20,000 for a new van. The new van had a fair market value of $10,000, and Leker also received $3,000 in cash.

What was Leker's tax basis in the acquired van?

Review Question

Amount Realized:

Van	10,000	
Cash	3,000	
		13000
Adjusted Basis		<20,000>
Realized Loss		<7,000>
Recognized Loss	0	

Like-Kind Exchanges - Basis

The basis of like-kind property received can be computed as follows:

FMV of property received 10,000

- Postponed gain

+ Postponed loss + 7,000

17,000

Like-Kind Exchanges

Basis of non-like kind property received is the property's FMV, since gain has been recognized to that extent.

Holding period of like-kind property surrendered tacks on to the holding period of like-kind property received.

Involuntary Conversions

An involuntary conversion includes **destruction, theft, seizure, and condemnation** of property.

Replacement property must be "*similar or related in service or use*" to the involuntarily converted property.

Property must be replaced within 2 years after the close of the taxable year in which the conversion took place (3 years for condemned business or investment real property).

Involuntary Conversions

Amount realized from conversion
- Adjusted basis of old property
Realized gain/loss

Amount realized from conversion
- Cost of replacement property
Recognized gain, limited to realized gain

Losses are **NEVER** deferred under these rules.

Review Question

Mr. N's business building was destroyed by a hurricane. The building had an adjusted basis to Mr. N of $200,000 and a fair market value immediately before the hurricane of $300,000.

Mr. N received a reimbursement of $270,000 from his insurance company and immediately spent $268,000 for a new business building.

What amount must Mr. N include in his gross income?

Involuntary Conversion Solution

Amount realized from conversion	270,000
- Adjusted basis of old property	<200,000>
Realized gain/loss	70,000
Amount realized from conversion	270,000
Cost of replacement property	<268,000>
Recognized gain, limited to realized gain	2,000

Involuntary Conversion - Basis

The basis of new property received is computed as follows:

FMV of property received
- Postponed gain
+ Postponed loss

If a gain is deferred, the holding period of the converted property tacks on to the holding period of the replacement property.

OTHER NONRECOGNITION TRANSACTIONS

Wash Sales

If a taxpayer sells **stock or securities** and has a realized loss, and the taxpayer acquires substantially identical stock or securities within 30 days before or after the date of the sale, the loss is disallowed.

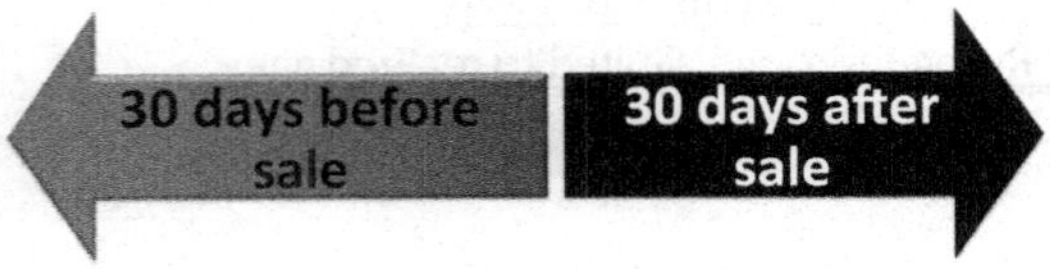

Wash Sales

Basis of the newly acquired stock or securities = Cost + Disallowed Loss

Holding period of the new stock or securities includes the holding period of the old stock or securities.

Wash Sale Example

Smith, an individual calendar-year taxpayer, purchased 100 shares of Core Co. common stock for $15,000 on December 15, Year 1, and an additional 100 shares for $13,000 on December 30, Year 1

On December 31, Year 1 Smith sold the shares purchased on December 15, Year 1, for $13,000

What amount of loss from the sale of Core's stock is deductible on Smith's Year 1 income tax return?

Wash Sale Solution

	Shares	Basis
12/15	100	$15,000
12/30	100	$13,000
12/31	(100)	

Amount Realized
Adjusted Basis
Realized Loss

Recognized Loss

Basis in remaining shares:
Cost
+ Disallowed Loss

Related Party Losses

Realized losses from sales or dispositions of property between related taxpayers is not recognized.

Related parties include:

- spouse
- descendants – children, grandchildren, great-grandchildren, etc.
- ancestors – parents, grandparents, great-grandparents, etc.
- siblings – brothers and sisters, including half brothers and sisters

Related Party Losses

In-laws are not considered related parties, although they are eligible to be claimed as a dependent.

Aunts and uncles and cousins are not related parties.

The amount of disallowed loss is called a **right of offset**.

Related Party Losses

The right of offset can be used to offset any gain recognized when the current owner disposes of the property in the future (unless the property was personal use property to the original seller).

The right of offset can only reduce a gain to zero; it cannot create a loss.

Holding period of original buyer does not include holding period of the seller. Begins on date of purchase of property from related party.

Related Party Losses

Related Parties also include:

- A corporation and a more than 50% shareholder
- A partnership and a partner that owns more than 50% of the capital or profits interest of the partnership

Related Party Loss Problem

Fay sold 100 shares of Gym Co. stock to her son, Martin, for $11,000. Fay had paid $15,000 for the stock in 1990.

Two years later Martin sold the stock to an unrelated third party for $16,000.

What amount of gain from the sale of the stock to the third party should Martin report on his income tax return?

Related Party Loss Solution

	Fay	Martin
Amount Realized	11,000	16,000
Adjusted Basis	<15,000>	<11,000>
Realized Gain/Loss	<4,000>	5,000
Right of Offset		<4,000>
Recognized Gain/Loss	0	1,000

Sale of a Principal Residence

An individual can exclude up to **$250,000** of gain from the sale or exchange of a **principal residence**.

The individual must have **owned** and **occupied** the residence as a principal residence for at least two of the five years before the disposition.

Sale of a Principal Residence

This restriction does not apply in the event of a change in employment (exclusion is pro-rated).

Married couples filing jointly can exclude up to **$500,000** if:

- at least one meets the ownership requirement, and
- both meet the use requirement.

Frequency Test: The exclusion applies to only one sale or exchange every two years.

Installment Sales

The gross profit from the sale is recognized as cash is received:

Recognized gain = cash received x gross profit percentage

Review Problem

In year 1, a taxpayer sold real property for $200,000, receiving $100,000 at closing and $100,000 plus accrued interest at the prime rate in the next year. The buyer also assumed a $50,000 mortgage on the property. The taxpayer's adjusted basis was $75,000, and the taxpayer incurred $10,000 of selling expenses.

If this transaction qualifies for installment sale treatment, what is the gross profit on the sale?

Review Problem Solution

Cash	200,000	100,000
Liability relief	50,000	x 82.5%
Selling expenses	<10,000>	82,500
Amount Realized	240,000	
Adjusted Basis	<75,000>	
Gross Profit	165,000	

Gross profit % = Gross Profit/Contract Price = 82.5%

165,000 / 200,000

Installment Sales

- Does not apply to losses.
- Dealers cannot use installment method for sales of inventory.
- All depreciation recapture must be recognized in the year of sale.
- The entire gain will be recognized immediately if the installment note is sold.
  The installment obligation must have a market interest rate or a portion of the gain will be treated as imputed interest.
- Can elect to recognize gains currently.

Among which of the following related parties are losses from sales and exchanges not recognized for tax purposes?

- [ ] **A. Father-in-law and son-in-law.**
- [ ] **B. Brother-in-law and sister-in-law.**
- [ ] **C. Grandfather and granddaughter.**
- [ ] **D. Ancestors, lineal descendants, and all in-laws.**

In 2012, Joan Reed exchanges commercial real estate that she owns for other commercial real estate, plus $50,000 cash. The following additional information pertains to this transaction:

<u>Property given up by Reed.</u>	
Fair market value.	**$500,000**
Adjusted basis.	**$300,000**
<u>Property received by Reed.</u>	
Fair market value.	**$450,000**

What amount of gain should be recognized in Reed's 2012 income-tax return?

- [ ] A. **$200,000**
- [ ] B. **$100,000**
- [ ] C. **$50,000**
- [ ] D. **$0**

REG 6-4

INCOME 1

Gross Income - Concepts, Interest and Dividends

Gross Income - Other Inclusions

Selected Questions (4)

GROSS INCOME – CONCEPTS, INTEREST, AND DIVIDENDS

Gross Income

Gross income is **broadly defined**. All income is considered to be taxable unless the income is specifically excluded by the tax law.

Taxable Income differs from Accounting Income.

Income is not limited to cash receipts.

Bartering can also produce income.

Income Principles

Constructive Receipt: Constructive receipt requires a cash basis taxpayer to include the value of property in income in the period in which the right to the property is acquired.

Income has been constructively received if:

- The amount is readily available to the taxpayer, and
- Actual receipt is **not** subject to substantial restrictions.

Review Question

Dowd, a cash-basis engineering consultant, wanted to defer income to Year 2. A client who was in Dowd's office on December 31, Year 1, offered to pay his $2,000 bill immediately, ~~but~~ Dowd told him to pay in January. A check for $5,000 from another client arrived in the mail on December 29 and Dowd told his office manager not to deposit it until January. Dowd also told his office manager not to send a client a bill for $3,000 for services performed in Year 1 until January. **How much income from these transactions should Dowd report in Year 2?**

YR 1 = $7,000 $3,000

Income Principles

Assignment of Income: Income is taxed to the individual who earned the income. Income cannot be assigned to others.

Tax Benefit Rule: The tax benefit rule requires a taxpayer to include an expense reimbursement in income if the expense was deducted in a prior period and the deduction reduced the taxpayer's taxable income.

Tax Benefit Rule Problem

Clark filed Form 1040EZ for the Year 1 taxable year. In July Year 2, Clark received a state income tax refund of $900, plus interest of $10, for overpayment of Year 1 state income tax.

What amount of the state tax refund and interest is taxable in Clark's Year 2 federal income tax return?

$900 X NO TAX BENEFIT $10

Income Principles

Claim of Right Doctrine: The claim of right rule requires the taxpayer to include property in income in the period in which an apparent claim to the property materializes.

A later repayment of the property generates a deduction but does not influence the earlier recognition of the income.

Interest Income

In general, all interest income is taxable except for **municipal interest**, which is interest paid on bonds owned by state and local governments.

Interest earned from mutual funds is also tax-free to the extent that that the funds own municipal bonds.

However, gain from the sale of municipal bonds is taxable.

Prepaid interest income is always taxed when received.

Interest Income

Common sources of taxable interest that individuals often have are:

- United States Treasury notes and bonds
- Federal and state tax refunds, and
- Mortgages

Series EE Bonds

Interest is paid and taxed at maturity.

Taxpayer can elect to tax annually.

Interest at maturity or redemption can be excluded if:

- Owner of the bond is at least 24 years old.
- Proceeds used to pay **higher education expenses (tuition and fees)** in the year of redemption.
- Higher education expenses are for taxpayer, spouse, or dependents.
- Exclusion is phased-out at higher income levels.

Interest Income Example

Charles and Marcia are married cash-basis taxpayers. This year they had interest income as follows:

✓$ 500 interest on federal income tax refund
✓$ 600 interest on state income tax refund
✓$ 800 interest on federal government obligations
$1,000 interest on state government obligations

What amount of interest income is taxable on Charles and Marcia's joint income tax return? $1,900

Bond Premium Amortization

If a taxpayer buys a taxable bond at a **premium**:

- An election can be made to amortize the premium.
- The amortization reduces the basis of the bond.
- The amortization offsets the interest income from the bond.
- The amortized bond premium is computing using the **constant yield to maturity method.**

Premiums on tax-exempt bonds must be amortized, but the amortization cannot be deducted.

Bond Discount Amortization

Bond **discounts** are amortized using the **effective interest rate** method.

The amortization increases interest income.

For short-term bonds, the discount is taxed at maturity as ordinary income for cash basis taxpayers. It is reported as earned for accrual basis taxpayers.

Short-term bonds: maturity of one-year or less.

Dividends Tax Rate

Dividend income is not taxed (0%) if the taxpayer is in the 10% or 15% bracket.

For higher tax brackets, dividend income is taxed at 15%.

To qualify for this lower rate, the dividend must be received from a **domestic corporation** or a foreign corporation whose stock is tradable on an established U.S. securities market.

Dividend Income

Dividends received by a taxpayer are taxed in the following order:

- Dividend income to extent of E&P
- Reduction of basis in stock
- Capital Gain

Dividend Income Problem

How much income does the taxpayer have if:

Distribution to Shareholder = $10,000 — 10,000

Shareholder's share of E&P = $ 4,000 — E&P <4,000>

6,000

Stock Basis = $5,000 — BASIS <5,000>

CG 1,000

Dividend Income

Stock dividends on common stock are not taxable.

Stock dividends on preferred stock are taxable.

The taxpayer's basis in the stock is spread over all shares owned after the dividend.

Stock dividend is taxable:

- if the dividend is not proportionate, or
- if the shareholder has the option of receiving some of the dividend in cash.

Dividend Income Example

Greller owns 100 shares of Arden Corp., a publicly-traded company, which Greller purchased on January 1, Year 1, for $10,000. On January 1, Year 3, Arden declared a 2-for-1 stock split when the fair market value (FMV) of the stock was $120 per share. Immediately following the split, the FMV of Arden stock was $62 per share. On February 1, Year 3, Greller had his broker specifically sell the 100 shares of Arden stock received in the split when the FMV of the stock was $65 per share.
What is the basis of the 100 shares Arden sold?

Dividend Income Solution

Pre-split basis
$10,000 / 100 shares = $100

Post-split basis
$10,000 / 200 shares = $50

Basis in shares sold
100 shares x $50 = $5,000

GROSS INCOME – OTHER INCLUSIONS

Alimony

- Alimony is taxed to the recipient and the payor is granted a deduction ("for AGI").
- Child support is not taxed to the recipient and is not deductible by the payor.
- Property transfers between spouses are not taxable and basis stays the same.

To qualify as alimony

1. The payment must be in cash or via expense payment (such as a mortgage payment).
2. The payment must be contingent upon the life of the recipient (payments cease upon the recipient's death).
3. The payment must be required by a written agreement or decree.
4. The payment is not child support or specifically identified as "non-alimony".

Alimony Example

Ed and Ann Ross were divorced in January Year 2. In accordance with the divorce decree, Ed transferred the title in their home to Ann in Year 2.

The home, which had a fair market value of $150,000, was subject to a $50,000 mortgage that had 20 more years to run.

Monthly mortgage payments amount to $1,000.

Alimony Example

Under the terms of settlement, Ed is obligated to make the mortgage payments on the home for the full remaining 20-year term of the indebtedness, regardless of how long Ann lives. Ed made 12 mortgage payments in Year 2.

What amount is taxable as alimony in Ann's Year 2 return?

0

Damages & Insurance Benefits

1. Payments for **physical injury or physical sickness are excluded**, as is worker's compensation.
2. Unemployment compensation is taxable.
3. Benefits from accident and health policies are generally excluded from income.
4. Benefits from disability plans are excluded unless premiums were paid by employer and not taxed to employee.

Damages & Insurance Benefits

5. Medical insurance premiums paid by the employer are excluded from income.
6. Damages received for emotional distress, employment or age discrimination, or injury to reputation must be included in gross income.
7. Benefits received under long-term care insurance are excludible from income.
8. Punitive damages in general must be included in gross income.

Annuities

- If a taxpayer has basis in the annuity/retirement plan and receives a stream of payments, then the annuity rules are used to determine the taxable portion of each payment.
- Each payment is part income/part return of capital
- For retirement payouts, expected return is annual annuity amount multiplied by life expectancy determined by IRS table.

Annuities

- Exclusion ratio stays the same until entire cost is fully recovered; additional payments are fully taxable.
- If annuitant dies before total cost is recovered, unrecovered cost is a deduction on taxpayer's final return.

Annuities

Each payment is part income/part return of capital.

$$\text{Excluded portion} = \frac{\text{Cost of Annuity}}{\text{Expected Return}} \times \text{Payment}$$

Annuity Problem

Mr. Kitten purchased an annuity contract for $50,000 from the XYZ Company on March 31, Year 1. He is to receive $1,000 per month starting April 1, Year 1 and continuing for life. He has a life expectancy of 10 years as of March 31, Year 1.

Mr. Kitten's reportable annuity income for Year 1 is:

Annuity Solution

50,000

$$\frac{\text{Cost of Annuity}}{\text{Expected Return}} \times \text{Pmt.}$$

9,000

$120 \times 1{,}000 = 120{,}000$

$= 3{,}750$

Includible Amount = 9,000 − 3750 = 5250

Jury Duty

Jury duty pay is includible in income.

If the jury pay is given to the juror's employer then a deduction for AGI is received to offset this income.

An individual received $50,000 during the current year pursuant to a divorce decree. A check for $25,000 was identified as annual alimony, checks totaling $10,000 as annual child support, and a check for $15,000 as a property settlement. What amount should be included in the individual's gross income?

- [ ] A. **$50,000**
- [ ] B. **$40,000**
- [ ] C. **$25,000**
- [ ] D. **$0**

Charles and Marcia are married cash-basis taxpayers. In 2012, they had interest income as follows:

- **$500 interest on federal income tax refund.**
- **$600 interest on state income tax refund.**
- **$800 interest on federal government obligations.**
- **$1,000 interest on state government obligations.**

What amount of interest income is taxable on Charles and Marcia's 2012 joint income tax return?

- [ ] A. **$500**
- [ ] B. **$1,100**
- [ ] C. **$1,900**
- [ ] D. **$2,900**

Dale received $1,000 in 2012 for jury duty.
In exchange for regular compensation from her employer during the period of jury service, Dale was required to remit the entire $1,000 to her employer in 2012.

In Dale's 2012 income tax return, the $1,000 jury duty fee should be

- [ ] **A. Claimed in full as an itemized deduction.**
- [ ] **B. Claimed as an itemized deduction to the extent exceeding 2% of adjusted gross income.**
- [ ] **C. Deducted from gross income in arriving at adjusted gross income.**
- [ ] **D. Included in taxable income without a corresponding offset against other income.**

REG 6-5

INCOME 2

Gross Income: Exclusions

Accounting Methods and Periods

Selected Questions (3)

GROSS INCOME : EXCLUSIONS

Prizes and Awards

The fair market value of these items must be included in income.

Prizes or awards can be excluded if they are for civic, artistic, educational, scientific, or literary achievement and the recipient is

- Selected without action on her part
- Not required to perform services, and
- The amount is paid directly to a tax-exempt or governmental organization.

Prizes and Awards Example

Joan accepted and received a $10,000 award for outstanding civic achievement. Joan was selected without any action on her part, and no future services are expected of her as a condition of receiving the award.

What amount should Joan include in her adjusted gross income in connection with this award?

$10,000

Scholarships

Amounts received as scholarships by a degree seeking student can be excluded from income to the extent that the funds are used for **tuition, fees, books, supplies, and equipment required** for courses.

Amounts received for **room and board** are treated as **earned income**.

Scholarship Example

Klein, a master's degree candidate at Briar University, was awarded a $12,000 scholarship from Briar in Year 3. The scholarship was used to pay Klein's Year 3 university tuition and fees. Also in Year 3, Klein received $5,000 for teaching two courses at a nearby college. WAGES

What amount is includible in Klein's Year 3 gross income?

$5,000

Life Insurance

Proceeds of life insurance received due to the **death** of the insured are excluded from income.

Accelerated death benefits from a life insurance policy can be excluded from income if the insured taxpayer is terminally or chronically ill.

Gifts and Inheritances

Gifts/inheritances are excluded from the income of the recipient; **intent of the donor** determines if the transaction is a gift.

No such thing as a gift between employer and employee (except for deminimus rules).

Income accrued up to time of gift is still taxed to the donor whereas income accruing after the gift is taxed to recipient (donee).

Social Security Benefits

Generally, SSB are not included in income. However, if the taxpayers provisional income (PI) exceeds a specified amount, up to 85% of the benefits may be included in income.

PI = AGI + tax-exempt interest + 50% (SSB)

Social Security Benefits

PI is compared to the following base amounts (BA):

	BA1		BA2	
Married filing joint	$32,000		$44,000	
	Not taxed	50% may be taxed	85% may be taxed	
Single	$25,000		$34,000	

Forgiveness of Debt

Generally, the forgiveness of debt results in income to the borrower unless the forgiveness is a gift.

If the taxpayer is **bankrupt or insolvent**:

- the debt forgiveness is not taxable, and
- the taxpayer must reduce tax attributes such as NOLs, credit carryovers, and the basis of property.

Forgiveness of Debt

A taxpayer that is insolvent, but not bankrupt, can exclude forgiveness of debt **only to the extent of the insolvency**.

INCOME – ACCOUNTING METHODS AND PERIODS

Cash Basis

Under the cash basis, a taxpayer has **no accounts receivable** because no accounting entry is made for sales on account (no property has been received).

Accrual Basis – Exceptions

Unearned income is usually recognized in the year received, rather than the year earned.

Taxpayers may elect to defer recognition of **service income** into the next year if the service is to be provided within the following year.

The taxpayer only has to include the payments in gross income in the year of receipt if they are also included in the taxpayer's financial statements.

Taxpayers may elect to defer recognition of **advance payments for goods** if the method of accounting for sales is the same for tax and financial reporting purposes.

Rental Income

Prepaid rent is taxed when received.

Lease deposits are not income when received if they can be returned to the lessee at the end of the lease term. They are taxed when the lessor receives an unrestricted right to them.

The fair value of **leasehold improvements** is income to the landlord if the improvements are made in **lieu of rent**.

Rental Income - Problem

Nare, an accrual-basis taxpayer, owns a building which was rented to Mott under a ten-year lease expiring August 31, Year 8. On January 2, Year 5, Mott paid $30,000 as consideration for canceling the lease. On November 1, Year 5, Nare leased the building to Pine under a five-year lease. Pine paid Nare $10,000 rent for the two months of November and December, and an additional $5,000 for the last month's rent.
What amount of rental income should Nare report in its Year 5 income tax return?

$45,000

Method of Accounting

The following entities cannot use the cash method of accounting:

- Regular C corporations
- Partnerships that have regular C corporations as partners
- Tax shelters

Method of Accounting

The following entities (but not tax shelters) can use the cash method of accounting:

- Any corporation or partnership whose annual gross receipts do not exceed $5 million. The test is satisfied for a given year if the average annual gross receipts for the previous three-year period does not exceed $5 million. Once the test is failed, the entity must use the accrual method for all future tax years.
- Certain farming businesses.
- Qualified personal service corporations.

Review Question

Which of the following taxpayers may use the cash basis as its method of accounting for tax purposes?

A. Partnership that is designated as a tax shelter
B. Retail store with a $2 million inventory
C. An international accounting firm
D. Office cleaning business with average annual income of $8 million

Inventory Accounting

In general, business with inventories must use the accrual method to report purchases (cost of goods sold) and sales.

LIFO can be used only if it is also used for financial reporting.

When prices are rising, LIFO results in:
- Higher cost of goods sold
- Lower taxable income

Inventory Accounting

Taxpayers can value inventory at the lower of cost or market unless they are using LIFO (in which case cost must be used).

Market is defined as replacement cost or reproduction cost.

Uniform Capitalization Method

Manufacturers and certain retailers and wholesalers are required to use the uniform capitalization method to capitalize all the **direct** and **indirect** costs allocable to property they produce and for property bought for resale.

Virtually all indirect production costs must be capitalized for tax purposes.

The uniform capitalization rules do not apply to **small personal property dealers** (those with $10 million or less in gross receipts during the preceding three years).

Uniform Capitalization Method

Included costs:
- Storage costs if off-site
- Quality control
- Taxes (except income taxes)
- Utilities, repairs, rent, depreciation

Costs not included:
- Marketing and Selling
- Research
- Advertising
- Distributions
- General and administrative expenses

Changes in Accounting Method

Any adjustment to income required due to a **voluntary change** in accounting method is spread over **four years** beginning with the year of change. A voluntary change includes changing from an incorrect to a correct method. If the adjustment is less than $25,000 the taxpayer can include all income in the year of change.

If the change in accounting method is initiated due to an IRS examination, any positive adjustment to income is included in the earliest tax year under examination.

Short-Year Returns

If a corporation files a short-year return for a period less than 12 months (e.g., 5 months):

- the income for that period is first multiplied by 12 months/5 months to annualize the income for 12 months;
- the corporate tax liability is then computed on this amount for the full 12 months; and
- that amount is then multiplied by 5/12 to prorate for the short tax year.

Lake Corp., an accrual-basis calendar year corporation, had the following 2011 receipts:

2012 advanced rental payments where the lease ends in 2012	**$125,000**
Lease cancellation payment from a 5-year lease tenant	**50,000**

Lake had no restrictions on the use of the advanced rental payments and renders no services. What amount of income should Lake report on its 2011 tax return?

- [ ] **A. $0**
- [ ] **B. $50,000**
- [ ] **C. $125,000**
- [ ] **D. $175,000**

Fred Zorn died on January 5, 2012, bequeathing his entire $2,000,000 estate to his sister, Ida.

The alternate valuation date was validly elected by the executor of Fred's estate. Fred's estate included 2,000 shares of listed stock for which Fred's basis was $380,000.

This stock was distributed to Ida nine months after Fred's death.

Fair market values of this stock were:

At the date of Fred's death	**$400,000**
Six months after Fred's death	**450,000**
Nine months after Fred's death	**480,000**

Ida's basis for the stock is:

- ☐ A. **$380,000**
- ☐ B. **$400,000**
- ☐ C. **$450,000**
- ☐ D. **$480,000**

Fuller was the owner and beneficiary of a $200,000 life insurance policy on a parent. Fuller sold the policy to Decker, for $25,000. Decker paid a total of $40,000 in premiums.

Upon the death of the parent, what amount must Decker include in gross income?

- A. **$0**
- B. **$135,000**
- C. **$160,000**
- D. **$200,000**

REG 6-6

INCOME 3

Taxation of Employee Benefits

Taxation of Retirement Plans

Selected Questions (3)

TAXATION OF EMPLOYEE BENEFITS

Employee Business Reimbursements

Reimbursements of employee business expenses are included in income of the employee.

However, note that reimbursements under an **accountable plan** are not required to be reported on the W-2.

Discrimination Rules

Employee Benefits are generally excluded from income as long as the benefit plans do not **discriminate** in favor of highly compensated employees.

If they do discriminate, highly compensated employees must include these benefits in income, but in general other employees do not.

Life Insurance

The limit on this exclusion is the amount of premiums necessary for a **group-term** policy of **$50,000** face value.

For amounts over $50,000, the insurance benefits are taxable based on the rates in an IRS table. The rates are based on the age of the taxpayer.

If an employer pays premiums on a **whole-life insurance policy** for an employee the value of those premiums are included in income.

Insurance Premiums

Health insurance premiums paid by an employer are **excluded from income**.

Employer paid premiums **for long-term care policies** are also excluded from income.

Employer paid premiums for **wage continuation insurance** are included in income.

Meals and Lodging

Meals and lodging are excluded if:

- Furnished for convenience of employer
- On employer's premises
- Meals must be in-kind
- Lodging must be a condition of employment

Employee Benefits

Following are excluded from income:

- No-additional cost **services**, employee discounts (limited to gross profit percentage; 20% for services), working condition fringes, de minimus fringes, nominal gifts (up to $25), payments for transportation and parking
- Employer provided retirement planning advice
- Payments from an employer for expenses that would be deductible as moving expenses

Employee Benefits Example

Mr. T has been a night watchman at Y Company for 10 years. This year he received the following payments from Y Company:

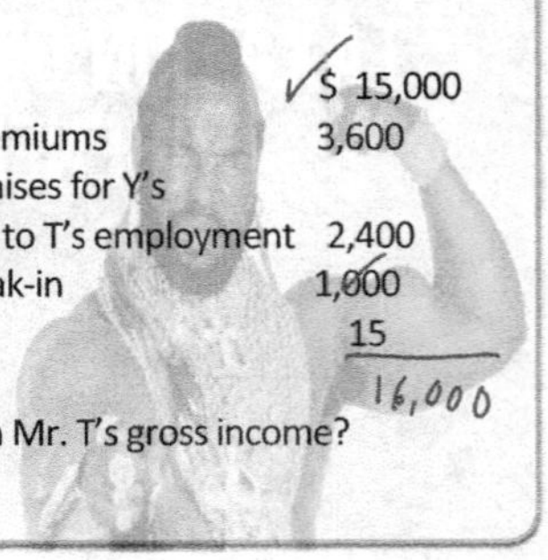

Salary	$ 15,000
Hospitalization insurance premiums	3,600
Required lodging on Y's premises for Y's convenience as a condition to T's employment	2,400
Reward for preventing a break-in	1,000
Christmas ham (value)	15
	16,000

What amount is includable in Mr. T's gross income?

Other Employee Benefits

Employees can exclude (up to $5,000; $2,500 if married filing separately) from gross income the value of **child and dependent care services** provided by the employer, if the services are provided so that the employee can work.

Employees can exclude (up to $5,250) from gross income the value of assistance provided by the employer **for *undergraduate and graduate* tuition, fees, books, and supplies.**

Tuition Waivers

Employees of **nonprofit educational institutions** can exclude **undergraduate tuition** waivers for themselves, their spouse, and dependent children from gross income if the institution has a qualified tuition reduction plan.

Graduate tuition waivers are excluded from income only for **graduate teaching/research assistants**.

Other Employee Benefits

Employees can exclude from gross income **expenses incurred to adopt a child**, if these expenses are reimbursed by the employer.

The exclusion is phased-out at higher AGI levels.

Cafeteria Plans

Under a cafeteria plan, an employee can choose between cash and certain "qualified benefits."

Cash is treated as wages.

Qualified benefits are tax-free benefits if they would have been tax-free if not offered through a cafeteria plan.

Cafeteria Plans

Qualified benefits include:

- Benefits/coverage under accident or health plans
- Long-term or short-term disability coverage
- Group-term life insurance coverage
- Dependent care assistance programs
- Section 401(k) plans
- Contributions through health savings accounts
- Adoption assistance

Stock Options

	Incentive Stock Option	Non-Qualified Stock Option
Grant Date	None	None
Exercise Date	None (except amt.)	Ordinary Income
Sale Date	Ordinary Income/ Capital Gain (amt. adj. reverses)	Capital Gain

Corporation receives deduction for ordinary income portion only.

Non-Qualified Stock Options

On the exercise date, the employee recognizes ordinary income equal to:

(FMV of Stock – Exercise Price) x # of shares exercised

Non-Qualified Stock Options Example

Greg received 100 non-qualified stock options to purchase E.com stock on October 17, Year 4. At the grant date the stock had a fair market value of $10, and an option price of $6. On December 12, Year 4 Greg exercised the stock options. The FMV of the stock was $14 at that time On January 5, Year 5 Greg sold the 100 shares for $15 per share.

How much income should Greg report on his Year 4 tax return?

Non-Qualified Stock Options Solution

Year 4:
(FMV of Stock - Exercise Price) x # of shares exercised
(14 - 6) x 100 =
$ 800 OI

Year 5:
Amount Realized 15
Adjusted Basis ‹14›
Short-term capital gain 1 x 100 = $100

Incentive Stock Options

The gain on sale is LTCG if acquired stock is:

- Held more than one year, and
- Not sold until after two years from the date the option was granted.

Incentive Stock Options

If these requirements are not met, the option is treated like a non-qualified stock option:

1. the gain on the stock sale is ordinary income, and the employer receives a deduction, equal to the stock's FMV on the exercise date over the exercise price, and
2. the difference in the FMV on the sale date and the FMV on the exercise date is capital gain or loss.

Incentive Stock Options Example

In Year 1 Jan received an incentive stock option from her employer with an exercise price of $10. The fair market value of the stock at that time was $10.

Jan exercised the option on December 30, Year 1, when the fair market value of the stock was $13. Jan sold the stock on May 15, Year 4 for $20.

How much income should Jan report on her Year 1 tax return?

Incentive Stock Options Solution (Sold in Year 4)

Grant Date	YR 1
Exercise Date	12/30/1
Sale Date	5/15/4

> 2 yr (grant to sale); > 1 yr (exercise to sale)

Year 4

Amount Realized	20
Adjusted Basis	(10)
Long-term Capital Gain	10

Incentive Stock Options Solution (Sold in Year 2)

Year 2

Ordinary Income =
(FMV of Stock - Exercise Price) x # of shares exercised

(13 - 10) = $3

Amount Realized	20
Adjusted Basis	(13)
Short-term Capital Gain	7

TAXATION OF RETIREMENT PLANS

Qualified Plans

Income for contributions of salary to "qualified" pension plans are deferred until distributions are made from the pension.

Earnings in the plan are not taxed until distributed.

For a plan to be "qualified," it must meet nondiscriminatory, funding, vesting, and certain participation/coverage requirements.

Early withdrawals (before age 59 1/2) trigger a penalty in addition to the taxation of the withdrawal.

Traditional IRAs

The limit for a traditional IRA contribution (deductible or nondeductible) is the lower of the annual ceiling amount or compensation.

If the taxpayer is not a participant in a qualified pension plan, the IRA contributions can be deducted "for" AGI.

IRA contributions can also be deducted by taxpayers who are active participants in qualified plans, but this deduction is phased out proportionately above a certain level of modified AGI.

Traditional IRAs

A married taxpayer who is not an active participant can deduct contributions even if the taxpayer's spouse is an active participant. However, this deduction is phased-out proportionately above a certain level of modified AGI.

All phase-outs are pro-rate over the phase-out range (usually $10,000 or $20,000 range).

Taxpayers who cannot deduct IRA contributions can nonetheless defer the income earned by **nondeductible IRA contributions** to traditional IRAs.

Traditional IRAs

IRA contributions must be made by the original due date of the return (April 15) to be deductible for the previous tax year.

Nondeductible contributions to traditional IRAs are reported on **Form 8606**.

Withdrawals from a traditional IRA must begin when the taxpayer reaches age 70 ½.

Roth IRAs

Contributions are **not deductible** but can only be made if modified AGI does not exceed certain levels.

Withdrawals of income accumulated in a Roth IRA are not taxed as income if the distribution:

1. occurred five years or more from the date of the initial contribution, and
2. is made on or after an individual attains age 59 ½.

Withdrawals are not required once the taxpayer reaches age 70 ½.

Withdrawals – IRAs

Withdrawals from an IRA may be subject to a **penalty tax of 10%**. This tax is not imposed if the taxpayer is disabled, age 59 ½, separated from service after age 55, or has died.

Also if:

- made in the form of certain periodic payments;
- for first-time homebuyers (up to $10,000);
- used to pay qualified higher education expenses;
- pay health insurance premiums if unemployed, or
- used to pay medical expenses in excess of 7.5% of AGI.

IRA Conversions

Taxpayers can convert a traditional IRA to a Roth IRA.

The taxpayer must recognize gain at the time of the conversion to the extent that the conversion amount exceeds the tax basis in the IRA.

This same rule applies to conversions of 401(k) plans into Roth plans.

These conversions are reported on Form 8606.

Distributions

Payments from retirement plans are included in income, except to the extent that the employee has "basis" in the plan.

An employee has **basis** to the extent that the employee made **nondeductible contributions** to the plan.

The following do not create basis:

1. Contributions made by employers
2. Tax deductible employee contributions
3. Tax-free earnings inside the plan.

Distribution Problem

John invested $5,000 a year into his retirement plan from his taxable earnings. His employer contributed $8,000 a year to John's retirement fund. After 20 years of contributions, John retires and receives a distribution, which is not tax-free, of $750,000, the balance in his retirement fund. John must include what amount in gross income:

Distribution	$750000
Basis	⟨100,000⟩ 20 x $5,000
Income	$650,000

Tax on Excess Accumulations

Distributions from qualified plans must begin by the "required beginning date" and the payment each year must be at least equal to the required minimum distribution.

If the required distribution is not made a tax equal to 50% of the required distribution not made must be paid.

Distributions must begin by April 1 of the later of:

- The year the taxpayer reaches age 70 ½, or
- The year the employee retires.

Keough Plans

Keogh plans are for **self-employed taxpayers.** Contributions are limited to the lesser of the annual limitation or 100% of earned income.

Earned income equals net earnings from self-employment less 50% of the self-employment tax less the allowable Keogh contribution.

Section 401(k) Plans

A 401(k) plan allows voluntary employee contributions to reduce taxable salary up to an annual limit, plus a catch-up amount for those age 50 and over.

Employers often match a certain percentage of employee contributions to these plans.

Simplified Employee Pension Plan (SEP)

A SEP is an individual retirement plan established by an employer.

Employer contributions for a year must be made to each SEP of each employee who has:

- reached age 21,
- performed service for the employer during at least three of the immediately preceding five years, and
- has received a certain level of compensation.

Simplified Employee Pension Plan (SEP)

Maximum allowable contributions made by an employer to a SEP cannot exceed the lower of:

- 25% of compensation, or
- the dollar limitation for defined contribution plans.

Contributions can be made up to the **extended due date of the return**.

Section 529 Plans

These plans are used to save for college expenses through a vehicle that allows the earnings to be excluded from gross income.

Contributions are not deductible, and a beneficiary must be specified for the plan.

States typically allow lifetime contributions to the plan of as much as $250,000.

Earnings in the plan are tax deferred.

Section 529 Plans

Distributions from the plans are excluded from income to the extent the distribution is used to pay for tuition, fees, book, etc., and reasonable room and board costs.

Distributions not used for a qualified purpose are subject to income taxation and a 10% penalty.

John invested $2,000 a year into his retirement plan from his before tax earnings (that is, he received a deduction for these contributions and was not taxed on the income). His employer contributed $3,000 a year to John's retirement fund. After 30 years of contributions, John retires and receives a distribution, which is not tax-free, of $350,000, the balance in his retirement fund. John must include what amount in gross income?

- [ ] A. **$0**
- [ ] B. **$200,000**
- [ ] C. **$260,000**
- [ ] D. **$350,000**

A 33-year-old taxpayer withdrew $30,000 (pretax) from a traditional IRA. The taxpayer has a 33% effective tax rate and a 35% marginal tax rate. What is the total tax liability associated with the withdrawal?

- A. **$10,000**
- B. **$10,500**
- C. **$13,000**
- D. **$13,500**

Easel Co. has elected to reimburse employees for business expenses under a non-accountable plan.

Easel does not require employees to provide proof of expenses and allows employees to keep any amount not spent. Under the plan, Mel, an Easel employee for a full year, gets $400 per month for business automobile expenses.
At the end of the year, Mel informs Easel that the only business expense incurred was for business mileage of 12,000 at a rate of 30 cents per mile, the IRS standard mileage rate at the time. Mel encloses a check for $1,200 to refund the overpayment to Easel.

What amount should be reported in Mel's gross income for the year?

- [ ] A. **$0**
- [ ] B. **$1,200**
- [ ] C. **$3,600**
- [ ] D. **$4,800**

REG 7-1

DEDUCTIONS 1

Deductions: Basic Principles

Deductions for AGI

Selected Questions (2)

DEDUCTIONS - BASIC PRINCIPLES

Individual Deductions

Deductions can be divided into two broad categories:

1. Deductions for AGI
2. Deductions from AGI (i.e., itemized deductions)

Activities for Tax Purposes

Activities/transactions can be divided into three mutually exclusive categories:

1. Trade or Business
2. Investment
3. Personal

Types of Deductions

Expenses related to one's personal activities cannot be deducted unless specifically provided for in the IRC (e.g., charitable contributions, mortgage interest).

Expenses related to **trade or business** activities are deductible if they are related to the business operations and are ordinary, necessary, and reasonable.

Types of Deductions

Expenses related to investment activities or other activities that produce income are deductible if ordinary, necessary, and reasonable.

Expenses related to the management or maintenance of property and in connection with the determination of any tax are deductible.

Types of Deductions

Definition: "Ordinary and necessary" are usually interpreted to mean the nature of the expenditure is customary and appropriate under the circumstances.

The expenditure must be "reasonable" in amount.

Review Question

Rich is a cash basis self-employed air-conditioning repairman with Year 5 gross business receipts of $20,000. Rich's cash disbursements were as follows:

Air conditioning parts	$2,500 ✓
Yellow Pages listing	2,000 ✓
Estimated federal income taxes on self-employment	1,000
Business long-distance telephone calls	400 ✓
Charitable contributions	200

What amount should Rich report as net self-employment income? 20,000 − 4,900 = $15,100

Disallowed Deductions

Executive compensation for the CEO and the four other most highly compensated officers that exceeds $1 million per person is not deductible unless the income is based on a performance based compensation plan.

Disallowed Deductions

Lobbying expenses at the state and federal level; deductions are permitted at the city and county government level.

No expenses can be deducted if the expense is used to **generate tax-exempt income**.

Political contributions.

Expenses Against Public Policy

No expenses can be deducted if the expenditure is against public policy (e.g., illegal). Examples include bribes, fines, penalties, and expenses of operating an illegal drug business.

However, cost of goods sold can be deducted for an illegal drug business.

Note that the ordinary, necessary, and reasonable expenses of operating other illegal businesses are permitted (as long as the expense itself is not against public policy).

Prepaid Expenses

For prepaid expenses under the cash method, an immediate deduction can be taken when paid as long as the benefits from the expenditure do not extend beyond the earlier of:

- 12 months after benefits first begin, or
- The end of the year after the year in which the payment was made.

If the **12 month rule** is not met then the expenses are amortized over the benefit period.

Prepaid interest must always be amortized over the life of the loan.

Accrual Method Exceptions

The taxpayer can deduct refunds, rebates, awards, prizes, provision of warranty work or service contracts, taxes, and insurance premiums only when actually paid.

Vacation pay and bonuses are deducted only if paid within two and one-half months after the close of the tax year.

DEDUCTIONS FOR AGI

Business and Rental Expenses

Income from Sole Proprietorships is reported on Schedule C net of business deductions.

The net income is transferred to page 1 of Form 1040 so these deductions are for AGI.

Similarly, deductions from Rental Property reported on Schedule E are also deductions for AGI; and for farming operations on Schedule F.

Moving Expenses

Deductible if related to work at a **new job** (even if this is first job).

Qualified moving expenses include reasonable expenses for:

- moving household goods and personal items, and
- traveling (lodging is included, but not meals) from the former residence to the new residence.

If the mileage rate is used for automobile expenses, a special rate is provided for moving expenses.

Moving Expenses

Distance Test: The new job location must be at least 50 miles farther from the taxpayer's old residence than the old residence was from the previous place of employment. If no former job, the new job must be at least 50 miles from the former residence.

Moving Expenses

Time Test: The employee must be employed on a full-time basis at the new location for 39 weeks in the 12-month period following the move (78 weeks during 24 months if self-employed, and 39 weeks must fall within first 12 months).

Moving Expenses

Barlow moved from Chicago to Miami to start a new job, incurring costs of $1,200 to move household goods and $2,500 in temporary living expenses. Barlow was not reimbursed for any of these expenses.

TIME?

What amount should Barlow deduct for moving expenses?

$1,200

Interest on Education Loans

Individuals can deduct interest paid on education loans.

The maximum deduction is **$2,500**.

Interest on Education Loans

Education loan is defined as a loan to pay higher education expenses for the taxpayer and the taxpayer's spouse and dependents.

The deduction is phased out for certain higher-income taxpayers.

A taxpayer will not be allowed a deduction if she can be declared as a dependent by someone else.

Other Deductions for AGI

Alimony is deductible by the payor as a deduction for AGI

One-half of self employment taxes as computed on Schedule SE is allowed as a deduction for AGI

100% of the costs of **health insurance premiums** are deductible by self-employed workers as long as the amount does not exceed the taxpayer's net earnings from self-employment

IRA and other retirement plan contributions

Other Deductions for AGI

Forfeiture penalties

Repayment of jury duty fees to employer

Alimony Example

Rick and Stacy were divorced in February of the current year. Requirements of the divorce decree and Stacy's performance follow:

- Transfer title to their residence to Rick. Stacy's basis was $95,000. The fair market value was $105,000, and the residence was subject to a mortgage of $90,000. Make the mortgage payments of $1,000 per month (beginning in March) for the remaining 20 years or until Rick dies, if sooner.
- Pay Rick $500 per month (beginning in March) for 6 years or until Rick dies, if sooner. Of this amount, $200 is designated as child support.

How much is Stacy's alimony deduction?

In the current year, an unmarried individual with modified adjusted gross income of $25,000 paid $1,000 interest on a qualified education loan entered into on July 1.

How may the individual treat the interest for income tax purposes?

- [ ] **A. As a $500 deduction to arrive at AGI for the year.**
- [ ] **B. As a $1,000 deduction to arrive at AGI for the year.**
- [ ] **C. As a $1,000 itemized deduction.**
- [ ] **D. As a nondeductible item of personal interest.**

Tom owns a fast-food restaurant which he reports as a sole proprietorship for tax purposes. Which of the following expenses is allowed as a deduction on Tom's Schedule C for the current year?

- [ ] A. **Wages of $20 per week to his 14 year-old daughter who cleans the restaurant on Saturdays.**
- [ ] B. **Speeding ticket of $75 that he incurred while picking up supplies to bring to the restaurant.**
- [ ] C. **A bribe of $200 to the city inspector charged with inspecting whether restaurants have met all city health requirements.**
- [ ] D. **State income taxes paid during the year of $1,650.**

REG 7-2

DEDUCTIONS 2

Itemized Deductions - Medical, Taxes, Interest

Itemized Deductions - Other

Selected Questions (3)

ITEMIZED DEDUCTIONS – MEDICAL, TAXES, INTEREST

Standard Deduction

Individuals deduct the greater of the standard deduction or itemized deductions.

Standard deduction amounts vary according to filing status.

Medical Expenses

Deductible for taxpayer, spouse, and **dependent** (gross income and joint return tests do not apply for this purpose).

Deductible Items:

- Dental, medical, and hospital care
- Prescription drugs
- Equipment such as wheelchairs, crutches, eyeglasses, hearing aids, contacts
- Transportation for medical care
- Medical insurance premiums
- Qualified long-term care expenses and insurance;
- Alcohol and drug rehabilitation
- Weight-reduction programs if as part of medical treatment

Non-deductible Items

- Funeral, burial, and cremation expenses
- Nonprescription drugs (except insulin)
- Bottled water
- Toiletries
- Cosmetics
- Health spas, stop smoking clinics
- Unnecessary cosmetic surgery

Formula for Medical Expenses

Qualified Medical Expenses

\- Reimbursements from Insurance

\- 7.5% of AGI

Deductible Medical Expenses

Medical Expenses Problem

Smith paid the following unreimbursed medical expenses:

Dentist and eye doctor fees	$ 5,000
Contact lenses	500
Facial cosmetic surgery to improve Smith's personal appearance (surgery is unrelated to personal injury or congenital deformity)	10,000
Premium on disability insurance policy to pay him if he is injured and unable to work	2,000

What is the total amount of Smith's tax-deductible medical expenses before the adjusted gross income limitation?

Real Estate Taxes

Real estate taxes on property used for personal purposes are itemized deductions.

State, local, and foreign taxes on real property are deductible, but only by the person legally liable for the tax.

Income Taxes

Foreign, state and local income taxes are itemized deductions, even if partially due to business income.

Taxes

Personal property taxes based on the value of the property (*ad valorem*) are deductible.

Other property taxes are not deductible.

Special assessments are not deductible.

Fees, licenses (dog, automobile, hunting and fishing, etc.) are not deductible.

Taxes Example

George Burke, a salaried taxpayer, paid the following taxes which were not incurred in connection with a business:

Federal income tax (withheld by employer)	$1,500
State income tax (withheld by employer)	1,000
FICA tax (withheld by employer)	700
State sales taxes	900
Federal auto gasoline taxes	200
Federal excise tax on telephone bills	50

What taxes are allowable deductions from Burke's adjusted gross income?

Interest Expense

Personal interest: Credit card interest, car loan interest, and interest on income tax underpayments are not deductible.

Investment interest expense is limited to net investment income (investment income less investment expenses).

Investment Interest Example

For the current year, David Roth, a married taxpayer filing a joint return, reported the following:

Investment income from dividends and interest	$24,000
LTCG on stock held for investment	25,000
Investment expenses	4,000
Interest expense on funds borrowed to purchase investment property	70,000

Assuming that David elects to treat the gain as investment income, what amount can Roth deduct as investment interest expense?

Investment Interest Example

Assuming that David elects to treat the gain as investment income, what amount can Roth deduct as investment interest expense?

Net investment income = Inv Inc - Inv Exp

49,000 − 4,000 = 45,000

Deduction = 45,000

Carryforward = 70,000 − 45,000 = 25,000

Mortgage Interest Expense

Interest paid or incurred on debt secured by a qualified residence (principal residence plus one other residence) is deductible. Debt is limited to $1,000,000.

Deductible interest also includes interest on the portion of **home equity loans** that does not exceed the lesser of:

The fair market value of the residence less the lower of remaining acquisition indebtedness, or $100,000.

Mortgage Interest Example

On January 2 of the current year the Philips paid $50,000 cash and obtained a $200,000 mortgage to purchase a home.

This year they borrowed $15,000 secured by their home, and used the cash to add a new room to their residence.

They also took out a $5,000 auto loan.

Mortgage Interest Example

The following information pertains to interest paid in the current year:

Mortgage interest	✓ $ 17,000
Interest on room construction loan	✓ 1,500
Auto loan interest	500

How much interest is deductible, prior to any itemized deduction limitations? $18,500

ITEMIZED DEDUCTIONS - OTHER

Charitable Contributions

- Must be made to a **qualified charitable organization**.
- Payments to individuals do not qualify.
- No deduction is allowed for a contribution of services.
- Overall deduction is **limited to 50% of AGI**.
- Carryover is 5 years - **no carryback!**

Charitable Contributions

LTCG and Section 1231 property: FMV is deductible

All other property, the deduction is the lesser of:
- The adjusted basis of the property, or
- The FMV of the property.

Charitable Contributions Example

Moore, a single taxpayer, had $50,000 in adjusted gross income this year. During the current year she contributed $18,000 to her church. She had a $10,000 charitable contribution carryover from her previous year church contribution.

What is the maximum amount of properly substantiated charitable contributions that Moore could claim as an itemized deduction for this year?

Charitable Contributions Solution

AGI 50,000

Limitation x50% $25,000

Contributions:

Current 18,000

Carryover 10,000 7,000 3,000

25,000

Casualty Losses

Casualties must be sudden and unexpected.

Typical casualties include natural disasters, thefts, and automobile accidents.

Damage caused from erosion is not sudden, and does not qualify as a casualty.

The deduction equals the lesser of:
- The decline in the FMV of the property, or
- The adjusted basis of the property

Casualty Losses

For **personal casualty** losses, the deduction is computed as follows:

Lower of decline in FMV or AB of property
- Insurance Reimbursements
- Casualty Floor
- 10% x AGI

Casualty loss deduction

Casualty Losses Example

The following two items are based on the following selected information pertaining to Sam and Ann Hoyt, who, filed a joint federal income tax return for the current calendar year.

The Hoyts had adjusted gross income of $34,000 and itemized their deductions this year. The Hoyts' cash expenditures follow.

What amount of fire loss were the Hoyts entitled to deduct as an itemized deduction on their return?

Casualty Losses Example

$2,500 repairs in connection with fire damage to the Hoyt residence.

This property has a basis of $50,000. Fair market value was $60,000 before the fire and $55,000 after the fire. Insurance on the property had lapsed in 1999 for nonpayment of premium.

$800 appraisal fee to determine amount of fire loss.

Casualty Loss Solution

Lower of decline in FMV or AB of property	5,000 / 50,000	5,000
- Insurance Reimbursements		-0-
- Casualty Floor		⟨100⟩
- 10% x AGI	34,000	⟨3400⟩
Casualty loss deduction		1500

2% Miscellaneous Itemized Deductions

The following deductions are, in the aggregate, allowed only to the extent that they exceed 2% of adjusted gross income:

- Unreimbursed employee expenses, and expenses reimbursed but not under an accountable plan
- Expenses relating to tax planning and return preparation (for all taxes)
- Investment expenses, including:
  - Fees paid for investment advice
  - Safe deposit box rental fees

Other Miscellaneous Deductions

Certain miscellaneous expenses are not subject to the 2% rules, including:

- Gambling losses to the extent of gambling winnings
- Certain expenses of short sales
- Unrecovered annuity costs

2% Miscellaneous Itemized Deductions Example

Mr. G, a construction worker, had adjusted gross income of $30,000. He incurred the following employment-related and investment-related miscellaneous expenses. He was not reimbursed for any of the employment-related expenses.

What is the amount of his miscellaneous expense deduction after any limitations?

2% Misc. Itemized Deductions Example

Safety shoes	✓$ 100
Union initiation fees	✓2,000
Union dues	✓ 300
Life insurance	800
Jeans and flannel shirts for work	200
Management fees on investments producing taxable income	INV ✓1,200
Legal expenses for drafting a will	200

2% Misc. Itemized Deductions Example

Total 2% Deductions:

Work related:	2400
Investment expenses:	1200
	3600
2% x Adjusted Gross Income 2% x 30,000	(600)
Allowable Deduction	3,000

Moore, a single taxpayer, had $50,000 in adjusted gross income for 2012. During 2012, she contributed $18,000 to her church. She had a $10,000 charitable contribution carryover from her 2011 church contribution.

What was the maximum amount of properly substantiated charitable contributions that Moore could claim as an itemized deduction for 2012?

- [ ] A. **$10,000**
- [ ] B. **$18,000**
- [ ] C. **$25,000**
- [ ] D. **$28,000**

Hall, a divorced person and custodian of her 12-year old child, filed her 2012 federal income tax return as head of a household. She submitted the following information to the CPA who prepared her 2012 return:

- The divorce agreement, executed in 2010, provides for Hall to receive $3,000 per month, of which $600 is designated as child support. After the child reaches 18, the monthly payments are to be reduced to $2,400 and are to be continued until remarriage or death. However, for the year 2012, Hall received a total of only $5,000 from her former husband. Hall paid an attorney $2,000 in 2012 in a suit to collect the alimony owed.
- In June 2012, Hall's mother gifted her 100 shares of a listed stock. The donor's basis for this stock, which she bought in 1995, was $4,000, and market value on the date of the gift was $3,000. Hall sold her stock in July 2012 for $3,500. The donor paid no gift tax.
- During 2012, Hall spent a total of $1,000 for state lottery tickets. Her lottery winnings in 2012 totaled $200.
- Hall earned a salary of $25,000 in 2012. Hall was not covered by any type of retirement plan, but contributed $2,000 to an IRA in 2012.
- In 2012, Hall sold an antique that she bought in 2005 to display in her home. Hall paid $800 for the antique and sold it for $1,400, using the proceeds to pay a court-ordered judgment.
- Hall paid the following expenses in 2012 pertaining to the home that she owns: realty taxes, $3,400; mortgage interest, $7,000; casualty insurance, $490; assessment by city for construction of a sewer system, $910; interest of $1,000 on a personal, unsecured bank loan, the proceeds of which were used for home improvements. Hall does not rent out any portion of the home.

The $2,000 legal fee that Hall paid to collect alimony should be treated as

- [ ] **A. A deduction in arriving at adjusted gross income.**
- [ ] **B. An itemized deduction subject to the 2% of adjusted gross income floor.**
- [ ] **C. An itemized deduction not subject to the 2% of adjusted gross income floor.**
- [ ] **D. A nondeductible personal expense.**

Carroll, an unmarried taxpayer with an adjusted gross income of $100,000, incurred and paid the following unreimbursed medical expenses for the year:

Doctor bills resulting from a serious fall	**$ 5,000**
Cosmetic surgery that was necessary to correct a congenital deformity	**15,000**

Carroll had no medical insurance. For regular income tax purposes, what was Carroll's maximum allowable medical expense deduction, after the applicable threshold limitation, for the year?

- A. **$0**
- B. **$12,500**
- C. **$15,000**
- D. **$20,000**

REG 7-3

DEDUCTIONS 3

Employee Business Expenses

Selected Questions (1)

EMPLOYEE BUSINESS EXPENSES

Accountable Plan

If employee business expenses are reimbursed under an **accountable plan**, then the reimbursement is **not taxable** (for FICA or income tax) and the employee gets **no deduction** for the expense.

If the expenses are reimbursed, but not under an accountable plan, the reimbursement must be included in income (for FICA and income tax) and the deduction is a **2% miscellaneous itemized deduction**.

Accountable Plan

If the expenses are not reimbursed by the employer, the employees deduction is a 2% miscellaneous itemized deduction.

For a plan to be accountable:

- Employees must substantiate all expenses to be reimbursed, and
- All excess reimbursements must be returned to the employer.

Review Question

Easel Co. has elected to reimburse employees for business expenses under a non-accountable plan. Easel does not require employees to provide proof of expenses and allows employees to keep any amount not spent. Under the plan, Mel, an Easel employee for a full year, gets $400 per month for business automobile expenses. At the end of the year Mel informs Easel that the only business expense incurred was for business mileage of 12,000 at a rate of 30 cents per mile, the IRS standard mileage rate at the time. Mel encloses a check for $1,200 to refund the overpayment to Easel.

What amounts should be reported in Mel's gross income for the year? 12 X $400 = $4,800

Transportation Expenses

Commuting between the taxpayer's residence and the place of business is never deductible.

However, travel from one job or work area to a second job or work area is deductible.

Also, travel from home to a "temporary work location" is deductible if the assignment is short-term in nature.

Transportation Expenses

Transportation costs include direct costs (airfare, tolls, gas, depreciation of a vehicle, insurance, etc.), or a mileage rate can be claimed for auto use.

If the mileage rate is used, the only costs added to this amount are for parking and tolls.

Travel Expenses

- Includes transportation expenses and meals and lodging while **away from your business home**
- Away from home means that the taxpayer must be **gone overnight** to be away from home.
- If the taxpayer is assigned to a new location for an indefinite period of time or for more than a year, the "tax home" shifts to the new location. Thus, there would be no travel expenses.
- The cost of **meals is reduced by 50%**

CPAexcel

Travel Expenses

For business travel that is mixed with personal travel, the transportation to the location is deductible **only if greater than 50% of the total days are business days**

If the 50% test is met, all of the transportation costs to the location are deductible. If not met, then none of the transportation costs are deductible.

If Friday and Monday are both business days, then the weekend can be counted as business days also.

No deduction is allowed for travel to "investment" seminars.

CPAexcel

Review Question

Baker, a sole proprietor CPA, has several clients that do business in Spain. While on a four-week vacation in Spain, Baker took a five-day seminar on Spanish business practices that cost $700. Baker's round trip airfare to Spain was $600. While in Spain, Baker spent an average of $100 per day on accommodations, local travel, and other incidental expenses, for total expenses of $2,800.
What amount of educational expense can Baker deduct on Form 1040 Schedule C, "Profit or Loss from Business"?

Travel Expense Solution

Business Days/Total Days: 5/28   AIR X

Deductible Expenses:
Seminar Costs   700

Daily Travel Expenses – 5 days x (100)   500

1,200

Entertainment Expenses

Only **50%** of meal and entertainment expenses are deductible.

A meal must be related to a clear business purpose to be deductible.

Entertainment Expenses

Dues to clubs organized for pleasure or recreation are not deductible. Dues for public service clubs (e.g., Kiwanis), professional organizations, and trade associations are deductible

The deduction for tickets to an entertainment activity is limited to the face value of the ticket (before the 50% disallowance)

Business gifts are limited to $25 per donee per year

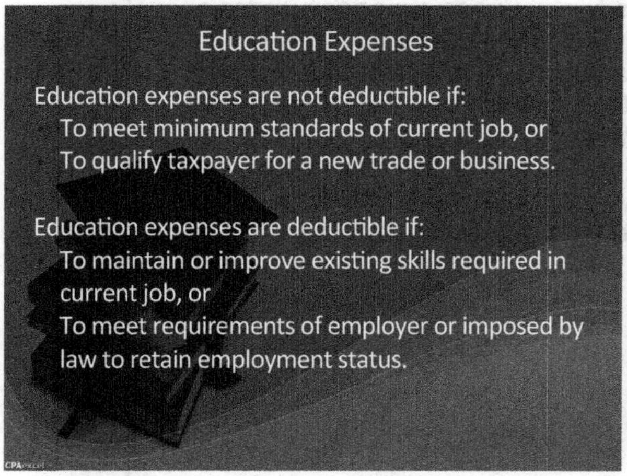
Education Expenses
Education expenses are not deductible if:
To meet minimum standards of current job, or
To qualify taxpayer for a new trade or business.
Education expenses are deductible if:
To maintain or improve existing skills required in current job, or
To meet requirements of employer or imposed by law to retain employment status.

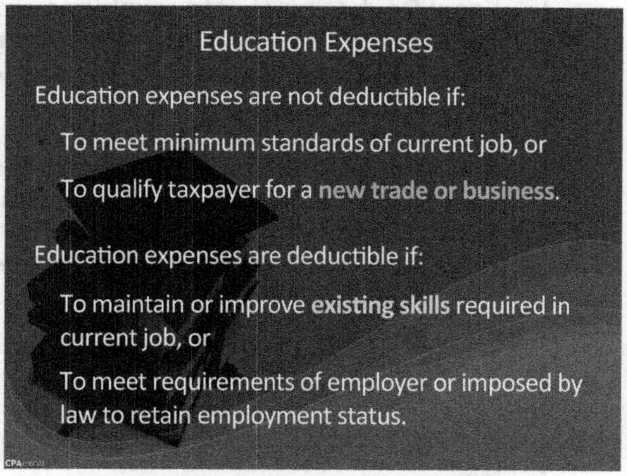
Education Expenses
Education expenses are not deductible if:
To meet minimum standards of current job, or
To qualify taxpayer for a new trade or business.
Education expenses are deductible if:
To maintain or improve existing skills required in current job, or
To meet requirements of employer or imposed by law to retain employment status.

Easel Co. has elected to reimburse employees for business expenses under a nonaccountable plan. Easel does not require employees to provide proof of expenses and allows employees to keep any amount not spent. Under the plan, Mel, an Easel employee for a full year, gets $400 per month for business automobile expenses. At the end of the year Mel informs Easel that the only business expense incurred was for business mileage of 12,000 at a rate of 30 cents per mile, the IRS standard mileage rate at the time. Mel encloses a check for $1,200 to refund the overpayment to Easel. What amounts should be reported in Mel's gross income for the year?

- [ ] A. **$0**
- [ ] B. **$1,200**
- [ ] C. **$3,600**
- [ ] D. **$4,800**

REG 7-4

DEDUCTIONS 4

Deductions - Losses and Bad Debts

Limitations on Business Deductions

Selected Questions (2)

DEDUCTIONS - LOSSES AND BAD DEBTS

Bad Debts

Bad debts are deductible only for **accrual basis** taxpayers that have previously recognized income, and therefore have basis in the receivable.

The **specific-charge off method** must be used (financial institutions can use the reserve method).

A business bad debt is deducted against ordinary income in the year that partial or total worthlessness occurs.

Non-Business Bad Debts

Nonbusiness bad debts include debts provided by a lender that is not in the business of lending money (e.g., loans to relatives and friends) and loans that are not directly related to a taxpayer's trade or business.

A NBD is always treated as a short-term capital loss.

No deduction is allowed until the debt becomes totally worthless.

Bad Debts Problem

Jason Budd, CPA, reports on the cash basis. In April Year 4, Budd billed a client $3,500 for the following professional services:

Personal estate planning	$ 2,000
Personal tax return preparation	1,000
Compilation of business financial statements	500

No part of the $3,500 was ever paid. In April Year 5, the client declared bankruptcy, and the $3,500 obligation became totally uncollectible.
What loss can Budd deduct on his tax return for this bad debt?

Worthless Securities

A worthless asset is treated as being sold for no consideration on last day of the year.

This rule applies to stocks and bonds.

In general, the security must be totally worthless.

NOLs

NOLs must be **carried back to the two** preceding tax years (beginning with the second prior year) unless an election is made in the year of the NOL to forego the carryback.

The **carryover period is 20 years**.

NOLs

NOLs are only allowed for **business losses and casualty** losses. Any nonbusiness losses or expenses must be added back to the taxable loss to determine the NOL.

NOL - Problem

Destry, a single taxpayer, reported the following on his U.S. Individual Income Tax Return Form 1040:

Income:

Wages $5,000 B

Interest on savings account 1,000 I

Net rental income 4,000 B

Deductions: P

Personal exemption: current year amount P

Standard deduction: current year amount B

Net business loss 16,000 I

Net short-term capital loss 2,000

What is Destry's net operating loss that is available for carryback or carryforward?

NOL - Solution

Wages	5,000
Non-Business Income 1,000 Less Non-Business Deductions (standard deduction)	Ø
Rental Income	4,000
Business Losses	(16000)
Net Operating Loss	(7000)

LIMITATIONS ON BUSINESS DEDUCTIONS

Hobby Losses

Losses from hobbies are personal expenses that are not deductible.

If the taxpayer clearly has a profit motive then the activity is not a hobby.

Profit-seeking is presumed if profit in **three of last five** years.

Otherwise is presumed to be a hobby.

Hobby Loss Deductions

Expenses from a hobby are deductible only to the extent of income.

Expenses related to the hobby are deducted in the following order:

1. Items that would have been deductible anyway
2. Other cash expenses
3. Depreciation

Hobby Loss Deductions

Revenue from a hobby is reported on page 1 of Form 1040.

Cash expenses and depreciation are reported as 2% miscellaneous itemized deductions.

Home Office Expenses

Expenses for a home office are deductible if it is used **exclusively** (i.e., solely) on a regular basis as either:

- The principal place of business for a trade/ business of the taxpayer, or
- A place of business used by clients, patients, or customers, and
- The use is for the **convenience of the employer** (if employed).

Home Office Expenses

Home office expense deduction is limited to income from the business less all other business expenses.

Expenses are deducted in the same order as for hobby losses.

Any disallowed expenses are carried forward to future years (indefinitely) and used when there is sufficient business income.

Vacation Homes

If rented for less than 15 days a year, it is treated as a **personal residence**.

Rent income is **excluded**.

Mortgage interest and property taxes are deductible on Schedule A.

Vacation Homes

It is treated as **rental property** if rented for 15 days or more, and if it is **not** used for personal purposes for more than the greater of

- 14 days or
- 10% of the total days rented.

Vacation Homes

All rent is taxable, net of all regular rental expenses, pro-rated for the percentage of rental days only.

A rental **loss is allowable**.

Vacation Homes

It is treated as a **personal/rental property** if rented for 15 days or more and if it is used for personal purposes for more than the greater of

- 14 days or
- 10% of the total days rented.

All regular expenses are pro-rated as above for rental days, but a rental **loss is not allowed**.

Expenses must be deducted in the same order as for a hobby.

Vacation Home - Problem

Adam owns a second residence that is used for both personal and rental purposes. This year, Jackson used the second residence for 50 days and rented the residence for 200 days.
Which of the following statements is correct?

50 200 Y

Rental Days: >= 15?

Personal Days: more than the greater of

14 days or

10% of the total days rented? 20 Y

(10% x 200 = 20)

Vacation Home - Problem

A. Depreciation may not be deducted on the property under any circumstances

B. A rental loss may be deducted if rental-related expenses exceed rental income

C. Utilities and maintenance on the property must be divided between personal and rental use

D. All mortgage interest and taxes on the property will be deducted to determine the property's net income or loss

Passive Losses

Losses from passive activities cannot offset earned income or portfolio income (i.e., investment income).

A passive activity is one in which the taxpayer does not "**materially participate**," most rental activities, and any limited partnership interest.

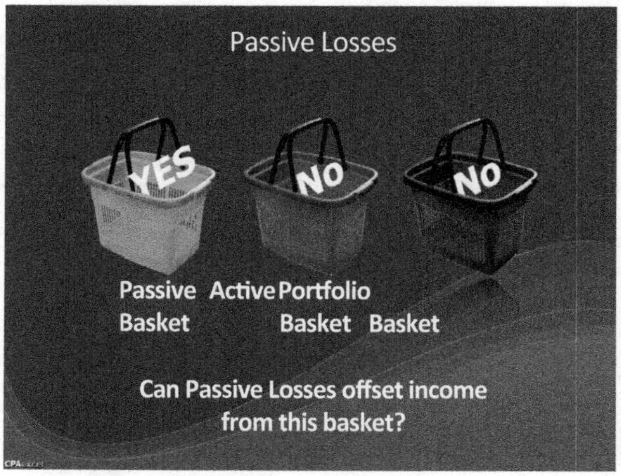

Passive Losses

If the taxpayer "**actively participates**" in a rental real estate activity, $25,000 of losses from such activities can offset active and portfolio income.

This deduction phases out between modified AGI of $100,000 and $150,000.

Disallowed passive losses can be carried forward to offset passive income in future years and to offset any gain or increase the loss when the passive activity is disposed of in a fully taxable transaction.

Barkley owns a vacation cabin that was rented to unrelated parties for 10 days during the year to unrelated parties for $2,500. The cabin was used personally by Barkley for 3 months and left vacant for the rest of the year. Expenses for the cabin were as follows:

Real Estate Taxes	**$1,000**
Maintenance and Utilities	**$2,000**

How much rental income (loss) is included in Barkley's adjusted gross income?

- A. **$0**
- B. **$ 500**
- C. **$ (500)**
- D. **$(1,500)**

Destry, a single taxpayer, reported the following on his 2012 U.S. Individual Income Tax Return Form 1040:

Income:	
Wages	**$ 5,000**
Interest on savings account	**1,000**
Net rental income	**4,000**
Deductions:	
Personal exemption	**$ 3,800**
Standard deduction	**5,950**
Net business loss	**16,000**
Net short-term capital loss	**2,000**

What is Destry's net operating loss that is available for carry back or carry forward?

- [ ] A. **$ 7,000**
- [ ] B. **$ 9,000**
- [ ] C. **$15,100**
- [ ] D. **$16,000**

REG 7-5

INDIVIDUAL TAX ISSUES

Personal and Dependency Exemptions

Filing Status

Alternative Minimum Tax and Other Taxes

Selected Questions (4)

PERSONAL AND DEPENDENCY EXEMPTIONS

Personal and Dependency Exemptions

Most taxpayers can claim an exemption in computing taxable income on their own return. No personal exemptions can be claimed for a taxpayer (or spouse) who is claimed as a dependent by another taxpayer.

Specific criteria must be met for one to claim another as a dependent. One can qualify as a dependent as either a **qualifying child or qualifying relative**.

Qualifying Child

A Qualifying Child can be claimed as a dependent if the following tests are met:

1. **Relationship test**: natural child, stepchild, adopted child, foster child, sibling, step-sibling, or a descendent of any of these.
   Note that this definition includes brothers, sisters, nieces and nephews.
2. **Residence test**: The dependent must have the same principal place of abode as the taxpayer for **more than one half of the tax year**. One could live with several individuals at the same time who potentially qualify to claim the individual as a dependent (mother, aunt, grandfather).

Qualifying Child

3. **Age test**: must be **less than 19** at the end of the tax year, or **less than 24** if a full-time student for at least five months of the tax year. There is no age limitation if the individual is permanently and totally disabled.
4. **Joint return test**: if the individual is married, he cannot be claimed as a dependent by another if he files a joint return with his spouse, unless there is no tax liability on the return.

Qualifying Child

5. **Citizenship/residency test**: the individual must be a U.S. citizen or resident, or a resident of Canada or Mexico.
6. **Not self-supporting test**: To be claimed as a dependent the individual must **not have provided more than 50%** of her own support.

Qualifying Relative

The qualifying relative rule defines "relative" very broadly, including all common relatives except for cousins.

The term also includes any person who lives in the taxpayer's home for the entire tax year.

Qualifying Relative

The following tests must be met to claim a qualifying relative as a dependent:

1. **Relationship test**
2. **Support test**: The taxpayer must provide more than 50% of the dependent's total support
3. **Joint return test**
4. **Citizenship/residency test**
5. **Gross income test**: The dependent's gross income must be less than the exemption amount for the year. Gross income is defined as only income that is taxable.

Qualifying Relative

There are two exceptions to the gross income test. These apply for a **child/stepchild** (adopted and foster also):

1. That is less than 19 at the end of the tax year, or
2. That is less than 24 at the end of the tax year and is a full-time student for at least five months during the tax year.

Review Question

Sam Dunn provided more than half the support for his wife, his father's brother, and his cousin. Sam's wife was the only relative who was a member of Sam's household. None of the relatives had any income, nor did any of them file an individual or a joint return. All of these relatives are U.S. citizens.

Which of these relatives should be claimed as a dependent or dependents on Sam's return?

UNCLE

Exemptions - Problem

Jim and Kay Ross contributed to the support of their two children, Dale and Kim, and Jim's widowed parent, Grant. Dale, a 19-year old full-time college student, earned $4,500 as a baby-sitter. Kim, a 23-year old bank teller, earned $12,000. Grant received $5,000 in dividend Income and $4,000 in nontaxable social security benefits. Grant, Dale, and Kim are U.S. citizens and were over one-half supported by Jim and Kay.
How many exemptions can Jim and Kay claim on their joint income tax return? 2+1=3

Multiple Support Agreement

If no one person provides more than 50% of an individual's support, but a group of individuals does, the group can file **a multiple support agreement** designating which person will claim the individual as a dependent.

The person designated must:

- Provide more than 10% of the support for the individual, and
- Meet the other dependency tests.

Divorced Parents

The parent with **custody** (over half the year) is entitled to dependency exemption in the absence of any written agreement.

The custodial parent can waive the exemption to other parent by signing **Form 8332**.

The non-custodial parent must attach this form to the return to claim the exemption.

FILING STATUS

Filing Status

Marital status is determined on the **last day** of the taxable year.

If one spouse dies, a joint return can be filed for the year of death.

A **surviving spouse** (i.e., qualifying widow(er)) may continue to use the rates for **married filing joint for two years** after the year of the spouse's death, if:

- the spouse provides more than half of the cost of maintaining the household,
- for a dependent child (also step, adopted),
- who uses the home as a principal residence.

Filing Status

Maintaining the household includes rent, mortgage interest, taxes, home insurance, repairs, food consumed in the house, utilities, etc.

Maintaining household does not include clothing, education, medical, vacations, and transportation.

Head of Household Status is used by:

- an unmarried person,
- that provides more than half of the cost of maintaining the household,
- for a qualifying child or a qualifying relative (a non-relative living in the home for the entire tax year does not qualify),
- who uses the home as a principal residence for more than half the tax year.

Head of Household

Two exceptions to these rules:

1. If the qualifying child is an unmarried child the child need not qualify as a dependent.
2. If the qualifying relative is a parent, the parent need not live with the taxpayer, but the taxpayer must provide more than 50% of the cost of maintaining the parent's home.

Head of Household Exceptions

	Dependent	Live in Home
CHILD	No	Yes
PARENT	Yes	No

Dependents' Returns

If someone is a dependent on another return, but is required to file his own return, then for the dependent's return:

- No personal exemption is allowed, and
- The standard deduction is limited to a statutory amount that can be increased if the dependent has earned income.

Review Question

Al and Mary Lew are married and filed a joint income tax return in which they validly claimed the personal exemption for their dependent 17 -year old daughter, Doris. Since Doris earned $5,400 this year from a part-time job at the college she attended full-time, Doris was also required to file an income tax return.

What amount was Doris entitled to claim as a personal exemption in her individual income tax return?

Kiddie Tax

The kiddie tax includes all children who are under 18.

It also includes children who are 18, or between 19 and 23 who are full-time students, if their earned income does not exceed 50% of their total support for the year.

Net unearned income in excess of a statutory amount is taxed at the parent's tax rate, while the remaining taxable income is taxed at child's tax rate.

Kiddie Tax Problem

	One	Two	Three
Unearned Income	$1,950	$500	$3,000
Earned Income	250	800	5,600
	2,200	1,300	8,600
Standard Deduction	(950)	(1,100)	(5,800)
Personal Exemption	0	0	0
Taxable Income	$1,250	$ 200	$2,800
	====	=====	=====
Taxed at Parent's Rate (Unearned Income > $1,900)	$ 50	$ 0	$1,100
Taxed at Child's Rate	$1,200	$ 200	$1,700

Standard Deduction

Standard Deduction amounts are provided for each filing status and are indexed for inflation.

The standard deduction can be increased if the taxpayer (or spouse if filing jointly) is blind at year end or is at least age 65.

These additions do not apply to dependents.

ALTERNATIVE MINIMUM TAX & OTHER TAXES

Alternative Minimum Tax

Must pay the greater of the regular tax or the tentative minimum tax.

An AMT exemption is provided which prevents many taxpayers from being impacted by the AMT.

Formula for computing AMT

Regular taxable income
+/- Adjustments
\+ Preferences
AMT Income
\- Exemption
AMT Base
x Rate
Tentative Minimum Tax before Credits
\- Certain Credits
Tentative Minimum Tax
\- Regular Tax Liability
AMT (if positive)

AMT Adjustment Items

The AMT adjustment applies only to MACRS 3-, 5-, 7-, and 10-year property that is depreciated using the 200 percent declining balance method.

For AMT, the 150% declining-balance method is used over the MACRS life.

No AMT adjustment is required for property that was depreciated using bonus depreciation.

AMT Adjustment Items

For itemized deductions:

1. Medical deduction is allowed only to extent it exceeds 10% of AGI.
2. No deduction is allowed for taxes (so must be added back to taxable income).
3. 2% miscellaneous deductions are not allowed.
4. Home equity interest not used for the residence.
5. Personal exemptions and the standard deduction (if used) are added back.
6. The compensation element on the exercise date for an incentive stock option.

Tax Preference Items

For real property and leased personalty purchased before 1987, excess of accelerated over straight-line depreciation.

Tax-exempt interest on private activity bonds (less related expenses).

AMT Credit

The AMT credit is limited to the amount of AMT generated from **timing differences**, and this credit is available in a year in which the tentative tax is less than regular tax.

The AMT credit may be **carried forward indefinitely**.

AMT - Problem

Don Mills, a single taxpayer, had $70,000 in taxable income before personal exemptions. Mills had no tax preferences. His itemized deductions were as follows:

State and local income taxes	$5,000
Home mortgage interest on loan to acquire residence	6,000
Miscellaneous deductions that exceed 2% of adjusted gross income	2,000

What amount did Mills report as alternative minimum taxable income before the AMT exemption?

Self-Employment Tax

Self employment income includes:

- gross income from self employment less deductions associated with the activity
- director's fees
- allocations of income to general partners (but not limited partners)
- guaranteed payments paid to both general and limited partners.

Self-employment tax is **NOT** due on allocations to S corporation shareholders.

Self-Employment Tax - Problem

Freeman, a single individual, reported the following income in the current year:

Guaranteed payment from services rendered to a partnership ✓
$50,000
Ordinary income from a S corporation $20,000

What amount of Freeman's income is subject to self-employment tax? $50,000

In 2012, Don Mills, a single taxpayer, had $70,000 in taxable income before personal exemptions. Mills had no tax preferences. His itemized deductions were as follows:

State and local income taxes	**$5,000**
Home mortgage interest on loan to acquire residence	**6,000**
Miscellaneous deductions that exceed 2% of adjusted gross income	**2,000**

What amount did Mills report as alternative minimum taxable income before the AMT exemption?

- **A. $72,000**
- **B. $75,000**
- **C. $77,000**
- **D. $83,000**

Baum, an unmarried optometrist and sole proprietor of Optics, buys and maintains a supply of eyeglasses and frames to sell in the ordinary course of business. In 2012, Optics had $350,000 in gross business receipts and its year-end inventory was not subject to the uniform capitalization rules. Baum's 2012 adjusted gross income was $90,000 and Baum qualified to itemize deductions.

During 2012, Baum recorded the following information:

Business expenses:		
Optics cost of goods sold		**$35,000**
Optics rent expense	**$28,000**	
Liability insurance premium on Optics		**$ 5,250**
Other expenditures:		
Baum's self-employment tax	**$29,750**	
Baum's self-employment health insurance		**$ 8,750**
Insurance premium on personal residence		
In 2012, Baum's home was totally destroyed by fire. The furniture had an adjusted basis of $14,000 and a fair market value of $11,000. During 2012, Baum collected $3,000 in insurance reimbursement and had no casualty gains during the year.	**$ 2,625**	
Qualified 2012 mortgage interest on a loan to acquire a personal residence		**$52,500**
Annual interest on a $70,000, 5-year home equity loan. The loan was secured by Baum's home, obtained January 2, 2012. The fair market value of the home exceeded the mortgage and the home equity loan by a substantial amount. The proceeds were used to purchase a car for personal use.	**$ 3,500**	
Points prepaid on January 2, 2012 to acquire the home equity loan		**$ 1,400**
Real estate taxes on personal residence	**$ 2,200**	
Estimated payments of 2012 federal income taxes		**$13,500**
Local property taxes on the car value, used exclusively for personal use	**$ 300**	

What amount should Baum report as 2012 net earnings from self-employment?

- [ ] **A. $243,250**
- [ ] **B. $252,000**
- [ ] **C. $273,000**
- [ ] **D. $281,750**

Parker, whose spouse died during the preceding year, has not remarried. Parker maintains a home for a dependent child. What is Parker's most advantageous filing status?

- [ ] **A. Single**
- [ ] **B. Head of household**
- [ ] **C. Married filing separately.**
- [ ] **D. Qualifying widow(er) with dependent child.**

Jim and Kay Ross contributed to the support of their two children, Dale and Kim, and Jim's widowed parent, Grant. For 2012, Dale, a 19-year old full-time college student who lives at home when not at college, earned $4,500 as a baby-sitter.

Kim, a 23-year old bank teller, earned $12,000. Kim provided more than 50% of her support during 2012. Grant received $5,000 in dividend income and $4,000 in nontaxable social security benefits.

Grant, Dale, and Kim are U.S. citizens and Grant and Dale were over one-half supported by Jim and Kay.

How many exemptions can Jim and Kay claim on their 2012 joint income tax return?

- [ ] **A. Two**
- [ ] **B. Three**
- [ ] **C. Four**
- [ ] **D. Five**

REG 8-1

TAX CREDITS

Personal Tax Credits

Business and Energy Tax Credits

Selected Questions (2)

PERSONAL TAX CREDITS

Personal Tax Credits

Credits reduce tax liability dollar for dollar.

More valuable than deductions.

Do not focus on phase-out amounts if indexed for Inflation.

Refundable credits allow a taxpayer to receive payments from the federal government in excess of her federal income tax withholding for the year.

Child Credit

The taxpayers are entitled to a **$1,000** tax credit for each **qualifying child under the age of 17**.

Qualifying children include a dependent child, stepchild, grandchild, siblings, and nieces and nephews.

The credit is phased-out for higher income taxpayers.

A portion of the credit may be refundable for some taxpayers.

American Opportunity Tax Credit

If enrolled in one of the first **four years** of post-secondary education, a credit of $2,500 is allowable.

- A 100% credit is allowed for the first $2,000 of **tuition, fees and course materials** paid.
- A 25% credit is allowed for the next $2,000 paid.
- The expenses must relate to an academic period beginning in the current tax year, or the first three months of the next tax year.

American Opportunity Tax Credit

Student must be enrolled in a degree program.

The credit is phased out for higher income taxpayers.

Lifetime Learning Credit

The lifetime learning credit allows a credit of **20%** of qualified tuition expenses for years for which the American Opportunity credit is not available.

The maximum credit is $2,000 per taxpayer. (**regardless of the number of students for which tuition is paid**). Student does not need to be at least half-time for expenses to qualify.

Credit applies for tuition paid for the taxpayer, taxpayer' s spouse, and taxpayer's dependents.

The credit is phased out for higher income taxpayers.

American Opportunity Tax Credit

The $2,500 credit is allowed for each eligible student.

Credit applies for tuition paid for the taxpayer, taxpayer's spouse, and taxpayer's dependents carrying at least one-half of the normal load of a full time student.

Education Credit

The American opportunity credit, the lifetime learning credit, and other tax benefits for higher education are mutually exclusive in that an educational expenditure can never simultaneously qualify for more than one benefit (e.g., no double "dipping").

Child and Dependent Care Credit

Credit is a specified percentage (between 20% and 35%) of **qualified expenses** incurred for care for a qualified individual to enable the taxpayer to work.

A **qualified individual** is:

- A qualifying child (as defined for dependency rules) under age 13, or
- A dependent or spouse who is physically or mentally incapacitated and has the same abode as the taxpayer for more than half the tax year.

Child and Dependent Care Credit

Qualified expenses are limited to the lower of

- earned income of the lowest paid spouse, or
- $3,000 ($6,000 for two or more qualified individuals).

Credit percentage is 35% if AGI is $15,000 or less. It is reduced by 1% for each $2,000 (or portion thereof) of AGI in excess of $15,000 (but not below 20%).

Review Question

Robert and Mary Jason, filing a joint tax return, had a tax liability of $9,000 based on their tax table income and three exemptions. Robert and Mary had earned income of $20,000 and $12,000, respectively

In order for Mary to be gainfully employed, the Jasons incurred the following employment-related expenses for their four year old son John:

Child and Dependent Care Credit – Problem

Payee	Amount
Union Day Care Center	$ 2,500 ✓
Acme Home Cleaning Service	500
Wilma Jason, babysitter (Robert Jason's mother)	1,000 ✓
	3,500

Assuming that the Jasons do not claim any other credits against their tax, what is the amount of the child care tax credit they should report on their tax return?

Child and Dependent Care Credit - Solution

Lowest of: Qualified expenses 3500
Statutory limits 3000
Earned income of lowest paid spouse 12,000

3,000
X26%
780

AGI 32,000
Phase-out threshold ⟨15,000⟩
17,000 / 2000 = 8.5 → 9
35% − 9% = 26%

Allowable %

Earned Income Credit

The credit is generated by earning income.

The credit percentage increases if the taxpayer maintains a home with qualifying children.

The credit is phased out based on earned income or AGI (if greater) exceeding a threshold that also depends upon the number of qualifying children.

EIC – Earned Income

The most common sources of **earned income** that qualify for the credit are wages, salaries, tips, and earnings from self-employment.

Combat pay can also be included as earned income.

Taxable disability payments from an employer plan qualify as earned income until the taxpayer reaches normal retirement age.

Earned Income Credit

The credit is disallowed if **disqualified income**, such as interest, dividends, tax exempt interest and other investment income exceeds a threshold.

Taxpayers between the ages of 25 through 64 without qualifying children are also eligible if they are not claimed as a dependent on another's return.

EIC – Qualifying Children

"**Qualifying child**" is defined as it is for the dependency exemption rules - - - a natural child, stepchild, adopted child, foster child, sibling, step-sibling, or descendants of these.

The descendants must be under the age of 19, students under 24, or permanently disabled dependents.

The qualifying child must also be younger than the taxpayer.
Information on qualifying children is reported on Form 1040 Schedule EIC.

EIC – Qualifying Children

The qualifying child also must have lived in the taxpayer's home for more than half of the tax year in the United States.

A qualifying child can only be used by one taxpayer to claim the EIC. If more than one person qualifies to claim the qualifying child the tie breaker rules are similar to those used for dependency exemptions.

The individual who claims the qualifying child as a dependent must be the same individual who claims the EIC.

EIC – Form 8867

A paid preparer must also complete Form 8867 which provides a checklist to insure that the preparer met all due diligence requirements for taking the EIC on the return.

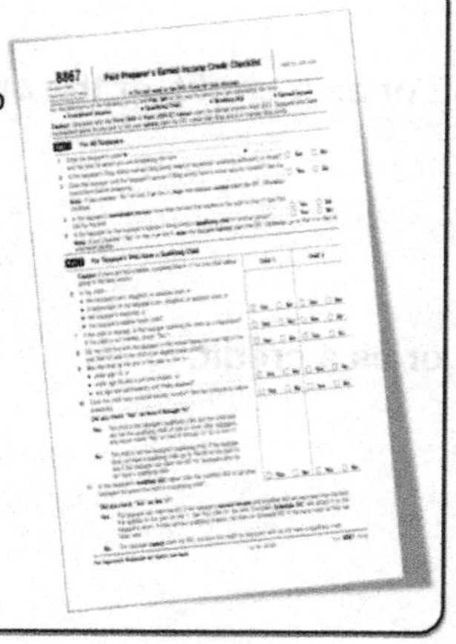

There is a $500 penalty for each failure to meet these requirements.

BUSINESS TAX CREDITS

Foreign Tax Credit

The credit is limited to the lower of the foreign tax paid, or the proportion of U.S. tax allocable to foreign source income, which is equal to:

$$\text{U.S. Tax} \times \frac{\text{Foreign taxable income}}{\text{Worldwide taxable income}}$$

Excess foreign tax credits **carryback 1 year and forward 10 years**.

Review Question

The following information pertains to Wald Corp.'s operations:

Worldwide taxable income	$ 300,000
U.S. source taxable income	180,000
U.S. income tax before foreign tax credit	96,000
Foreign source taxable income	120,000
Foreign income taxes paid on foreign source taxable income	39,000

What amount of foreign tax credit may Wald claim?

Review Question

Lower of:

$39,000

Foreign tax paid, or

$$\text{U.S. Tax} \times \frac{\text{Foreign taxable income}}{\text{Worldwide taxable income}}$$

$$\$96,000 \times \frac{120,000}{300,000} = \$38,400$$

General Business Credit

The General Business Credit consists of a combination of credits designed to subsidize certain activities. While each credit is calculated independently, the combination of credits is subject to an overall limit.

The business credit cannot offset all of the regular tax if the liability exceeds $25,000.

Unused credits are **carried back one year and then forward 20 years**.

Foreign income taxes paid by a corporation

- ☐ A. **May be claimed either as a deduction or as a credit, at the option of the corporation.**
- ☐ B. **May be claimed only as a deduction.**
- ☐ C. **May be claimed only as a credit.**
- ☐ D. **Do not qualify either as a deduction or as a credit.**

In 2012, to qualify for the child care credit on a joint return, at least one spouse must

	Have an adjusted gross income of $15,000 or less	Be gainfully employed when related expenses are incurred
☐	Yes	Yes
☐	No	No
☐	Yes	No
☐	No	Yes

REG 8-2

CORPORATE TAXATION 1

Formation of a Corporation

Corporate Income

Special Corporate Deductions

Selected Questions (4)

FORMATION OF A CORPORATION

Formation of a Corporation

No gain or loss is recognized to the shareholder or corporation if the following conditions are met:

1. The **only** property received from the corporation is **stock** (stock does **not** include stock rights, stock warrants, or debt),
2. The stock is received in exchange for **property or cash** (i.e., not services), and
3. The group (can include more than one person) transferring property and receiving stock as part of this exchange collectively **own at least 80%** of a) the voting power, and b) each nonvoting class of stock.

Stock for Services

If stock is received in exchange for **services**:

- The transferor has **wage income** equal to the fair market value of the stock received (and basis in the stock equal to that amount), and
- The corporation has a salary expense deduction (unless the services rendered were an organizational expense).

Boot Received

If anything other than stock is received, it is called **boot**.

If boot is received, the gain recognized to the shareholder is the **lower** of:

- Realized gain, or
- The fair market value of the boot received.

Review Question

Dole, the sole owner of Enson Corp., transferred a building to Enson. The building had an adjusted tax basis of $35,000 and a fair market value of $100,000.

In exchange for the building, Dole received $40,000 cash and Enson common stock with a fair market value of $60,000.

What amount of gain did Dole recognize?

Review Question

Amount Realized:	Cash	40,000
	Stock	60,000
		100,000
Adjusted Basis		(35,000)
Realized Gain		65,000

Recognized Gain: lower of:

1. realized gain, or — 65,000
2. boot received — 40,000 (circled)

Liability Assumption

If the total liabilities assumed by the corporation exceed the total adjusted basis of property transferred by the shareholder, then gain must be recognized as follows:

Gain Recognized =
Liabilities Assumed – Basis of Property Transferred

Review Question

Anna transferred land with an adjusted basis to her of $20,000 and a fair market value of $56,000, to Elm Corporation in exchange for 100% of Elm Corporation's only class of stock.

The land was subject to a liability of $26,000 which Elm assumed for legitimate business purposes. The fair market value of Elm's stock at the time of the transfer was $30,000.

What is the amount of Anna's recognized gain?

Review Question

Amount Realized	30,000+26,000 = 56,000
Adjusted Basis	<20,000>
Realized Gain	36,000

Debt assumed	26,000
Adj. basis of assets contributed	<20,000>
Recognized Gain	6,000

Shareholder's Basis

The shareholder's basis in the stock received from the corporation is:

Basis of all property transferred to the corporation 20,000

- \+ Gain recognized by shareholder 6,000
- \- Boot received by shareholder
- \- Liabilities assumed by corporation <26,000>

0

Corporation's Basis

The corporation's basis in the property received is:

Shareholder's basis in the property 20,000
+ Gain recognized by the shareholder 6,000

26,000

Holding Period

The shareholder's holding period for the stock is determined as follows:

1. **Capital asset or Section 1231 asset** transferred to corporation - property holding period is tacked on to stock holding period.
2. All other property - holding period of property does not tack on. Holding period for stock begins on day after the transfer.

The **corporation's** holding period in the property received always includes the period that the transferor held the property before the exchange.

CORPORATE INCOME

Corporate Income Computation

The general income and deduction rules for corporations are the same as those for individuals.

The due date for a corporate return (Form 1120) is the 15th day of the 3rd month following the end of the tax year.

There is a six-month extension to file granted upon request.

Estimated corporate tax payments are required if the tax liability exceeds $500.

Capital Losses

Deductible capital losses are offset against recognized capital gains, but there is **no deduction** for a net capital loss.

Rather, a net capital loss is **carried back 3 years/ forward 5 years** to offset against capital gains in other years.

2 ½ Month Rule

Corporations using the accrual method can deduct unpaid bonuses and charitable contributions only if:

1. Approved by the board before the end of the tax year, and
2. Paid within 2 ½ months after the end of the tax year.

Definitions

A **personal service corporation** is a corporation whose principal activity is the performance of personal services performed by employees who own substantially all of the stock.

A corporation is a closely held corporation if at any time during the last half of the taxable year, more than 50 percent in value of its outstanding stock is owned, directly or indirectly, by or for not more than 5 individuals.

Passive Losses

Passive loss limits do not apply to corporations. **Closely held corporations** can use passive losses to offset active corporate income but **not portfolio income**.

Personal service corporations cannot offset passive losses against either active income or portfolio income.

Permitted Year-Ends

Corporations can choose a fiscal year unless the corporation makes an "S" election or qualifies as a "personal service corporation".

Personal service corporations generally must use a calendar year-end.

Book/Tax Income Reconciliation

Schedule M-1 is a reconciliation of book income to taxable income.

Nondeductible expenses are added to book income (federal tax expense, net capital loss, expenses in excess of limits, etc.).

Income that is taxable but not included in book income is added to book income (for example, prepaid income included in taxable income).

Book/Tax Income Reconciliation

Nontaxable income that is included in book income is subtracted from book income (municipal interest, life insurance proceeds, etc.)

Deductions not expensed from book income are subtracted from book income (dividends received deduction, Section 179 election to expense, etc.)

Review Question

Starke Corp., an accrual-basis calendar year corporation, reported book income of $380,000. Included in that amount was $50,000 municipal bond interest income, $170,000 for federal income tax expense, and $2,000 interest expense on the debt incurred to carry the municipal bonds

What amount should Starke's taxable income be as reconciled on Starke's Schedule M-1 of Form 1120, U.S. Corporation Income Tax Return?

M-1 Items - Solution

Book income	380,000
Municipal interest	(50,000)
Federal income tax	+ 170,000
Interest expense	+ 2,000
Taxable income	502,000

Schedule M-3 Requirement

Corporations that report total assets of $10 million or more must complete and file Schedule M-3 instead of Schedule M-1.

Schedule M-3 provides much more detail than Schedule M-1.

SPECIAL CORPORATE DEDUCTIONS

Charitable Contributions

Charitable contribution rules are the same as for **individuals, with the following exceptions**:

- A contribution **of inventory**, by corporations only, to charities that use the property in a manner related to the exempt purpose and solely for the care of the **ill, needy, or infants**, or where the property is used for research purposes under specified conditions are subject to special rules.
- The deduction is the lower of:
  AB of property + 50% x (FMV - AB), or
  2 x AB

Charitable Contributions

The corporation can elect to deduct accrued contributions if the contributions are actually paid in first 2 and one-half months following the year-end.

The limit on the deduction is **10 percent of taxable income** (before special deductions for charity, dividends received, and carryovers).

Any excess charitable contribution (above the 10 percent limit) **carries forward for 5 years** (there is no carryback).

Dividends Received Deduction

The dividends-received deduction (DRD) is a percent (%) of domestic dividends.

If the corporation owns less than 20% of the stock of another corporation, then the dividends-received deduction (DRD) is 70% of the dividends received.

If the corporation owns 80% or more, then the DRD is 100% of the dividends received.

All ownership levels between these two extremes are entitled to an 80% DRD.

Dividends Received Deduction

The DRD is **limited** to:

- Taxable income multiplied by the same % used to compute the DRD.
- This limitation is not required if the full dividends-received deduction would create or add to a net operating loss.

Review Question

Best Corp., an accrual-basis calendar year C corporation, received $100,000 in dividend income from the 5% common stock interest that it held in an unrelated domestic corporation. The stock was not debt-financed, and was held for over a year.

Best recorded the following information:

Loss from Best's operations	($ 10,000)
Dividends received	100,000
Taxable income	
(before dividends received deduction)	$ 90,000

Dividends Received Deduction - Solution

Best's dividends-received deduction was:

Step 1: Full DRD

100,000 x 70% = 70,000

Step 2: Taxable Income Limitation

90,000 x 70% = 63,000

Step 3: Income/Loss with full DRD

90,000 – 70,000 = 20,000

Organization Expenses

Typical **organizational expenses** are legal services incident to organization, accounting services, organizational meetings of directors and shareholders, and fees paid to incorporate.

$5,000 of these expenses may be deducted, but the $5,000 is reduced by the amount of expenditures incurred that exceed $50,000.

Expenses not deducted must be capitalized and amortized over 180 months, beginning with the month that the corporation begins its business operations (unless an election is made to not do so).

Organization Expenses

They must be **incurred** before the end of the taxable year that business begins (but they do not have to be paid, even if on the cash basis).

Costs of issuing and selling stock (**syndication expenses**) must also be capitalized, but cannot be amortized.

Review Question

Brown Corp., a calendar-year taxpayer, was organized and actively began operations on July 1, Year 4, and incurred the following costs:

Legal fees to obtain corporate charter	$40,000
Commission paid to underwriter	$25,000
Other stock issue costs	$10,000

Brown wishes to amortize its organizational costs over the shortest period allowed for tax purposes. **In Year 4, what amount should Brown deduct for organizational expenses?**

Organization Expense Solution

Current year expense: 40,000

Legal Fees 5,000

Current year amortization:

Legal Fees

35,000 ÷ 180 months = 164.44

x 6 months = x 6

1167

Total 6167

Start-Up Costs

Same rules apply for start-up costs.

Start-up costs are expenditures that would be deductible as trade or business expenses (ordinary, necessary, and reasonable) except that the corporation has not yet started its trade or business operation.

Domestic Production Deduction

Corporations engaged in production activities within the United States qualify for a deduction equal to, 9% times the lower of:

- **Qualified production activity income**, or
- **Taxable income**.

This deduction may not exceed 50% of the wages allocable to domestic production income.

Domestic Production Deduction

Qualified production activity income is equal to:
Gross receipts from domestic production, less:

1. Cost of Goods Sold
2. Direct expenses allocated to this income, including wages
3. A pro-rate share of indirect expenses allocated to this income

John Budd is the sole stockholder of Ral Corp., an accrual basis taxpayer engaged in wholesaling operations. Ral's retained earnings at January 1, 2012 amounted to $1,000,000. For the year ended December 31, 2012, Ral's book income, before federal income tax, was $300,000. Included in the computation of this $300,000 were the following:

Dividends received on 500 shares of stock of a taxable domestic corporation that had 1,000,000 shares of stock outstanding (Ral had no portfolio indebtedness)	**$ 1,000**
Loss on sale of investment in stock of unaffiliated corporation (this stock had been held for two years; Ral had no other capital gains or losses)	**(5,000)**
Keyman insurance premiums paid on Budd's life (Ral is the beneficiary of this policy)	**3,000**
Group term insurance premiums paid on $10,000 life insurance policies for each of Ral's four employees (the employees' spouses are the beneficiaries)	**4,000**
Amortization of cost of acquiring a perpetual dealer's franchise (Ral paid $48,000 for this franchise on July 1, 2012, and is amortizing it over a 48-month period)	**6,000**
Contribution to a recognized, qualified charity (this contribution was authorized by Ral's board of directors in December 2012, to be paid on January 31, 2013)	**75,000**

On December 1, 2012, Ral received advance rental of $27,000 from a tenant for a three-year lease commencing January 1, 2013 to cover rents for the years 2013, 2014, and 2015. In conformity with GAAP, Ral did not include any part of this rental in its income statement for the year ended December 31, 2012. With regard to Ral's contribution to the recognized, qualified charity, Ral

- [ ] **A. Can elect to deduct in its 2012 return any portion of the $75,000 that does not exceed the deduction ceiling for 2012.**
- [ ] **B. Cannot deduct any portion of the $75,000 in 2012 because the contribution was not paid in 2012.**
- [ ] **C. Can deduct the entire $75,000 in its 2012 return because Ral reports on the accrual basis.**
- [ ] **D. Can elect to carry forward indefinitely any portion of the $75,000 not deducted in 2012 or 2013.**

In 2012, Best Corp., an accrual-basis calendar year C corporation, received $100,000 in dividend income from the common stock that it held in an unrelated domestic corporation.
The stock was not debt-financed, and was held for over a year. Best recorded the following information for 2012:

Loss from Best's operations	**($ 10,000)**
Dividends received	**100,000**
Taxable income (before dividends-received deduction)	**$ 90,000**
	========

Best's dividends-received deduction on its 2012 tax return was

- **A. $100,000**
- **B. $80,000**
- **C. $70,000**
- **D. $63,000**

Don Wolf became a general partner in Gata Associates on January 1, 2012 with a 5% interest in Gata's profits, losses, and capital.

Gata is a distributor of auto parts. Wolf does not materially participate in the partnership business. For the year ended December 31, 2012, Gata had an operating loss of $100,000. In addition, Gata earned interest of $20,000 on a temporary investment. Gata has kept the principal temporarily invested while awaiting delivery of equipment that is presently on order. The principal will be used to pay for this equipment.

Wolf's passive loss for 2012 is

- [ ] A. **$0**
- [ ] B. **$4,000**
- [ ] C. **$5,000**
- [ ] D. **$6,000**

Adams, Beck, and Carr organized Flexo Corp. with authorized voting common stock of $100,000. Adams received 10% of the capital stock in payment for the organizational services that he rendered for the benefit of the newly formed corporation. Adams did not contribute property to Flexo and was under no obligation to be paid by Beck or Carr.
Beck and Carr transferred property in exchange for stock as follows:

	Adjusted basis	Fair market value	Percentage of Flexo stock acquired
Beck	5,000	20,000	20%
Carr	60,000	70,000	70%

What amount of gain did Carr recognize from this transaction?

- [ ] A. $40,000
- [ ] B. $15,000
- [ ] C. $10,000
- [ ] D. $0

REG 8-3

CORPORATE TAXATION 2

Corporate Alternative Minimum Tax

Penalty Taxes

Taxation of Related Corporations

Selected Questions (3)

CORPORATE ALTERNATIVE MINIMUM TAX

Corporate AMT

The corporate AMT formula is very similar to the individual formula in that taxable income is modified by adding "tax preferences" and adding or subtracting "adjustments" to income.

Corporate AMT

Taxable Income Before the NOL Deduction
+/- Adjustments (excluding ACE adjustment)
+ Preferences

AMTI before ACE and NOL
+/- ACE adjustment

AMTI before NOL
- NOL deduction (limited to 90% of AMTI before NOL)

AMTI
- Exemption

AMT Base

Corporate AMT

AMT Base
x 20%

Tentative Minimum Tax before the FTC
- Foreign Tax Credit

Tentative Minimum Tax
- Regular Tax Liability

Alternative Minimum Tax (if positive)
===

Corporate AMT Applicability

For new corporations the **TMT is always zero** for its first year of operations.

The corporate AMT doesn't apply to small corporations meeting a **gross receipts test**.

The tentative minimum tax (TMT) is zero if the corporation's average annual gross receipts for all three-year-tax periods ending before the tax year doesn't exceed $7,500,000 ($5,000,000 for first testing period).

If a corporation fails this test for any year, then it will be subject to the AMT for ALL future years.

Corporate AMT Applicability

Assume that Corp. ABC is formed in Year 1

Year 1 - exempt from AMT for first year
Year 2 - testing period is Year 1
Year 3 - testing period is average for Years 1 and 2
Year 4 - testing period is average for Years 1, 2, & 3

ACE Adjustment

AMTI is increased by 75% of the excess of ACE over pre-ACE AMTI.

Or AMTI is reduced by 75% of the excess of pre-ACE AMTI over ACE.

The negative adjustment is limited to the aggregate of the positive adjustments under ACE for prior years reduced by any previously claimed negative adjustments.

Adjusted Current Earnings

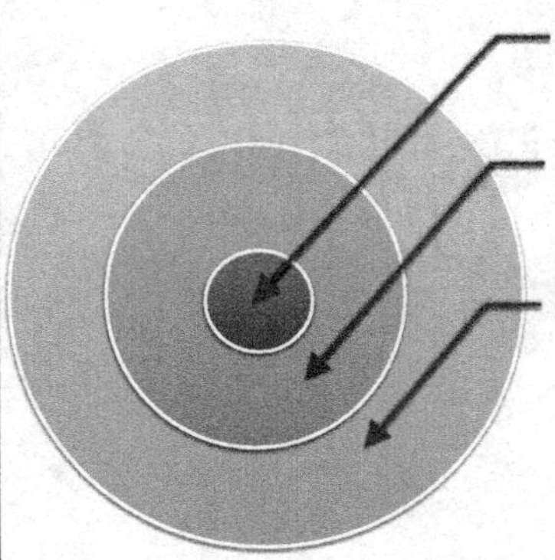

Review Question

Green Corp. was incorporated and began business in Year 2. In computing its alternative minimum tax for Year 4, it determined that it had adjusted current earnings (ACE) of $400,000 and alternative minimum taxable income (prior to the ACE adjustment) of $300,000. For Year 5, it had adjusted current earnings of $100,000 and alternative minimum taxable income (prior to the ACE adjustment) of $300,000.

What is the amount of Green Corp.'s adjustment for adjusted current earnings that will be used in calculating its alternative minimum tax for Year 5?

Review Question

	Year 4	Year 5
ACE	400,000	100,000
AMTI	(300,000)	(300,000)
Difference	100,000	(200,000)
x 75%	x75%	75%
ACE Adjustment	+75000	(150,000)
		75,000

AMT Exemption

The **AMT exemption for corporations** is $40,000, and it is phased out for AMTI over $150,000 (25% of the amount of AMTI over this trigger).

An exemption for the corporate AMT is completely phased out when AMTI equals $310,000.

This is $160,000 over the phase-out trigger of $150,000.

AMT Credit

The AMT credit is limited to the amount of AMT generated from timing differences, and this credit is available in a year in which the tentative tax is less than regular tax.

The AMT credit may be carried forward indefinitely.

PENALTY TAXES FOR CORPORATIONS

Penalty Taxes - Corporations

Accumulated Earnings Tax: Accumulated Taxable Income represents earnings that are retained in the business for which there is **no reasonable business need** to retain the earnings for the future.

Personal Holding Company Tax: PHC tax for a previous year can be **avoided by paying a deficiency dividend** within 90 days after a determination by the IRS that the tax applied.

Penalty Taxes - Corporations

Both penalty taxes operate to force corporations to distribute dividend income to shareholders.

The rate of the penalty tax is the **current top tax rate** on dividend income.

The two penalty taxes are mutually exclusive - only one will apply in any year.

Accumulated Taxable Income

	Taxable Income
+	Dividends received deduction
+	NOL deduction
-	Federal income taxes
-	Excess charitable contributions
-	Net capital loss
	Adjusted Taxable Income
-	Dividends paid
-	Accumulated earnings credit
	Accumulated Taxable Income
x	Tax rate on dividend income
	Accumulated Earnings Tax

Accumulated Earnings Tax Credit

A credit is allowed which represents the amount of earnings that can be accumulated for reasonable business needs.

The **accumulated earnings credit is the greater** of:

1. Earnings needed for reasonable business needs, or
2. Minimum credit of $250,000 ($150,000 for service corporations) less accumulated earnings and profits at the beginning of the year.

Review Question

Daystar Corp., which is not a mere holding or investment company, derives its income from retail sales. Daystar had accumulated earnings and profits of $145,000 at December 31, Year 2. For the year ended December 31, Year 3, it had earnings and profits of $115,000 and a dividends-paid deduction of $15,000 for a dividend paid in June Year 3. It has been determined that $20,000 of the current and accumulated earnings and profits for Year 3 is required for the reasonable needs of the business.

How much is the allowable accumulated earnings credit at December 31, Year 3?

Review Question

Greater of:

1. Earnings needed for reasonable business needs, or $20,000
2. $250,000 less accumulated earnings and profits at the beginning of the year

$250,000 − $145,000 =
$105,000

Personal Holding Company Tax

Two tests must be met for a corporation to fall within the PHC provisions.

1. More than 50% of the value of the outstanding stock must be owned directly or indirectly by five or fewer individuals at any time during the last half of the tax year.
2. A substantial portion (60% or more) of the corporate income must consist of **passive income** such as dividends, interest, rents, and royalties.

Personal Holding Company Tax

An individual indirectly owns stock if it is owned by the individual's family.

Family includes the individual's brothers, sisters, spouse and lineal descendants and ancestors.

An individual will not be considered to be the constructive owner of the stock owned by nephews, cousins, uncles, aunts, and any of his/her spouse's relatives.

Constructive ownership also may exist if the individual is a partner in a partnership or the beneficiary of an estate that is a shareholder.

The Personal Holding Company Tax Formula

Taxable Income
plus or minus Adjustments:
- corporate income tax
- excess charitable contributions
- net capital gain (after tax)
+ dividends received deduction
+ net operating loss carryover

Adjusted Taxable Income
- Dividends paid or deemed paid

Undistributed PHC Income

Review Question

Tax Corp. calculated the following taxes for the year:

Regular tax liability	$210,000 ✓
Tentative minimum tax AMT = $30,000	$240,000
Personal holding company tax	$ 65,000

What is Tax's total tax liability for the year?

$210,000 + $30,000 + $65,000 =
$305,000

TAXATION OF RELATED CORPORATIONS

Taxation of Related Corporations

There is a tax incentive to create multiple corporations to avoid the limits placed on individual corporations.

Congress created limits on related corporations to mitigate these incentives and create a mechanism for identifying and taxing related economic entities.

These related corporations are know as **controlled groups**.

Controlled Groups

Controlled groups are **parent-subsidiary corporations, brother-sister groups, and certain insurance companies.**

A controlled group of corporations is entitled to one $250,000 accumulated earnings tax credit and is limited to taxable income in each of the first two brackets as though the group was one corporation.

A group also receives only one Sec 179 expense deduction and one AMT exemption.

Parent-Subsidiary Group

A parent-subsidiary controlled group exists if:

- Stock possessing at least 80% of the voting power of all classes of stock entitled to vote **OR** at least 80% of the total value of shares of all classes of stock of each of the corporations, except the common parent, is owned by one or more of the other corporations, and
- The common parent owns stock possessing at least 80% of the total combined voting power of all classes of stock entitled to vote OR at least 80% of the total value of shares of all classes of stock of at least one of the other corporations.

Review Question

Ape Corporation owns 80% of Bear Corporation and 92% of Cat Corporation. Bear Corporation owns 79% of Eel Corporation and 60% of Dog Corporation. Cat Corporation owns 20% of Dog Corporation. All corporations are domestic C corporations having a single class of stock outstanding.

Which corporations form a controlled group?

Parent-Subsidiary Group - Solution

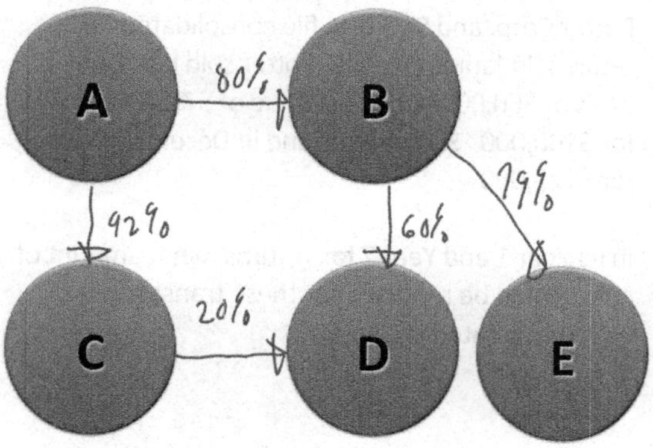

Brother-Sister Controlled Group

A brother-sister controlled group exists if:

1. Two or more corporations are owned by **five or fewer** persons (individuals, estates, or trusts), who have a common ownership of **more than 50%** of the total combined voting powers of all classes of stock entitled to vote or **more than 50%** of the total value of shares of all classes of stock of each corporation, **and**
2. who possess stock representing at least 80% of the total combined voting power of all classes of stock entitled to vote or at least 80% of the total value of shares of all classes of each corporation.

Brother-Sister Controlled Group

The 80% test no longer applies for determining brother-sister corporations in the following circumstances:

- corporate tax brackets,
- the accumulated earnings credit, and
- the minimum tax exemption.

Brother-Sister Controlled Group - Problem

The only class of outstanding stock of Corporations N, O, P, Q, and R is owned by the following unrelated individuals:

Corporations/Percent of Stock Owned

Individual	N	O	P	Q	R	50%
V	40%	40%	40%	40%	40%	40
W	20%	-0-	10%	20%	30%	0
X	10%	10%	20%	20%	10%	10
Y	30%	-0-	30%	10%	-0-	0
Z	-0-	50%	-0-	10%	-0-	0
						50%

Which corporations are members of a brother-sister controlled group? FAILED

Brother-Sister Controlled Group - Problem

The only class of outstanding stock of Corporations N, O, P, Q, and R is owned by the following unrelated individuals:

Corporations/Percent of Stock Owned

Individual	N	P	Q	50%
V	40%	40%	40%	40
W	20%	10%	20%	10
X	10%	20%	20%	10
Y	30%	30%	10%	10
~~Z~~	~~-0-~~	~~-0-~~	~~10%~~	0
	100%	100%	90%	70% ✓

Which corporations are members of a brother-sister controlled group?

Affiliated Groups

An "**affiliated group**" exists when one corporation owns at least 80 percent of the voting power of another corporation **and** holds shares representing at least 80 percent of its value.

This test must be met on **every day** of the year.

An affiliated group can **elect to file a consolidated tax return** (insurance companies, S corporations, and foreign corporations are not eligible).

Affiliated Groups

Dividends between the affiliated corporations are eliminated on the consolidated tax return.

Gains and losses on intercompany sales are deferred until disposition outside the group.

The parent adjusts the basis of the stock of a consolidated subsidiary for allocable portion of income, losses, and dividends.

The members of the group must conform their tax year to the parent's tax year.

Affiliated Groups - Problem

Potter Corp. and Sly Corp. file consolidated tax returns. In January Year 1, Potter sold land, with a basis of $60,000 and a fair value of $75,000, to Sly for $100,000. Sly sold the land in December Year 2 for $125,000

In its Year 1 and Year 2 tax returns, what amount of gain should be reported for these transactions in the consolidated return?

Affiliated Groups - Solution

	Year 1	Year 2
Amount Realized	75,000	125,000
Adjusted Basis	<60,000>	<60,000>
Realized Gain	15,000	65,000
Recognized Gain	Ø	65,000

Controlled vs. Affiliated Groups

While the rules for Parent-Subsidiary controlled groups are similar to those for affiliated groups, there are two important differences:

1. The affiliated group rules must be met every day of the year, while the P-S rules must only be met on the last day of the tax year, and
2. The 80% test for affiliated groups is for voting power AND value, whereas the 80% test for P-S is for voting power OR value.

Jans, an individual, owns 80% and 100% of the total value and voting power of A and B Corps., which in turn own the following (both value and voting power):

	Ownership	
Property	A Corp	B Corp
C Corp	80%	-
D Corp	-	100%

All companies are C corporations except B Corp., which had elected S status since inception. Which of the following statements is correct with respect to the companies' ability to file a consolidated return?

- [ ] A. A, C, and D may file as a group.
- [ ] B. A and C may not file as a group, and B and D may not file as a group.
- [ ] C. A and C may file as a group, and B and D may file as a group.
- [ ] D. A and C may file as a group, but B and D may not file as a group.

With regard to consolidated tax returns, which of the following statements is correct?

- [ ] **A. Operating losses of one group member may be used to offset operating profits of the other members included in the consolidated return.**
- [ ] **B. Only corporations that issue their audited financial statements on a consolidated basis may file consolidated returns.**
- [ ] **C. Of all intercompany dividends paid by the subsidiaries to the parent, 70% are excludable from taxable income on the consolidated return.**
- [ ] **D. The common parent must directly own 51% or more of the total voting power of all corporations included in the consolidated return.**

Kari Corp., a manufacturing company, was organized on January 2, 2012. Its 2012 federal taxable income was $400,000 and its federal income tax was $100,000.

What is the maximum amount of accumulated taxable income that may be subject to the accumulated earnings tax for 2012 if Kari takes only the minimum accumulated earnings credit?

- A. **$300,000**
- B. **$150,000**
- C. **$50,000**
- D. **$0**

REG 8-4

CORPORATE TAXATION 3

Distributions from a Corporation

Corporate Redemptions and Liquidations

Corporate Reorganizations

Selected Questions (4)

DISTRIBUTIONS FROM A CORPORATION

Ordinary Distributions

Step 1: Taxable as **dividend income** to extent of the shareholder's pro-rata share of E&P.

Step 2: Excess is **tax-free** to extent of shareholder's basis in stock (and reduces the basis).

Step 3: Remaining distribution amount is taxed as a **capital gain**.

Ordinary Distributions: Example

If Pat receives a corporate distribution of $10,000 and has the following tax characteristics:

Earnings and Profits	$3,000
Basis in Stock	4,000

The tax consequences would be as follows:

Distribution	10,000
E&P (dividend income)	(3,000)
	7,000
Basis in stock (tax-free)	(4,000)
Capital Gain	3,000

Property Distributions

Amount distributed = FMV - liabilities on property.

Basis of the property to the shareholder is the **fair market value**.

Earnings & Profits

Conceptually, E &P measures the corporation's economic ability to pay a dividend.

Computed by making adjustments to taxable income.

E & P is increased for all items of income, including tax-exempt income, and is decreased for both deductible and nondeductible expenses and losses.

The alternative depreciation system (straight-line) must be used for E&P purposes.

E&P – Reduction for Dividends

The E & P of the distributing corporation is reduced by:

- For **cash distributions** - the amount of money distributed.
- For **property distributions** - by
  1. The greater of the fair market value or the adjusted basis of the property distributed,
  2. Less the amount of any liability on the property.

E&P – Property Distributions

If Corporation Mouse distributes property with a FMV of $1,000 and a basis of $1,200 to shareholder Cat, and Cat assumes a liability attached to the property of $300:

E&P is reduced by $900 ($1,200 - $300).

Earnings & Profits

Current	Accumulated	Results
+	+	Dividend=both
-	-	Not a dividend
+	-	Dividend=current
-	+	Net first

Earnings & Profits - Problem

On January 1, Year 4, Kee Corp., a C corporation, had a $50,000 deficit in earnings and profits.

For Year 4 Kee had current earnings and profits of $10,000 and made a $30,000 cash distribution to its stockholders

What amount of the distribution is taxable as dividend income to Kee's stockholders?

Earnings & Profits - Solution

Amount of Distribution: $30,000

Earnings & Profits

Current	Accumulated
$10,000	($50,000)

$10,000

Corporate Gain

Gain but not loss is recognized to a corporation that distributes property as a dividend, as if the property were sold to the shareholder at its fair market value.

Corporate Gain - Problem

Dahl Corp. was organized and commenced operations in Year 1. At December 31, Year 5, Dahl had accumulated earnings and profits of $9,000 before dividend declaration and distribution. On December 31, Year 5 Dahl distributed cash of $9,000 and a vacant parcel of land to Green, Dahls' only stockholder. At the date of distribution, the land had a basis of $5,000 and a fair market value of $40,000

What was Green's taxable dividend income in Year 5 from these distributions?

Corporate Gain - Solution

Amount of Distribution:

Cash	9,000
Land	40,000
	49,000

Gain from Distribution:

FMV	40,000
Adjusted Basis	(5,000)
	35,000

Earnings and Profits:

Accumulated	9,000
Gain	35,000
Dividend Income	44,000

CORPORATE REDEMPTIONS AND LIQUIDATIONS

Redemptions

A redemption is a **sale of stock back to the issuing corporation**.

The redemption **qualifies for sale or exchange treatment** (i.e., capital gain treatment) if the shareholder owns :

- After the distribution, less then 80% of his or her total interest in the corporation before the distribution, and
- Less than 50% of the total combined voting power of all classes of stock entitled to vote.

Redemptions

Bill owns 60% of Buc Corporation before a redemption, and 49% after a redemption. Does the redemption qualify for sale or exchange treatment?

50% TEST ✓

60% X 80% = 48% ≯ 49% FAILED

Review Question

Elm Corp. is an accrual-basis calendar-year C corporation with 100,000 shares of voting common stock issued and outstanding as of December 28, Year 2. On Friday, December 29, Year 2, Hall surrendered 2,000 shares of Elm stock to Elm in exchange for $33,000. Hall had no direct or indirect interest in Elm after the stock surrender.

Hall's adjusted basis in 2,000 shares of Elm on December 29, Year 2 ($8 per share)	$16,000
Elm's accumulated earnings and profits at January 1, Year 2	25,000
Elm's Year 2 net operating loss	(7,000)

What amount of income did Hall recognize from the stock surrender?

Redemption - Solution

Amount Realized	33,000
Adjusted Basis	(16,000)
Capital Gain	17,000

Redemptions

A redemption also qualified as a sale or exchange if:

- It is not essentially equivalent to a dividend.
- Complete termination of interest (family attribution rules are waived).
- Partial liquidation:
  - At least two active businesses for last five years and one is liquidated.
- Redemption used to pay death taxes (stock must be at least 35% of adjusted gross estate).

Liquidations

A liquidation occurs when an entity ceases to be a going concern and it distributes its assets.

Expenses incurred in the liquidation are deducted on the last corporate return.

Consequences to corporation: Gain or loss is recognized to a liquidating corporation on the distribution of property in complete liquidation.

For purposes of computing gain/loss the fair market value of the property will not be less than any liability that is attached to the property.

Liquidations

Losses may not be recognized if:

- The property had been contributed in last five years, or
- The property is distributed to a related party.

Liquidations

Consequences to shareholder: Shareholders treat the distribution as a sale/exchange; capital gain or loss is recognized.

The basis of assets received by the shareholder will be the fair market value on date of distribution.

Review Question

Under a plan of complete liquidation, Len Corporation distributed land, having an adjusted basis to Len of $26,000, to its sole shareholder.

The land was subject to a liability of $38,000 which the shareholder assumed for legitimate business purposes. The fair market value of the land on the date of distribution was $35,000.

What is the amount of Len Corporation's recognized gain or (loss)?

Review Question

Liability > FMV of Property

38,000 > 35,000

Amount Realized	38,000
Adjusted Basis	(26,000)
Sec. 1231 Gain	12,000

Review Question

Mintee, Corp., an accrual-basis calendar-year C corporation, had no corporate shareholders when it liquidated. In cancellation of all their Mintee stock, each Mintee shareholder received a liquidating distribution of $2,000 cash and land with a tax basis of $5,000 and a fair market value of $10,500. Before the distribution, each shareholder's tax basis in Mintee stock was $6,500.

What amount of gain should each Mintee shareholder recognize on the liquidating distribution?

Liquidations – Solution

Amount Realized:

Cash	2,000
Land	10,500
	12,500
Adjusted Basis	(6,500)
Capital Gain	6,000

Liquidation of Subsidiary

When a corporation liquidates a subsidiary, in general **no gain or loss is recognized** on the liquidation.

Basis in the subsidiary's assets will stay the same.

CORPORATE REORGANIZATIONS

Corporate Reorganizations

A corporate reorganization is where two corporations (acquiring corporation and target corporation) choose to either merge or consolidate, or where one corporation spins off part of its operations into a separate corporation.

Corporate Reorganizations - Summary

Stock for Asset Reorgs are "A" and "C".

Stock for Stock Reorgs are "B".

Divisive Reorgs are "D".

If the transaction does not meet one of the reorganization classifications, all gains and losses are recognized.

A Reorganization

- Stock for Asset.
- Known as a statutory merger since the requirements of state law must be met.
- Target corporation must dissolve.
- **Voting or non-voting stock** can be used by Acquiring.
- At least 50% or the consideration given to Target by Acquiring must be stock.

B Reorganization

- Stock for Stock.
- Acquiring must own **at least 80%** of Target after the transaction.
- **Only voting stock** can be used by Acquiring.
- No boot is allowed.

C Reorganization

- Stock for Asset.
- Does not have to be a statutory merger.
- **Only voting stock** can be used by Acquiring.
- Boot is allowed but it cannot exceed 20% of the consideration provided by Acquiring.
- Acquiring must acquire **substantially all** of Target's assets (90% of net asset value and 70% of gross asset value).

Consequences to Shareholders

No gain or loss is recognized to the shareholders of the corporations involved in a tax-free reorganization if they receive only stock in exchange for property of the acquiring organization.

If they receive other property in addition to stock, it is treated as boot and gain is recognized equal to the lower of:

- **Boot received, or**
- **Realized gain**

Consequences to Corporations

Gain or loss generally is not recognized to the corporations involved in the reorganization.

If the **acquiring corporation** transfers appreciated property to target corporation, gain (but not loss) will be recognized.

If the **target corporation** transfers appreciated property to its shareholders, gain (but not loss) will be recognized.

Basis in Stock

The **basis to the shareholder** in the stock received is:

Basis in stock surrendered
\+ Gain recognized
\- Boot received

Corporate Basis

The **basis for the acquiring corporation** in the transferor's assets is:

Transferor's basis in asset
\+ Gain recognized by Transferor

Reorganization - Problem

In connection with a recapitalization of Yorktown Corporation, Robert Moore exchanged 1,000 shares of stock which cost him $95,000 for 1,000 shares of new stock worth $108,000 and bonds in the principal amount of $10,000 with a fair market value of $10,500

What is the amount of Moore's recognized gain?

Reorganization - Solution

Amount Realized:
Stock 108,000
Bonds – Boot 10,500
118,500

Adjusted Basis <95,000>

Realized Gain 23,500

Recognized Gain – Lower of:

1. Realized gain 23,500
2. Boot received 10,500

Basis in Stock - Solution

The basis to the shareholder in the stock received is:

Basis in stock surrendered 95,000
10,500
\+ Gain recognized <10,500>
95,000

\- Boot received

Reorganization - Problem

Jaxson Corp. has 200,000 shares of voting common stock issued and outstanding. King Corp. has decided to acquire 90 percent of Jaxson's voting common stock solely in exchange for 50 percent of its voting common stock and retain Jaxson as a subsidiary after the transaction. **Which of the following statements is true?**

A. King must acquire 100 percent of Jaxson stock for the transaction to be a tax-free reorganization
B. The transaction will qualify as a tax-free reorganization
C. King must issue at least 60 percent of its voting common stock for the transaction to qualify as a tax-free reorganization
D. Jaxson must surrender assets for the transaction to qualify as a tax-free reorganization

Tax Attributes

The tax attributes of Target normally carryover to Acquiring, including adjusted basis of assets, E&P, carryovers (including net operating loss, capital loss, and excess charitable contributions), accounting methods (including depreciation methods), and tax credit carryovers.

Same rules apply to the tax-free liquidation of a subsidiary.

Limitations may be placed on the use of Target's NOLS and negative E&P by Acquiring.

Pursuant to a plan of corporate reorganization adopted in July 2012, Gow exchanged 500 shares of Lad Corp. common stock that he had bought in January 2012 at a cost of $5,000 for 100 shares of Rook Corp. common stock having a fair market value of $6,000.

Gow's recognized gain on this exchange was

- [ ] **A. $1,000 long-term capital gain.**
- [ ] **B. $1,000 short-term capital gain.**
- [ ] **C. $1,000 ordinary income.**
- [ ] **D. $0.**

Elm Corp. is an accrual-basis calendar-year C Corporation with 100,000 shares of voting common stock issued and outstanding as of December 28, 2012.

On Friday, December 29, 2012, Hall surrendered 2,000 shares of Elm stock to Elm in exchange for $33,000 cash. Hall had no direct or indirect interest in Elm after the stock surrender. Additional information follows:

Hall's adjusted basis in 2,000 shares of Elm on December 29, 2012 ($8 per share)	**$16,000**
Elm's accumulated earnings and profits at January 1, 2012	**25,000**
Elm's 2012 net operating loss	**(7,000)**

What amount of income did Hall recognize from the stock surrender?

- [ ] **A. $33,000 dividend.**
- [ ] **B. $25,000 dividend.**
- [ ] **C. $18,000 capital gain.**
- [ ] **D. $17,000 capital gain.**

Dahl Corp. was organized and commenced operations in 1930. At December 31, 2012, Dahl had accumulated earnings and profits of $9,000 before dividend declaration and distribution.
On December 31, 2012 Dahl distributed cash of $9,000 and a vacant parcel of land to Green, Dahl's only stockholder. At the date of distribution, the land had a basis of $5,000 and a fair market value of $40,000.

What was Green's taxable dividend income in 2012 from these distributions?

- [ ] A. **$9,000**
- [ ] B. **$14,000**
- [ ] C. **$44,000**
- [ ] D. **$49,000**

Tank Corp., which had earnings and profits of $500,000, made a nonliquidating distribution of property to its shareholders in 2012 as a dividend in kind. This property, which had an adjusted basis of $20,000 and a fair market value of $30,000 at the date of distribution, did not constitute assets used in the active conduct of Tank's business.

How much gain did Tank recognize on this distribution?

- A. **$30,000**
- B. **$20,000**
- C. **$10,000**
- D. **$0**

REG 9-1

MULTIJURISDICTIONAL TAX ISSUES

State and Local Taxation

Taxation of Foreign Income

Selected Questions (3)

STATE AND LOCAL TAXATION

Types of SALT

State Income Taxes – starting point is usually Federal taxable income and then adjustments are made.

Sales Taxes – levied on tangible personal property and some services; exemptions vary by state but usually include items bought for resale and that are used in manufacturing.

Types of SALT

Use Taxes – levied on the use of tangible personal property that was not purchased in the state.

Property Taxes – ad valorem taxes based on value of real property (realty taxes) and personal property (personalty taxes). There are usually many exemptions for property such as inventory. A few states also tax intangible property. Usually levied for property owned at a specific date.

Types of SALT

Franchise Tax – levied on the privilege of doing business in a state. Based on the value of the capital used in the jurisdiction (common stock, paid-in-capital, and retained earnings).

Excise Tax – levied on the quantity of an item or sales price. Examples include tax on gasoline, cigarettes, and alcohol. Can be charged to manufacturer or consumer.

Types of SALT

Unemployment Tax – levied on taxable wages with a per employee limit (usually $7,000). Rate varies based on experience of employer.

Incorporation fees are charged for incorporating in a state or registering to do business in a state.

Jurisdiction to Tax

Domestic corporations are entities incorporated under the laws of a particular state.

A **foreign corporation** is a corporation incorporated in another state.

Difficult to determine the degree of power to tax foreign corporations.

Jurisdiction to Tax

Supreme Court developed four tests to determine jurisdiction to tax (**Complete Auto Transit v. Brady**):

- Activity must have substantial nexus with state
- Fairly apportioned
- Not discriminate against interstate commerce
- Fairly related to services that the state provides

Nexus

Nexus for taxing a corporation's income does not exist if activity in the state is limited to:
- Soliciting sales of tangible personal property that are approved and shipped outside the state
- Advertising
- Determining reorder needs of customers
- Furnishing autos to sales staff

State Taxable Income

The starting point for computing state income taxes is federal taxable income, increased by adjustments such as (specific rules depend on state):
- Dividends received deduction
- Expenses related to interest earned on U.S. bonds
- State income taxes
- Depreciation in excess of that allowed for state
- Municipal interest taxed for state purposes

State Taxable Income

Decreased by:

- Federal income taxes paid
- Expenses related to municipal interest income
- Interest on U.S. bonds
- Depreciation in addition to that allowed for federal purposes

Business and Nonbusiness Income

Business income is apportioned among all the states in which the corporation does business.

Nonbusiness income is apportioned only to the corporation's home state (determined in various ways) or the state in which the income is earned.

Thus, designating income as business or nonbusiness is very important.

Business and Nonbusiness Income

Business Income is generally:
- Generated from business's regular operations **(transactional test)**, or
- From the sale of property that is an integral part of the business (**functional test**).

Nonbusiness income generally includes investment income and income from transactions not part of regular operations.

If investment income is generated by regular business operations it is business income.

Apportionment

Business income is apportioned among the states in which it is earned based on apportionment factors such as **sales, property, and payroll**.

Some states use only one apportionment factor; others vary in how they weight the factors.

Different types of factors are used for financial institutions and service businesses.

Apportionment Factors

Sales Factor is computed as:

- Total Sales in State/Total Sales

Property Factor is computed as:

- Average value of property in state/All property

Payroll Factor is computed as:

- Compensation paid or accrued in state/Total compensation paid or accrued

Review Question

BIG Corporation has business operations in five states (A, B, C, D, E). Taxable income is $110,000 of which $10,000 is from income from specific transactions in A. Sales, property, and payroll are apportioned as 10%, 30%, 20%, 15%, and 25%, respectively

How is the taxable income apportioned among the states?

Apportionment - Solution

	A	B	C	D	E
Allocated	10,000				
Apportioned	10,000	30,000	20,000	15,000	25,000
Total Income	20,000	30,000	20,000	15,000	25,000

Pass-Thru Entities

Note that some states do not recognize the Federal S Corporation election.

Some states also tax partnerships at the entity level.

TAXATION OF FOREIGN INCOME

General Rules

Treaties between the U.S. and other countries generally override the tax provisions in the U.S. tax law or foreign tax law.

Foreign taxpayers are usually taxed only on U.S. source income.

U.S. taxpayers are taxed on all income earned anywhere in the world.

Source of Income

Earned income is foreign source if earned in a foreign country and U.S. source if earned domestically.

This also includes employee benefits.

Unearned income is foreign source if received from a foreign resident or for property that is used in a foreign country.

Source of Gain from Sales

Income from the sale of **personalty** is determined based on the residence of the seller, except:

- Inventory is sourced where title transfers
- For depreciable property, recapture is sourced where depreciation was claimed; remaining gain is sourced where title transfers.

Source of Gain from Sales

Income from the sale of **intangibles** is sourced where the amortization was claimed.

Income from the sale or exchange of **real property** is sourced based on the location of the property.

Source of Interest Income

Interest income is U.S. source if received from:

- U.S. government
- Noncorporate U.S. residents
- Domestic corporations

If a U.S. corporation receives 80% or more of its active business income from foreign sources over the previous three years then interest received is foreign source.

Source of Dividends

Dividends from U.S. corporations are U.S. source and from foreign corporations are foreign source.

If a foreign corporation receives 25% or more of gross income from income connected with a U.S. business for the three previous tax years then dividend is U.S. source.

Source of Income Producing Property

Source of income from the use of **tangible property** is determined by the country in which the property is located.

Source of income from the use of **intangible property** is determined by the country in which the property is used.

Deductions

Deductions must be allocated or apportioned as U.S. source or foreign source.

The IRS has the authority to change allocation of income and deductions if it determines that the taxpayer's methods do not clearly reflect income.

Outbound Transactions

The transfer of assets from the U.S. to a foreign country may trigger income (depreciation recapture applies). If assets are used in a trade or business outside the U.S. gain is deferred unless the property is:

1. Inventory or unrealized receivables
2. Installments obligations
3. Foreign currency

Controlled Foreign Corporations (CFC)

A CFC is a foreign corporation for which **more than 50% of the voting power or value of stock is owned by U.S. shareholders** (limited to those who own, direct and indirect, 10% or more of the foreign corporation) on **any day** of the tax year of the foreign corporation.

U.S. shareholders may be taxed on CFC income as a constructive dividend.

Only certain income from a CFC is taxed to the U.S. shareholder as a constructive dividend.

Controlled Foreign Corporations (CFC)

The main types of income is that which is

1. not connected economically to the country in which it is organized, and
2. income from insuring the risk of loss from outside the county in which it is organized.

CFC - Problem

Bottom, Inc. is a CFC for the entire tax year.

Top, Inc., a U.S. based corporation, owns 75% of Bottom for the entire year. Both are calendar year corporations. Subpart F income is $50,000 and no distributions have been made.

What is Top's constructive dividend for the tax year?

$50,000 x 75% = $37,500

Worldwide Income

U.S. taxpayers are taxed on all income earned anywhere in the world.

Three provisions mitigate the potential double taxation of this income:

1. Foreign income taxes paid are an itemized deduction for individuals.
2. Alternatively, a credit may be claimed for foreign taxes paid.
3. Certain individuals can elect to exclude foreign-earned income.

Foreign Tax Credit

The credit for foreign taxes paid is limited if the U.S. effective tax rate exceeds the foreign effective rate.

Limit =

$$\text{U.S. tax on worldwide income} \times \frac{\text{Foreign source taxable income}}{\text{Worldwide taxable income}}$$

Individuals must add personal exemptions to worldwide income.

Foreign Tax Credit

Excess foreign tax credits can be carried back one year and carried forward 10 years.

Individuals who have passive foreign income that does not exceed $300 ($600 for joint returns) can elect to be exempt from the foreign tax credit limitation.

Planning

A foreign tax credit usually provides a greater benefit that a deduction.

The deduction may be preferable when the foreign effective tax rate is high and foreign income, as compared to worldwide income, is small.

Foreign Income Exclusion

Qualifying individuals must **meet one of two tests** to benefit from this exclusion:

- During a continuous period that includes an entire tax year the individual is a bona fide resident of at least one foreign country, or
- The individual has a tax home in a foreign country and was present in one or more foreign countries for at least 330 days during any 12 consecutive months.

Qualifying individuals can exclude:

- Foreign-earned income from personal services
- Employer provided foreign housing income

Foreign Income Exclusion

Exclusion is subject to a limit that is indexed for inflation.

Taxpayers must file an election to take the exclusion which is binding for future years until revoked.

Foreign Currency Gains and Losses

Foreign currency exchange gains and losses resulting from the **normal course of business** operations are **ordinary**.

Foreign currency exchange gains and losses resulting from **investment or personal** transactions are **capital**.

Mr. Travel is a U.S. citizen who has been a resident of Spain for five years. In 2012, he has the following income from Spanish sources:

	Salary	Interest Income
Gross amount	$90,000	$20,000
Spanish income tax (20%)	(18,000)	(4,000)
Net cash received (80%)	$72,000	$16,000

The interest income was from a Spanish money market account. Mr. Travel also was provided housing from his employer that had a fair market value of $30,000 (not subject to Spanish tax). Total U.S.-source earned income for Mr. Travel was $60,000. What is Mr. Travel's minimum includible United States gross income from these transactions?

- [ ] A. **$ 60,000.**
- [ ] B. **$ 96,686.**
- [ ] C. **$110,000.**
- [ ] D. **$200,000.**

Machine Corporation buys a business van in State V and pays 6% sales tax. The van is used in State W by Machine. State W has a 9% sales tax. Because of this transaction, State W is likely to impose which of the following taxes on Machine?

- [ ] **A. Sales tax.**
- [ ] **B. Income tax.**
- [ ] **C. Use tax.**
- [ ] **D. Franchise tax.**

Clock Corporation owns 80%, 90%, and 100%, respectively, of its three subsidiaries, Lamp, Chair, and Table. The corporations have elected to file a consolidated tax return for U.S. federal income tax. The corporations have nexus as follows:

	Nexus
Clock	**States M and N**
Lamp	**States M and N**
Chair	**State N**
Table	**States M and N**

If a consolidated state income tax return is filed in State M, which corporations will be included in the return?

- ☐ A. **Clock**
- ☐ B. **Clock and Table.**
- ☐ C. **Clock, Lamp, and Table.**
- ☐ D. **Clock, Lamp, Chair, and Table.**

REG 9-2

TAX-EXEMPT ENTITIES

Tax-Exempt Organizations

Selected Questions (2)

TAX-EXEMPT ORGANIZATIONS

Tax-Exempt Organizations

Tax-exempt organizations include charities, labor organizations, social clubs, pension and profit-sharing trusts, political organizations, and private foundations.

An exempt organization (EO) may be in the form of a corporation or trust, and it must apply for and receive an **exemption from taxation** (Form 1023 or Form 1024).

A private foundation is a tax-exempt organization which receives less than one-third of its annual support from the general public, governmental units, churches, charitable organizations, etc.

Annual Filing Requirement

EO must file an information return (**Form 990**) if gross receipts exceed $50,000. This form reports income, expenses, and substantial contributors.

Churches do not file Form 990.

Private foundations file Form 990-PF.

Acceptable Activities

To qualify as an EO the organization must operate exclusively for a tax-exempt purpose.

Influencing legislation or political parties is not an acceptable purpose.

Section 501(c)(3) organizations can participate in **lobbying efforts** if an election is made and lobbying expenditures do not exceed certain ceilings.

Review Question

Maple Avenue Assembly, a tax-exempt religious organization, operates an outreach program for the poor in its community. A candidate for the local city council has endorsed Maple's anti-poverty program. Which of the following activities is (are) consistent with Maple's tax-exempt status?

I. Endorsing the candidate to members

II. Collecting contributions from members for the candidate

A. I only
B. II only
C. Both I and II
D. Neither I nor II

Unrelated Business Income

An exempt organization is taxed on its unrelated business income (UBI).

To be UBI, income must:

1. Be from a **business regularly carried on**, and
2. **Not be substantially related** to the EO exempt purposes.

Unrelated Business Income

Related income includes:

1. An activity where substantially all work is performed for no compensation.
2. A business carried on for the convenience of students or members of a charitable, religious, or scientific organization.
3. Sale of merchandise received as contributions.
4. In general, **investment income.**
5. **Rents from real property.**

Unrelated Business Income

Income from **advertising in journals** of the EO is UBI.

Qualified corporate sponsorship income is not UBI.

UBI is **taxed (only if it exceeds $1,000) at regular corporate rates** if the organization is a corporation; at trust rates if it is a trust.

Review Question

Which of the following activities conducted by a tax exempt organization will result in unrelated business income?

I. Selling articles made by handicapped persons as part of their rehabilitation, when the organization is involved exclusively in their rehabilitation

II. Operating a grocery store almost fully staffed by emotionally handicapped persons as part of a therapeutic program

A. I only
B. II only
C. Both I and II
D. Neither I nor II

Which of the following activities conducted by a tax exempt organization will result in unrelated business income?

I. Selling articles made by handicapped persons as part of their rehabilitation, when the organization is involved exclusively in their rehabilitation.
II. Operating a grocery store almost fully staffed by emotionally handicapped persons as part of a therapeutic program.

- A. **I only.**
- B. **II only.**
- C. **Both I and II.**
- D. **Neither I nor II.**

Hope is a tax-exempt religious organization. Which of the following activities is (are) consistent with Hope's tax-exempt status?

I. Conducting weekend retreats for business organizations.

II. Providing traditional burial services that maintain the religious beliefs of its members.

- [ ] **A. I only.**
- [ ] **B. II only.**
- [ ] **C. Both I and II.**
- [ ] **D. Neither I nor II.**

REG 9-3

PARTNERSHIP TAXATION 1

Formation and Basis

Selected Questions (3)

FORMATION AND BASIS

Partnerships - Introduction

General partners can participate in management and have **joint and several liability** for the partnership's debts. All partnerships must have at least one general partner.

Limited partners are only liable up to their investment, but they cannot participate in management without losing their limited liability status.

LLC Members have limited liability.

Entities Taxed as Partnerships

General Partnerships – all GPs

Limited Partnerships – at least one GP and at least one LP

Limited Liability Companies – all members have limited liability

Limited Liability Partnerships – liability protection may be more limited than for LLC members

Check-the-Box Regulations

Non-incorporated entities (i.e., partnerships, limited liability companies) are taxed as follows:

- If only **one business owner**, the default classification is that the entity is disregarded for tax purposes.
- If more than one owner, the default classification is partnership.
- However, the owners can elect to be **taxed as a corporation** if they wish.

Advantages of Partnerships

Partnerships provide business owners substantial flexibility.

Limited liability companies are popular because all members have limited liability.

Partners can usually get into and out of a partnership without recognizing a gain.

Single taxation.

Formation of a Partnership

A partner and a partnership will not recognize gain or loss from the contribution of property in exchange for a partnership interest.

This provision does **not apply to partnership interests received for services**, for which wage income is recognized equal to the fair market value of the partnership interest .

Almost all **tax elections** are made by the partnership as opposed to by the partners.

Basis

The **partner takes a substituted basis** in his partnership interest (i.e., basis she had in property transferred), and the **partnership takes a carryover basis** in assets it receives.

Once the partnership begins operations, a partner's adjusted basis for her partnership interest must be adjusted to reflect the results of operations.

Holding Period

Partner's holding period in partnership interest:

- Holding period tacks for contributions of **capital assets and Section 1231 assets.**
- For **other assets**, the holding period starts when the contribution is received by the partnership.

Partnership's holding period in property received always includes holding period partner had in property.

Basis Adjustments

The initial basis is increased by:

- The partner's share of **taxable and nontaxable income,**
- Increases in the partner's share of **partnership debt**, and
- Additional **contributions** the partner makes to the partnership.

Basis Adjustments

The basis is reduced by:

- Share of the **deductions, losses, nondeductible and noncapitalizable expenditures** of the partnership,
- Decreases in the partner's share of partnership **debt**, and
- Any **distributions** from the partnership to the partner.

Basis - Problem

Gray is a 50% partner in Fabco Partnership. Gray's tax basis in Fabco on January 1 was $5,000. Fabco made no distributions to the partners during this year, and recorded the following:

Ordinary income	$ 20,000
Tax exempt income	8,000
Portfolio income	4,000

What is Gray's tax basis in Fabco on December 31 of the current year?

Basis - Solution

Initial Basis	5,000
Ordinary Income	10,000
Tax-Exempt Interest	4,000
Portfolio Income	2,000
Basis, December 31	21,000

Liabilities – Recourse Debt

Partners increase/decrease basis as their share of partnership debt changes.

For **recourse debt**, each partner's share of debt is measured by his/her **economic risk of loss** assuming a "constructive liquidation scenario" occurred.

Limited partners are not allocated any share of recourse debt.

Liabilities – Nonrecourse Debt

Nonrecourse debt is debt for which the lender's only recourse, in the event of default, is to take back the property.

Nonrecourse debt is often allocated based on the partners' **profit sharing ratios**.

In contrast with recourse debt, **both general and limited** partners are allocated nonrecourse debt.

Liabilities and Basis - Problem

Bailey contributed land with a fair market value of $75,000 and an adjusted basis of $25,000 to the ABC Partnership in exchange for a 30% interest.

The partnership assumed Bailey's $10,000 recourse mortgage on the land.

What is Bailey's basis for his partnership interest?

Liabilities and Basis - Solution

Beginning Basis	25,000
Partner's Debt Assumed	<10,000>
Partners' share of P'ship Debt	+3,000
Basis in Partnership Interest	18,000

Year-Ends

Partnerships use the same year-end as its **majority interest partner(s)** (more than 50% capital interest and profits interest).

If the partnership has no single year for the majority test, then the partnership uses same year-end as all of its **principal partners** (5% or more profits interest).

Year-Ends

Least Aggregate Deferral method.

Section 444 election allows a year-end different from required year-end but deferral cannot exceed three months.

Dean is a 25 percent partner in Target Partnership. Dean's tax basis in Target on January 1, 2012, was $20,000. At the end of 2012, Dean received a nonliquidating cash distribution of $8,000 from Target. Target's 2012 accounts recorded the following items:

Municipal bond interest income	**$12,000**
Ordinary income	**40,000**

What was Dean's tax basis in Target on December 31, 2012?

- A. **$15,000**
- B. **$23,000**
- C. **$25,000**
- D. **$30,000**

Strom acquired a 25 percent interest in Ace Partnership by contributing land having an adjusted basis of $16,000 and a fair market value of $50,000. The land was subject to a $24,000 mortgage, which was assumed by Ace. No other liabilities existed at the time of the contribution.

What was Strom's basis in Ace?

- [ ] A. **$0**
- [ ] B. **$16,000**
- [ ] C. **$26,000**
- [ ] D. **$32,000**

Kerr and Marcus form KM Partnership with a cash contribution of $80,000 from Kerr and a property contribution of land from Marcus. The land has a fair market value of $80,000 and an adjusted basis of $50,000 at the date of the contribution. Kerr and Marcus are equal partners.

What is Marcus's basis immediately after formation?

- [ ] A. **$0**
- [ ] B. **$50,000**
- [ ] C. **$65,000**
- [ ] D. **$80,000**

REG 9-4

PARTNERSHIP TAXATION 2

Flow-Through of Income and Losses

Transactions with Partners

Selected Questions (4)

FLOW-THROUGH OF INCOME AND LOSSES

Allocations of Income

All income, expenses, loss, credits, etc. flow to the partners and are taxed on each partner's return.

A partnership pays no taxes.

Allocations of Income

The partnership must file **Form 1065** to report the results of its operations.

Profits and losses are allocated to each partner based on each partner's **profit and loss sharing ratio**.

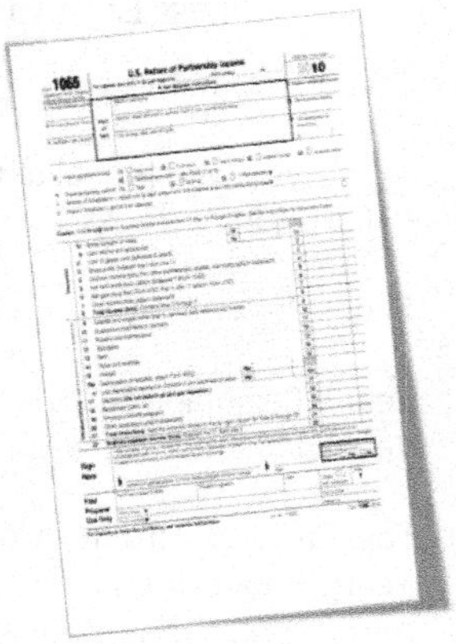

Allocations of Income

All items of income, gain, deduction, loss, or credit which are required to be **separately stated**, or which are specially allocated, are removed from the partnership's ordinary income or loss determination.

Each partner's proportionate share of these items is reported on **Schedule K-1**.

The remaining items are lumped together to produce the ordinary business income or loss, which is also proportionately reported to each partner.

Income Flow-Through

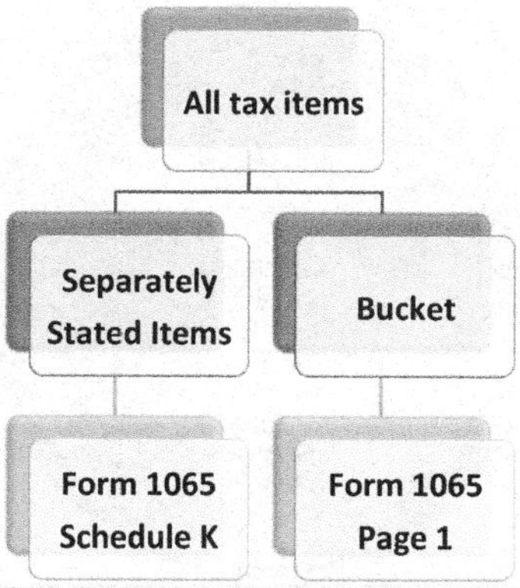

Income - Problem

Partnership M, a law partnership, had the following items this year:

		SS	Bucket
Income from clients	$200,000		✓
Repairs	1,000		✓
Depreciation	2,000		✓
Dividends on capital stock	500	✓	
Other operating expenses	125,000		✓
Charitable contribution	1,500	✓	
Sec. 1231 gain on sale of office furniture	1,200	✓	
Sec. 1245 gain on sale of office furniture	1,000		✓

What is Partnership M's ordinary income? $73,000

Flow-Through Effects

Distributive Share of Tax Item

10,000 INT INC → 5,000

Flows Through As Income

Flows Through To Basis

Partnership Losses

A partner can deduct partnership losses on her tax return only to the extent of her **basis in her partnership interest**.

A partnership loss will be a **passive loss** to a limited partner.

A partnership loss may be a passive loss to a general partner depending upon whether the partner meets the material participation test.

Loss Limitations - Problem

Linda and Mark each have a 50% interest in the LM Partnership. The partnership and the individuals file on a calendar year basis. For its Year 4 tax year, LM Partnership had a $30,000 loss. Linda's adjusted basis in her partnership on January 1, Year 4, was $8,000. In Year 5, LM Partnership had a profit of $28,000.

Assuming there were no other adjustments to Linda's basis in the partnership in Years 4 and 5, what amount of partnership income (loss) would Linda show on her Years 4 and 5 individual income tax return?

Loss Limitations - Solution

Year 4 Distributive Loss	30,000 x 50%	15,000
Loss Allowed (equal to basis)		<8,000>
Carryforward Loss		7,000
Ending basis is	0	
Year 5 Beginning Basis		0
Year 5 Income	28,000 x 50%	14,000
		14,000
Loss Carryforward from Year 4		<7,000>
Year 5 Ending Basis		7,000

Loss Limitations

Three hurdles must be cleared for a loss to be deducted:

- **Basis** in Partnership Interest
- **At-Risk** Amount (generally basis less share of nonrecourse debt)
- **Passive** Income (if the loss is passive)

Loss Limitations

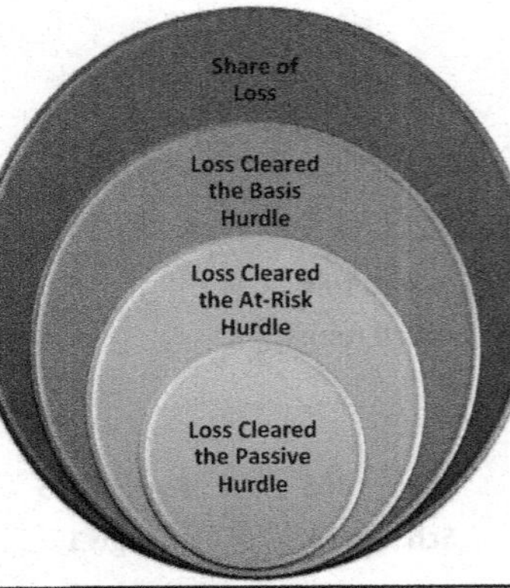

Loss Limitation Problem

Jose's share of Partnership JAK's loss is $50,000

Other relevant tax information is as follows:

Basis in partnership interest	$ 40,000
At-Risk amount	35,000
Passive income	20,000

How much loss from the partnership can Jose deduct on this year's tax return?

Loss Limitation Solution

50,000

	Cleared Hurdle	Carry-forward
Basis	40,000	10,000
At-Risk amount	35,000	5,000
Passive income	20,000	15,000
		30,000

Loss Limitations

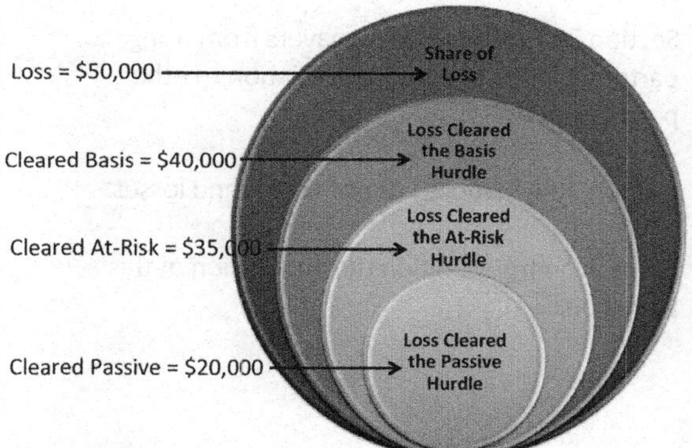

Organization and Start-Up Costs

Organization Costs: $5,000 of these expenses may be deducted, but the $5,000 is reduced by the amount of expenditures incurred that exceed $50,000.

Expenses not deducted must be capitalized and amortized over 180 months, beginning with the month that the corporation begins its business operations (unless an election is made to not do so).

Same rules apply for **start-up costs**.

TRANSACTIONS WITH PARTNERS

Guaranteed Payments

Guaranteed payments are determined **without regard to partnership income** and are paid to the partner in his or her role as a partner (i.e., salaries).

Guaranteed payments are taxable as ordinary income to the partner and are deductible by the partnership.

They are taxed as if they were paid on the **last day of the partnership's taxable year**.

Review Question

Evan, a 25% partner in Vista partnership, received a $20,000 guaranteed payment in Year 3 for services rendered to the partnership. Guaranteed payments were not made to any other partner. Vista's Year 3 partnership income consisted of:

Net business income before guaranteed payments	$ 80,000
Net long-term capital gains	10,000

What amount of income should Evan report from Vista Partnership on his Year 3 tax return?

Review Question

Net Income before Guar. Payment
Guaranteed Payment
Ordinary Business Income

Income Reported on Tax Return:
- Ordinary Income
- Capital Gains
- Guaranteed Payment

Built-In Gains/Losses

If a partnership disposes of an asset that was contributed by a partner and at the time of contribution the asset had a **built-in gain or built-in loss**, the recognized gain/loss is allocated back to the contributing partner to the extent of the built-in gain/loss.

If asset contributed has:

- FMV = $10,000
- Adjusted Basis = $7,000
- BIG = $3,000

Built-In Gains/Losses

Section 704(c) prevents taxpayers from using partnerships to transfer appreciation to other partners.

Section 704(c) applies to both gains and losses.

There is no time limit on the application of this provision.

Review Question

Art, Bart, and Dart decide to form the equal ABD partnership at the beginning of Year One. Art contributed depreciable assets that he has owned for two years that have a basis of $15,000 and a value of $20,000. Bart contributed $20,000 cash. Dart contributed $12,000 in cash and land with a basis of $5,000 and a value of $8,000.

What are the tax consequences if the partnership sells the land contributed by Dart for 11,000?

Review Question

	Land
FMV	
Adjusted Basis	
Built-in Gain	

Land Sale:

Amount Realized – Adjusted Basis = Recognized Gain

Built-in Gain — Dart

Remaining Gain — Dart, Art, Bart

Related Party Losses

Losses disallowed between a partnership and **person** owning **more than 50%** of capital or profits interest.

Losses disallowed between two partnerships if same **person** owns more than 50% of capital or profits interest.

Note application of constructive ownership rules.

Review Question

The FAD partnership is an equal partnership. F and D are father and daughter and F sells a business asset, with an adjusted basis of $12,000, to the FAD partnership for $8,000.

What are the tax consequences of this transaction?

What if FAD later sells the asset to an unrelated third-party for $10,000?

Related Party Losses - Solution

Father's ownership interest: (1/3 + 1/3) 67% >50%

Amount Realized	8,000
Adjusted Basis	<12,000>
Realized Loss	<4,000>
Recognized Loss	0
Right of Offset	4,000

Related Party Losses - Solution

FAD SALE

Amount Realized	10,000
Adjusted Basis	<8,000>
Realized Gain	2,000
Right of Offset	<2,000>
Recognized Gain	0

Under the Internal Revenue Code sections pertaining to partnerships, guaranteed payments are payments to partners for

- [ ] **A. Payments of principal on secured notes honored at maturity.**
- [ ] **B. Timely payments of periodic interest on bona fide loans that are not treated as partners' capital.**
- [ ] **C. Services or the use of capital without regard to partnership income.**
- [ ] **D. Sales of partners' assets to the partnership at guaranteed amounts regardless of market values.**

Peters has a one-third interest in the Spano Partnership. During 2012, Peters received a $16,000 guaranteed payment, which was deductible by the partnership, for services rendered to Spano. Spano reported a 2012 operating loss of $70,000 before the guaranteed payment.

What is(are) the net effect(s) of the guaranteed payment?

I. The guaranteed payment increases Peters's tax basis in Spano by $16,000.

II. The guaranteed payment increases Peters's ordinary income by $16,000.

- [ ] **A. I only.**
- [ ] **B. II only.**
- [ ] **C. Both I and II.**
- [ ] **D. Neither I nor II.**

In computing the ordinary income of a partnership, a deduction is allowed for

- [ ] **A. Contributions to recognized charities.**
- [ ] **B. The first $100 of dividends received from qualifying domestic corporations.**
- [ ] **C. Short-term capital losses.**
- [ ] **D. Guaranteed payments to partners.**

A partnership had four partners. Each partner contributed $100,000 cash. The partnership reported income for the year of $80,000 and distributed $10,000 to each partner. What was each partner's basis in the partnership at the end of the current year?

- [ ] A. **$170,000**
- [ ] B. **$120,000**
- [ ] C. **$117,500**
- [ ] D. **$110,000**

REG 9-5

PARTNERSHIP TAXATION 3

Distributions

Sales and Terminations

Selected Questions (4)

DISTRIBUTIONS

Non-Liquidating Distributions

In general, **no gain or loss** is recognized by the partnership or the partner for a proportionate nonliquidating distribution.

Assets are assumed to be distributed in the following order:

- Cash
- **Unrealized receivables and inventory** (all assets except for cash, capital assets, and Section 1231 assets); and
- Capital assets and Section 1231 assets.

Non-Liquidating Distributions

The distributee partner recognizes **gain if the cash distributed exceeds the partner's outside basis** in the partnership immediately before the distribution.

Gain recognized by the partner is usually capital gain.

In general, **distributed property takes a carryover basis** to the distributee partner.

The partner **reduces his basis in his partnership interest by the basis of the property distributed**.

Review Question

The adjusted basis of Jody's partnership interest was $50,000 immediately before Jody received a current distribution of $20,000 cash and property with an adjusted basis to the partnership of $40,000 and a fair market value of $35,000.

What amount of taxable gain must Jody report as a result of this distribution?

What is Jody's basis in the distributed property?

Review Question

	Basis in Partnership Interest
	50,000
Cash	(20,000)
	30,000
Land: Lower of AB or Remaining basis in interest	(30,000)
Basis in Land to Jody	0

30,000

Liquidating Distributions

Rules are the same as for non-liquidating distributions, with the following exceptions:

1. Loss is **recognized if**:
   - The partner receives only cash, unrealized receivables and inventory from the partnership, and
   - The inside bases of these assets is less than the partner's outside basis in the partnership immediately before the distribution
2. The partner's basis **must be reduced to zero**.

Review Question

The adjusted basis of Vance's partnership interest in Lex Associates was $180,000 immediately before receiving the following distribution in complete liquidation of Lex:

	Basis to Lex	Fair market value
Cash	$100,000	$ 100,000
Real estate	70,000	96,000

What is Vance's basis in the real estate?

Review Question

	Basis in Partnership Interest
	180,000
Cash	(100,000)
	80,000
Land	(80,000)
	0
Basis in Land to Vance	$80,000

Review Question

	Basis in Partnership Interest
	180,000
Cash	(100,000)
	80,000
Inventory	(70,000)
	10,000
Loss	(10,000)
	0
Basis in Inventory to Vance	= 70,000

Partner Retirements

If a partner retires from the partnership, in general payments received are treated the same as for liquidating distributions.

If the partner is a **general partner in a service** oriented partnership, then:

1. Payments for unrealized receivables and unstated goodwill are taxed as ordinary income.
2. Remaining payments are treated as being in exchange for partnership property.

SALES AND TERMINATIONS

Sales of Partnership Interests

A partnership interest is a **capital asset**. Thus, gain/loss from the sale of a partnership interest is, in general, capital in nature.

However, to the extent the partnership has **hot assets**, gain will be recharacterized as ordinary income.

The "**look through**" rules may also affect the tax rates applied to a portion of the gain.

Sales of Partnership Interests

Hot assets are:

1. Unrealized receivables (receivables of a cash basis taxpayer; includes depreciation recapture), and
2. Inventory.

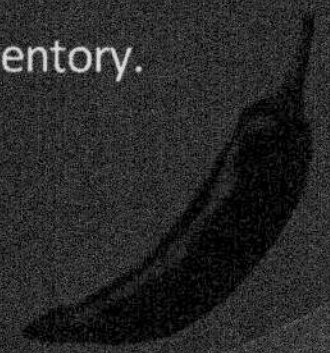

CPAexcel

Sales of Partnership Interests

If the partnership has hot assets at the time a partnership interest is sold, the selling partner must allocate a portion of the sale proceeds to these assets and recognize ordinary income.

Review Question

The personal service partnership of Allen, Baker & Carr had the following cash basis balance sheet at December 31, Year 4:

Assets

	Adjusted basis per books	Market value
Cash	$102,000	$102,000
Unrealized accounts receivable	-	$420,000
Totals	$102,000	$522,000

Review Question

Liability and Capital		
Note payable	$ 60,000	$ 60,000
Capital accounts:		
Allen	14,000	154,000
Baker	14,000	154,000
Carr	14,000	154,000
Totals	$ 102,000	$522,000

Carr, an equal partner, sold his partnership interest to Dole, an outsider, for $154,000 cash on January 1, Year 5. In addition, Dole assumed Carr's share of the partnership's liability.

What was the total amount and character of the gain recognized by Carr?

Review Question

	Total Sale
Amount Realized	
Cash	154,000
Debt Relief	+20,000
	174,000
Adjusted Basis (14,000 + 20,000)	(34,000)
Recognized Gain	140,000

Review Question

	If Hot Asset Sold
Amount Realized	420,000
Adjusted Basis	-0-
Ordinary Income	420,000
Allocated to Carr	× 1/3
	140,000

Total Gain	140,000
Ordinary Income	<140,000>
Capital Gain	0

Character of Gain on Sale

In addition to hot assets, if the partnership owns **collectibles or has Section 1250 assets**, these items may also impact the gain from the sale of a partnership asset.

Character of Gain on Sale

The selling partner's gain will be taxed at 28% to the extent it is due to collectibles, and any unrecaptured Section 1250 gain will be taxed at 25%.

Collectibles include coins, stamps, antiques, artwork, etc.

Partnership Terminations

No part of the business continues to be carried on by any partner in the partnership form.

There is a sale or exchange of **at least a 50% interest in both capital and profits** within a consecutive 12-month period.

Termination requires a closing of the partnership tax-year.

Partnership Terminations

When the partnership's business and financial operations are continued by other members, there is:

- a deemed distribution of assets to the remaining partners and the purchaser, and
- a hypothetical recontribution of assets to a new partnership.

Partnership Divisions

When a partnership divides into two or more partnerships, the original partnership is continued in each of the new partnerships which contain partners that controlled 50 percent or more of the partnership interest in the original partnership.

Curry's sale of her partnership interest causes a partnership termination. The partnership's business and financial operations are continued by the other members. What is (are) the effect(s) of the termination?

I. There is a deemed distribution of assets to the remaining partners and the purchaser.

II. There is a hypothetical recontribution of assets to a new partnership.

- [ ] **A. I only.**
- [ ] **B. II only.**
- [ ] **C. Both I and II.**
- [ ] **D. Neither I nor II.**

The personal service partnership of Allen, Baker & Carr had the following cash basis balance sheet at December 31, 2011:

	Adjusted basis per book	Market value
Assets		
Cash	$102,000	$102,000
Unrealized accounts receivable	--	420000
Totals	$102,000	$522,000
Liability and Capital		
Note payable	$ 60,000	$ 60,000
Capital accounts:		
Allen	14000	154,000
Baker	14000	154,000
Carr	14,000	154,000
	$102,000	$522,000

Carr, an equal partner, sold his partnership interest to Dole, an outsider, for $154,000 cash on January 1, 2012. In addition, Dole assumed Carr's share of the partnerships liability. What amount of ordinary income should Carr report in his 2012 income tax return on the sale of his partnership interest?

- A. $0
- B. $20,000
- C. $34,000
- D. $140,000

On June 30, 2012, Berk retired from his partnership.

At that time, his capital account was $50,000 and his share of the partnership's liabilities was $30,000. Berk's retirement payments consisted of being relieved of his share of the partnership liabilities and receipt of cash payments of $5,000 per month for 18 months, commencing July 1, 2012.

Assuming Berk makes no election with regard to the recognition of gain from the retirement payments, he should report income therefrom of

	2012	2013
☐	$13,333	$26,667
☐	$20,000	$20,000
☐	$40,000	-
☐	-	$40,000

Stone's basis in Ace Partnership was $70,000 at the time he received a nonliquidating distribution of partnership capital assets. These capital assets had an adjusted basis of $65,000 to Ace, and a fair market value of $83,000. Ace had no unrealized receivables, appreciated inventory, or properties which had been contributed by its partners.

What was Stone's recognized gain or loss on the distribution?

- [ ] **A. $18,000 ordinary income.**
- [ ] **B. $13,000 capital gain.**
- [ ] **C. $5,000 capital loss.**
- [ ] **D. $0.**

REG 10-1

S CORPORATION TAXATION

Eligibility, Elections, Terminations

Income and Basis

Distributions and Special Taxes

Selected Questions (2)

ELIGIBILITY, ELECTIONS, TERMINATIONS

S Corporations - Introduction

The S election can only be made by a corporation, and the corporation retains its legal corporate status after the election.

S corporations retain corporate status and their corporate characteristics:

- Shares can be freely transferred
- Shareholders are not liable for corporate debt
- Shareholders can be employees (separation of ownership and management).

S Corporations

Most rules are similar to corporate rules, except for flow-through rules, year-end rules, and basis rules.

Default rules for S Corporations are the regular corporation rules, not the partnership rules.

S Corporations - Eligibility

No more than **100 shareholders**.

Husbands and wives are treated as one shareholder (as are individuals and their estates).

A family may elect that all family members be treated as one shareholder.

Shareholders can **only be individuals, estates, and certain trusts**.

S Corporations - Eligibility

Non-resident aliens are not eligible to be shareholders.

Can only have **one class of stock** (voting and nonvoting stock is acceptable).

Banks and insurance companies are not eligible.

Election Requirements

To be effective for the current year, the S Corp. election must be filed **on or before the 15th day of the third month** of the taxable year.

All individuals owning stock any time during the taxable year must consent to the election.

Review Question

On February 10, Year 5, Ace Corp., a calendar year corporation, elected S corporation status and all shareholders consented to the election. There was no change in shareholders in Year 5. Ace met all eligibility requirements for S status during the pre-election portion of the year.

What is the earliest date on which Ace can be recognized as an S corporation?

JANUARY 1, YR 5

Termination of S Status

Once the election is terminated, must wait **five years** before re-electing S status.

Occurs if shareholders owning **more than 50% of voting and nonvoting stock** elect to revoke election.

If any eligibility requirements are violated.

Terminations - Problem

An S corporation has 30,000 shares of voting common stock and 20,000 shares of non-voting common stock issued and outstanding. The S election can be revoked voluntarily with the consent of the shareholders holding, on the day of the revocation,

	Shares of voting stock	Shares of nonvoting stock
A.	0	20,000
B.	7,500	5,000
C.	10,000	16,000
D.	20,000	0

30,000
20,000
50,000
x 50%
> 25,000

Termination of S Status

If **passive investment income** earned by the corporation

- Exceeds 25% of gross receipts for 3 consecutive taxable years, and
- The S corporation had accumulated earnings & profits,
- then the S election is terminated as of the beginning of the fourth year.

INCOME AND BASIS

Income Flow-Through

Any income, losses, deductions, and credits which can affect shareholders differently are **separately stated**, and each shareholder reports a pro-rata portion of each item.

Income Flow-Through

The nonseparately computed items are combined together and each shareholder reports a pro rata portion of this amount.

Items are pro-rated as follows:

allocation = item x ownership % x portion of year owned

Income Flow-Through

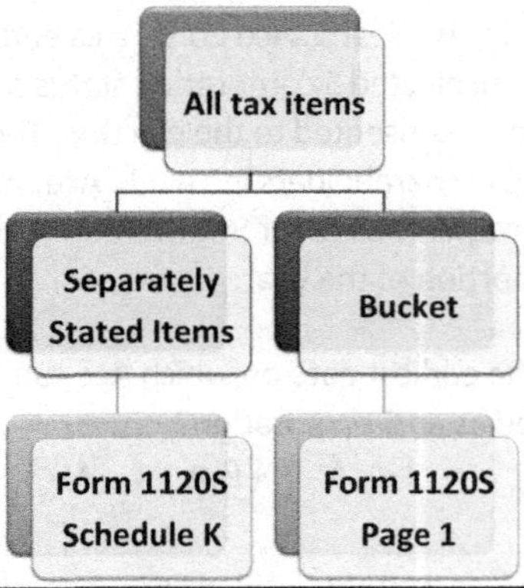

Special Rules

All items retain their character as they pass through to each shareholder. For example, tax-exempt income at the corporate level will be tax-exempt income at the shareholder level.

S corporations are not allowed a dividends received deduction.

Review Question

As of January 1, Year 2, Kane owned all the 100 issued shares of Manning Corp., a calendar year S corporation. On the 40th day of Year 2, Kane sold 25 of the Manning shares to Rogers. For the year ended December 31, Year 2 (a 365-day calendar year), Manning had $73,000 in non-separately stated income and made no distributions to its shareholders.

What amount of non-separately stated income from Manning should be reported on Kane's Year 2 tax return?

Review Question

Item x Ownership % x Time

40 days

73000 x 100% x 40/365 = 8,000

325 days

73000 x 75% x 325/365 = 48,750

56,750

Loss Limitations

Losses may flow through to the shareholder, but only to the extent of the **shareholder's stock and loan basis.**

Loan basis is created when the shareholder loans funds directly to the S corporation.

Disallowed losses are carried forward until there is basis to deduct them.

Loss Limitation - Example

Distributive Share of Losses – Sch. K-1	20,000
Stock Basis	10,000
Loan Basis	6,000
Allowed Loss on Form 1040	16,000 →
Carryforward Loss	4,000

Basis in Stock

The shareholder's basis in the S corporation is determined as follows:

Initial basis
\+ stock purchases
\+ taxable and tax-exempt income
\- deductible and non-deductible expenses
AAA distributions

AAA = (accumulated adjustments account)

Basis in Stock - Problem

Beck Corp. has been a calendar-year S corporation since its inception on January 2, Year 1. On January 1, Year 5, Lazur and Lyle each owned 50% of the Beck stock, in which their respective tax bases were $12,000 and $9,000. For the year ended December 31, Year 5, Beck had $81,000 in ordinary business income & $10,000 in tax-exempt income. Beck made a $51,000 cash distribution to each shareholder on December 31, Year 5.

What was Lazur's tax basis in Beck after the distribution?

Basis in Stock - Solution

Beginning Basis, 1/1/05	12,000
Ordinary Income	40,500
Tax-Exempt Income	+5,000
	57,500
Distribution	(51,000)
Ending Basis, 12/31/05	6,500

Flow-Through Effects

Distributive Share of Tax Item

Flows Through As Income | Flows Through To Basis

Fringe Benefits – Shareholders

S corporation shareholders who own more than 2% of the stock are treated as partners for fringe benefit purposes, meaning that the following are included in income:

- Employer paid premiums to health and accident plans;
- Benefits paid under employer-sponsored accident and health plans;
- Cost of up to $50,000 of employer paid group term life insurance; and
- Meals and lodging provided by employer.

DISTRIBUTIONS AND SPECIAL TAXES

Passive Investment Income Tax

If the S Corp's passive investment income **exceeds 25% of gross receipts** and the S Corp. has C corporation **AE&P**, a tax is imposed at the highest corporate rate.

Built-In Gains Tax

A C corporation that makes an S election and has unrealized **built-in gains** in its assets as of the election day must pay a built-in gains tax on this appreciation if it is recognized within the next **10 years**.

Gain is taxed at the highest corporate tax rate.

Built-In Gains Tax - Problem

Prail Corporation is a C corporation that on February 1, Year 2 elected to be taxed as a calendar-year S corporation. On June 15, Year 2, Prail sold land with a basis of $100,000 for $200,000 cash. The fair market value of the land on February 1, Year 2 was $150,000. Prail had no other income or loss for the year and no carryovers from prior years.

What is Prail's tax?

Built-In Gains Tax - Solution

Built-In Gain at Date of Election:

FMV	150,000	
Adjusted Basis	<100,000>	50,000

June 15 Sale:

Amount Realized	200,000
Adjusted Basis	<100,000>
Recognized Gain	100,000

Built-In Gains Tax to Corporation:

$50,000 x 35% = $17,500

Distributions with E&P

If the corporation has **earnings and profits**, distributions are taxed in the following order:

- Tax-free to the extent of AAA (Accumulated Adjustments Account)
- Ordinary dividend to the extent of accumulated E&P
- Tax-free to the extent of basis in stock
- Excess is treated as capital gain

Distributions if No E&P

If the corporation does **not have earnings and profits**, distributions are taxed in the following order:

- Tax-free to the extent of **basis in stock**
- Excess is treated as **capital gain**

Accumulated Adjustments Account

AAA reflects the cumulative income and losses for all of the S corporation years that have not been distributed.

Similar in concept to Earnings & Profits for C corporations.

Only tax-exempt income and the nondeductible expenses related to tax-exempt income are excluded in computing the amount in the AAA.

Distributions - Problem

JAS Corporation was formed in Year 1. It properly elected S corporation status on January 1, Year 4 when it had earnings and profits of $20,000. In Year 4, JAS earned $20,000 and made a cash distribution in December Year 4 of $50,000. JAS was founded by its sole shareholder, J.A. Stephens. His basis in JAS stock on January 1, Year 4 was $8,000.

How much capital gain will Stephens recognize from the distribution?

Distributions - Solution

Distribution Amount	50,000
AAA (not taxable)	<20,000>
	30,000
Earnings & Profits (dividend income)	<20,000>
	10,000
Basis in Stock	<8,000>
Long-Term Capital Gain	2,000

As of January 1, 2012, Kane owned all the 100 issued shares of Manning Corp., a calendar year S corporation. On the 40th day of 2012, Kane sold 25 of the Manning shares to Rodgers. For the year ended December 31, 2012 (a 365-day calendar year), Manning had $73,000 in nonseparately stated income and made no distributions to its shareholders.

What amount of nonseparately stated income from Manning should be reported on Kane's 2012 tax return?

- **A. $56,750**
- **B. $54,750**
- **C. $16,250**
- **D. $0**

B Corporation has been a calendar-year S electing corporation since its inception. S1 and S2 each own half of the stock with a basis of $12 and $9, respectively. This year B reported ordinary income of $81 and $10 of tax-exempt income. B also made a $51 cash distribution to each shareholder at year end. What is S1's basis after the distribution?

- [ ] A. **$ 1.5**
- [ ] B. **$ 6.5**
- [ ] C. **$52.5**
- [ ] D. **$57.5**

REG 10-2

ESTATE AND GIFT TAXATION

Federal Gift Tax

Federal Estate Tax

Selected Questions (1)

FEDERAL GIFT TAX

Introduction to Transfer Taxes

The gratuitous transfer of property during a taxpayer's life or upon the death of the taxpayer is subject to a federal transfer tax .

This tax is called a **gift tax** when it is imposed on lifetime transfers.

Introduction to Transfer Taxes

The tax is called an **estate tax** when it is imposed on transfers triggered by the death of the taxpayer.

The donor is primarily liable for the gift tax, while the decedent's estate is primarily liable for the estate tax.

Unified Credit

A unified credit provides an exemption for transfers from an estate so that most individuals are not subject to the estate tax at death.

The unified credit also applies to the gift tax.

Trusts

When a taxpayer transfers property to a trust, the taxpayer has made two gifts, the **income interest** and the **remainder interest**.

The beneficiary of the income interest receives the income from the trust each year.

The beneficiary of the remainder interest receives the **property (corpus)** of the trust when the trust terminates.

Trusts

The income and remainder interests are valued using actuarial tables provided by the IRS.

The rate used in the valuation is 120% of the applicable Federal midterm rate for the month in which the transfer is made.

Federal Gift Tax

Value of gifts for gift tax purposes is **fair market value.**

April 15 is the due date for gift tax returns (**Form 709**).

Each individual can give away an amount up to the **annual exclusion**, per donee, without having to pay any gift tax. Gift must be of a **present interest** for exclusion to apply.

Gift Splitting

Spouses can elect **gift-splitting**, which means that they could give away an amount up to twice the annual exclusion a year to a donee and pay no gift tax, regardless of which spouse actually made the gift.

A gift tax return must be filed to elect gift splitting.

Gift-Splitting - Problem

Steve and Kay Briar, U.S. citizens, were married for the entire Year 5 calendar year. In Year 5, Steve gave a $30,000 cash gift to his sister. The Briars made no other gifts in Year 5. They each signed a timely election to treat the $30,000 gift as made one-half by each spouse.

Disregarding the unified credit and estate tax consequences, what amount of the Year 5 gift is taxable to the Briars assuming the annual exclusion is $13,000?

Gift-Splitting - Solution

30,000

	Steve	**Kay**
	15,000	15,000
Exclusion	(13000)	(13000)
Taxable Gift	2,000	2,000

Gift Tax Exclusions

An unlimited exclusion exists for gifts to **spouses, charities**, and **political organizations.**

An unlimited exclusion exists for **educational tuition and medical expenses** paid on behalf of an individual if and only if the amounts are paid directly to the educational institution or medical provider.

Annual Exclusion - Problem

In Year 2, Blum, who is single, gave an outright gift of $50,000 to a friend, Gould, who needed the money to pay medical expenses.

In filing the Year 2 gift tax return, Blum was entitled to a maximum exclusion of how much?

$13,000

Gift Tax - Problem

Which of the following requires filing a gift tax return, if the transfer exceeds the available annual gift tax exclusion?

A. Medical expenses paid directly to a physician on behalf of an individual unrelated to the donor
B. Tuition paid directly to an accredited university on behalf of an individual unrelated to the donor
C. Payments for college books, supplies, and dormitory fees on behalf of an individual unrelated to the donor
D. Campaign expenses paid to a political organization

Gift Tax Formula

	Taxable gifts for current year
+	Taxable gifts for all prior years
	Total lifetime gifts
x	Unified tax rates
	Total gift tax
-	Gift tax paid in prior years (at current rates)
-	Unified tax credit (if elected)
	Gift tax due for current year

Unified Credit

Under the unified rate schedule,

A. Lifetime taxable gifts are taxed on a noncumulative basis
B. Transfers at death are taxed on a noncumulative basis
C. Lifetime taxable gifts and transfers at death are taxed on a cumulative basis
D. The gift tax rates are 5% higher than the estate tax rates

Gift Tax - Problem

Mr. C made the following gifts during the current year.

- $1,000 each month to a university to pay tuition costs for his niece
- An undeveloped tract of land to his sister that had an adjusted basis to Mr. C of $4,000 and a fair market value of $25,000
- Various shares of stock to his wife that had an adjusted basis to Mr. C of $15,000 and a fair market value of $40,000. Mr. C did not consent to gift-splitting

What is the total amount of taxable gifts for this year?

Gift Tax - Solution

Niece – tuition 0

Sister – land 25,000 − 13,000 = 12,000

Wife – Stock 0

FEDERAL ESTATE TAX

Federal Estate Tax

	Gross estate
-	Deductions
	Taxable estate
+	Taxable gifts made after 1976
	Total taxable transfers
x	Unified tax rates
	Tentative transfer tax
-	Gift tax paid after 1976 (at current rates)
-	Unified credit and other credits
	Estate tax due

Gross Estate

The gross estate includes the FMV of all property owned at the date of death.

An executor can elect to value certain realty used in farming or in connection with a closely held business at a "special use" **valuation**. The farm or business must continue to be used in that capacity for at least **five years during the eight year period** after the date of death.

Alternate Valuation Date

The FMV is measured at the date of death, unless the executor elects the **alternate valuation date**, which is **six months after the date of death**.

AVD can be elected only if the value of the gross estate will be less than the date of death value.

If the AVD is elected and the property is distributed before the AVD, the FMV is determined on the distribution date.

Jointly Owned Property

Husband and Wife: 50% of the property owned jointly by husband and wife goes into the estate of the first spouse to die. A tenancy by the entirety is a joint tenancy between husband and wife.

Jointly Owned Property

Joint-tenancy: property owned with a **right-of-survivorship**, meaning that at death the property immediately passes to the other owner that is still living.

For tax purposes, **100% of the property is included in the estate of the first owner to die**, unless it can be proven that the surviving owner contributed to the purchase of the asset.

Jointly Owned Property

Tenancy in common - there is no right of survivorship.

The decedent's share of property passes into the probate estate and its distribution is controlled by the decedent's will.

The **decedent's share of the property is included in the gross estate for tax purposes.**

Review Question

Following are the fair market values of Wald's assets at the date of death:

Personal effects and jewelry $ 150,000 ✓

Land bought by Wald with Wald's funds five years prior to death and held with Wald's sister as joint tenants with right of survivorship 800,000 ✓

The executor of Wald's estate did not elect the alternate valuation date. The amount includible as Wald's gross estate in the federal estate tax return is?

$950,000

Review Question

Which of the following items of property would be included in the gross estate of a decedent who died in the current year?

Clothes and jewelry of the decedent. ✓

Cash of $400,000 given to decedent's friend in Year 1. No gift tax was paid on the transfer. ✗

Land purchased by decedent and held as joint tenants with rights of survivorship with decedent's brother. ✓

Life Insurance

Proceeds are included in the gross estate under either of two conditions:

1. The decedent **had incidents of ownership** (e.g., the right to designate the beneficiary).
2. The **decedent's estate is the beneficiary** of the insurance policy.

Life insurance proceeds from buy-sell agreements are generally excluded from the gross estate.

Retained Interests

A retained life estate or the retention of a power to alter, amend, or revoke a transfer are retained interests that cause the property subject to the power to be included in the gross estate.

The **power to designate possession or enjoyment of property or income** (including power created by another that can be exercised in the decedent's favor) will also cause the property to be included in the gross estate.

Transfers Within 3 Years of Death

Transfers involving **retained interests and revocable** transfers where the retention or right to revoke was terminated within three years of death are included in the gross estate.

Transfers of **life insurance** are included in the decedent's gross estate if the transfer was made within three years of death.

Gift tax paid on transfers made within three years of death is included in the gross estate.

Deductions

- Marital Deduction
- Debts of the Estate
- Funeral and Administrative Expenses
- Charitable Contributions
- Casualty Losses

Estate Tax Return

The estate tax return **(Form 706)** is due 9 months after date of death.

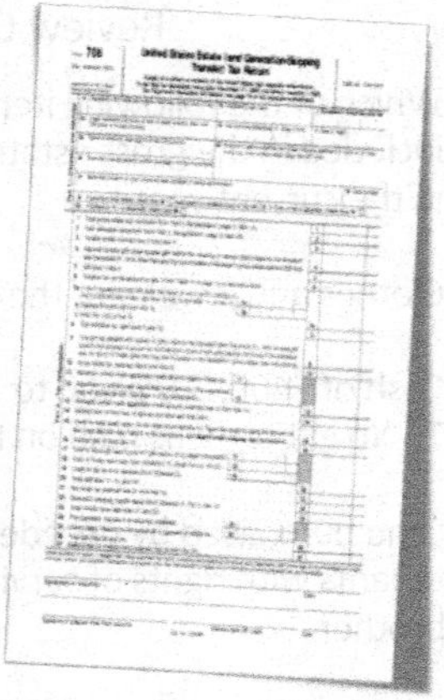

Unified Credit

The unified credit will offset a net estate of $5,120,000 in 2012.

Any unused credit from a spouse dying after 2010 may be used in the future by the **surviving spouse**.

Which of the following items of property would be included in the gross estate of a decedent who died in 2012?

I. Clothes and jewelry of the decedent.

II. Cash of $400,000 given to decedent's friend in 2009. No gift tax was paid on the transfer.

III. Land purchased by decedent and held as joint tenants with rights of survivor-ship with decedent's brother.

- [ ] A. **1, 2, and 3**
- [ ] B. **1 and 3**
- [ ] C. **1 and 2**
- [ ] D. **2 and 3**

REG 10 – 3

FIDUCIARY TAXATION

Income Taxation of Fiduciaries

Selected Questions (1)

INCOME TAXATION OF FIDUCIARIES

Filing Requirements

Trusts and Estates report their income on **Form 1041**.

Due on the 15th day of the 4th month after the close of the tax year.

Estates may adopt a calendar or any fiscal taxable year.

Trusts must use a calendar year.

Income Concepts

Income is taxed only once to **either the fiduciary or the beneficiary**.

A **distribution deduction** for fiduciary prevents double tax.

Income taxed to beneficiaries retains its character (a conduit approach).

Income Computation

The deductions and credits allowed (or disallowed) are similar to those allowed for an individual taxpayer, with some exceptions.

The **estate's administration costs and losses** during the administration of the estate may be deducted by the estate. If administration expenses are deducted on the fiduciary return they cannot also be deducted on the estate tax return (i.e., **no double deduction** is allowed).

Income Computation

State inheritance or estate taxes are not deductible for estates nor for individual taxpayers on their respective income tax returns.

State and local taxes that are deductible for estates and individual taxpayers include income taxes, personal ad valorem property taxes, and real property taxes

Extraordinary items are allocated to principal; that is, payments that are made irregularly such as proceeds from a fire.

Exemptions

Fiduciaries get a **personal exemption** depending on the type of fiduciary:

- $600 for estates,
- $300 for simple trusts and for complex trusts that distribute all of their income currently, and
- $100 for all other complex trusts.

Income in Respect of a Decedent

Gross income **includes income in respect of a decedent** (IRD).

IRD is income that was **earned by the decedent but not constructively received before death.**

IRD is included in the gross estate for estate tax purposes and is included in taxable income for the estate also.

Distributable Net Income

The estate/trust must pay tax on any income not distributed to the beneficiaries. Income that is distributed to beneficiaries is not taxed to the estate/trust.

Key concept is **distributable net income** (DNI).

DNI is the maximum amount that the entity can use as a **distribution deduction for the year and on which the beneficiaries can be taxed.**

The beneficiaries may be taxed on less than DNI since DNI includes tax-exempt interest.

DNI Computation

Taxable Income
+ net tax-exempt income
+ personal exemption
+ net capital loss
- net capital gains allocable to corpus

Distributable net income

Distributable Net Income

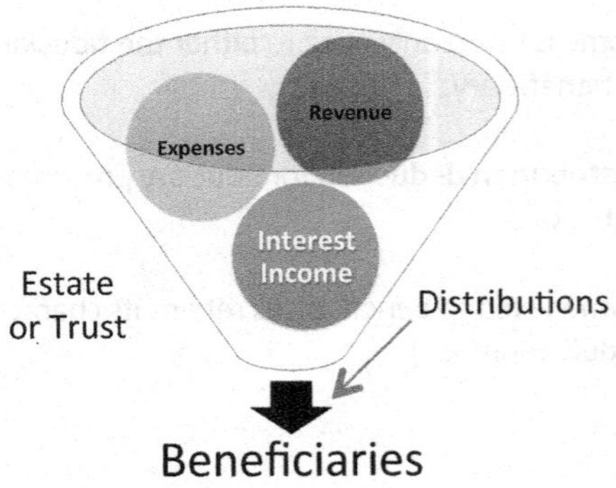

Review Question

Raff died in Year 4 leaving her entire estate to her only child. Raff's will gave full discretion to the estate's executor with regard to distributions of income. For Year 5, the estate's distributable net income was $15,000, of which $9,000 was paid to the beneficiary. None of the income was tax exempt.

MAX = DNI = 15,000

What amount can be claimed on the estate's Year 5 fiduciary income tax return for the distributions deduction?

9,000

Medical Expenses

Medical expenses incurred prior to the death of the taxpayer that are paid within one year of death have a special rule.

These expenses can be deducted either on the decedent's final Form 1040 or the estate tax return (Form 706).

Review Question

Bell, a cash basis calendar year taxpayer, died on June 1, Year 3. In Year 3, prior to her death, Bell incurred $2,000 in medical expenses. The executor of the estate paid the medical expenses, which were a claim against the estate, on July 1, Year 3. If the executor files the appropriate waiver, the medical expenses are deductible on:

A. The estate tax return
B. Bell's final income tax return
C. The estate income tax return
D. The executor's income tax return

Review Question

The charitable contribution deduction on an estate's fiduciary income tax return is allowable

A. If the decedent died intestate
B. To the extent of the same adjusted gross income limitation as that on an individual income tax return
C. Only if the decedent's will specifically provides for the contribution
D. Subject to the 2% threshold on miscellaneous itemized deductions

Lyon, a cash basis taxpayer, died on January 15, 2012. In 2012, the estate executor made the required periodic distribution of $9,000 from estate income to Lyon's sole heir. The following pertains to the estate's income and disbursements in 2012:

<u>2012 Estate Income</u>	
$20,000	**Taxable interest**
10,000	**Net long-term capital gains allocable to corpus**
2012 Estate Disbursements	
$ 5,000	**Administrative expenses attributable to taxable income**

For the 2012 calendar year, what was the estate's distributable net income (DNI)?

- [ ] A. **$15,000**
- [ ] B. **$20,000**
- [ ] C. **$25,000**
- [ ] D. **$30,000**

REG 10-4

TAX RESEARCH AND PRACTICE 1

Sources of Tax Authority and Research

Selected Questions (1)

SOURCES OF TAX AUTHORITY AND RESEARCH

Sources of Authority

Primary authority versus **secondary** authority.

Sources of primary authority

- Legislative Authority
- Administrative Authority
- Judicial Authority

Sources of Authority

Internal Revenue Code is the codification of the tax laws promulgated by Congress.

Statutory Law Development

House Ways and Means Committee
↓
House of Representatives
↓
Senate Finance Committee
↓
Senate
↓
Joint Conference Committee
↓
Back to House and Senate
↓
President – sign or veto

Legislative Authority

Constitution

Internal Revenue Code (IRC § 351)

Committee Reports

Barring certain exceptions (e.g., constitutional issues), Congress has the last word on what the Federal tax law should be.

Administrative Sources

Treasury Regulations (Treas. Reg. § 1.351 -1)
- Legislative, Interpretative, Procedural
- Proposed, Temporary, Final

Revenue Rulings (Rev. Rul. 2009-12)

Private Letter Rulings (PLR 200948009)

Revenue Procedures (Rev. Proc. 2008-23)

Technical Advice Memoranda (TAM 201003016)

Judicial Sources

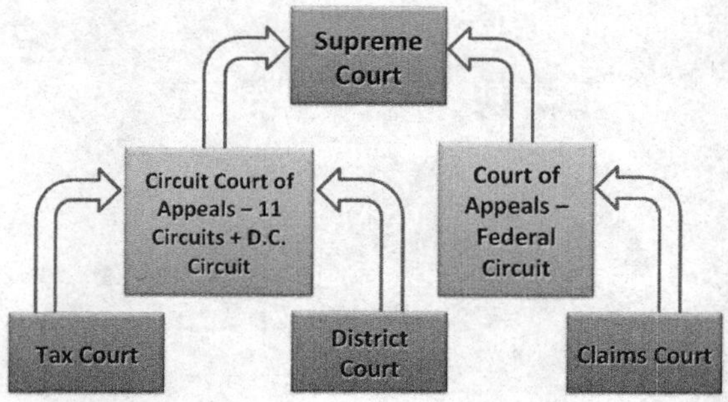

Courts of Original Jurisdiction

U. S. Tax Court - one court
Hears only tax cases

U. S. District Court - many courts
Jury trial possible
Must pay deficiency first

U. S. Court of Federal Claims - one court
Must pay deficiency first

U. S. Tax Court - Small Cases Division
$50,000 or less
No appeal

Precedents

Courts must follow previous decisions for future cases with the same controlling set of facts.

Tax Court will follow previous decisions in the Circuit that will have jurisdiction on appeal.

Weighting of Authority - Legislative

The highest source of tax authority is the U.S. Constitution.

The next highest source is the Internal Revenue Code.

Legislative regulations have almost as much weight as the IRC itself.

Weighting of Authority - Administrative

Other types of regulations have very significant authority within the context of administrative authority.

Revenue Rulings are the next highest source of authority.

Private Letter Rulings apply only to the taxpayer who requested the ruling.

Weighting of Authority - Judicial

The weighting of a judicial decision depends on:
- Level of Court
- Legal residence of the taxpayer
- Whether IRS has acquiesced to the decision
- The date of the decision
- Whether later decisions have concurred with opinion

Review Question

In evaluating the hierarchy of authority in tax law, which of the following carries the greatest authoritative value for tax planning of transactions?

A. Internal Revenue Code.
B. IRS regulations.
C. Tax court decisions.
D. IRS agents' reports.

Research Process

1. Identify all relevant facts
2. Clearly state problem to be solved
3. Locate applicable tax authority
4. Evaluate the relevance of the authorities
5. Determine alternative solutions
6. Determine most appropriate solution
7. Communicate results

Communicating Results

1. Document all relevant facts
2. Clearly describe the issue investigated
3. Report conclusions
4. Summarize rationale and authorities that support conclusions
5. Summarize key authorities used in research

In evaluating the hierarchy of authority in tax law, which of the following carries the greatest authoritative value for tax planning of transactions?

- [ ] **A. Internal Revenue Code.**
- [ ] **B. IRS regulations.**
- [ ] **C. Tax court decisions.**
- [ ] **D. IRS agents' reports.**

REG 10-5

TAX RESEARCH AND PRACTICE 2

Tax Practice and Procedure

Compliance Responsibilities

Selected Questions (1)

TAX PRACTICE AND PROCEDURE

Audit Process

Audit process begins with review of returns for error and matching information from W-2s, 1099s, etc.

Each return is given a score from formulas that are part of the Discriminant Function System (DIF). The DIF score is used to determine which returns to review for possible audit

Statute of Limitations

The IRS can assess additional tax **up to three years** from the later of:

- The date the return was filed or
- The due date for the return, with two exceptions:
  - The statute of limitations is 6 years if gross income omissions exceed 25% of the gross income stated on the return
  - There is no statute of limitations if the taxpayer willfully evaded tax in a fraudulent manner.

Statute of Limitations

A tax year may be reopened after the statute of limitations has expired if there is a determination for an open year that an earlier treatment was erroneous.

Review Question

A calendar-year taxpayer files an individual tax return for 2011 on March 20, 2012. The taxpayer neither committed fraud nor omitted amounts in excess of 25% of gross income on the tax return. What is the latest date that the Internal Revenue Service can assess tax and assert a notice of deficiency?

A. March 20, 2015
B. March 20, 2014
C. April 15, 2015
D. April 15, 2014

4/15/2012
+ 3
2015

Audit Process

A taxpayer may appoint qualified individuals to represent her before the IRS, usually a CPA, attorney, or enrolled agent

The IRS has the power to summon the taxpayer's records and witnesses to testify.

IRS reports findings in **an Income Tax Examination Changes** report.

Disagreements between the taxpayer and IRS may arise from questions of fact or from questions of law.

Audit Process

The IRS will take positions consistent with its administrative sources of the tax law.

The taxpayer and IRS can negotiate until the issues are resolved.

Revenue Agent's Report

If the taxpayer agrees to the audit changes proposed in the **Revenue Agent's Report**, he cannot pursue tax relief through the appeals process or through the Tax Court.

A signed agreement binds the IRS and taxpayer with regard to only items in the agreement.

Nevertheless, once the deficiency is paid the taxpayer can later pursue a claim for refund through the U.S. District Court or U.S. Claims Court.

30-Day Letter

If agreement is not reached through the audit process the taxpayer will receive a copy of the Revenue Agent's Report and a **30-day letter**.

The IRS encourages the taxpayer to agree to the RAR or request an appellate conference. However, the **taxpayer is not required to respond**.

If there is no response a 90-day letter is issued which includes a statutory notice of deficiency.

Appeals Process

To appeal, a written protest must be filed with the request for an appellate conference.

The protest must explain the taxpayer's position for each issue and provide the support on which the taxpayer is relying for questions of law.

The IRS is not required to grant an appeal in all cases.

Appeals Process

In general new issues may not be raised by the IRS during the appeal.

If the case is settled a **Form 870-AD** is signed, which means that the case will not be reopened unless there is a significant mathematical error or fraud.

If the IRS issues a "no change" report, the taxpayer still has the option to amend the return. However, the IRS cannot reopen the case unless fraud exists.

90-Day Letter

If a taxpayer does not respond to the **30-day letter** or does not reach agreement in the appeals process, a 90-day letter is issued.

The 90-day letter is significant in that this is the time that the taxpayer has to file a petition with the Tax Court. If the petition is not filed in a timely manner then the taxpayer's only judicial recourse is through U.S. District Court or U.S. Claims Court, both of which require the deficiency to be paid before the judicial process can begin.

Tax Court

Once a petition has been filed with the Tax Court, the IRS cannot enforce its assessment until the Tax Court's decision is finalized.

Other IRS Procedures

An **offer in compromise** may be agreed to by the IRS which allows a taxpayer to settle a tax liability for less than the actual amount owed.

The IRS may request the taxpayer to extend the statute of limitations period. While not required to do so, a refusal to extend will usually lead the IRS to assess a tax deficiency.

Privileged Communication

Any communication that would be **privileged** between a taxpayer and an attorney is also privileged between a taxpayer and any person who is authorized to practice before the IRS.

This privilege does not apply to **criminal tax matters** nor to corporate tax shelters.

Signing a Return

A taxpayer must sign a tax return for it to be complete. Both spouses must sign a joint return. This creates joint and several liability for each spouse.

A taxpayer can use an **electronic signature** to sign a return that is e-filed.

Signing a Return

A tax return is signed under the **penalty of perjury**. If a taxpayer knowingly signs a false tax return the taxpayer can be subject to civil and/or criminal penalties.

The tax preparer must also sign the tax return and provide a Personal Identification Number (PIN).

Failure to do so results in a **$50 penalty to the tax preparer for each failure** (maximum of $25,000 in any calendar year). The penalty applies separately to the failure to sign and failure to provide a PIN.

Circular 230

- IRS's rules of practice. The government may censure, fine, suspend, or disbar tax advisors from practice before the IRS if they violate Circular 230's standards of conduct.
- Subpart A: Rules Governing Authority to Practice
- Subpart B: Duties and Restrictions Relating to Practice before the IRS
- Subpart C: Sanctions for Violations

Who May Practice Before the IRS

- Attorneys
- CPAs
- Enrolled agents
- Enrolled actuaries enrolled by the Joint Board for the Enrollment of Actuaries. Practice is limited to issues related to qualified retirement plans
- Enrolled retirement plan agents. However, practice is limited to issues related to employee plans and to IRS forms in the 5300 and 5500 series
- Registered Tax Return Preparers (RTRP)

Additional Provisions for RTRPs

Practice is limited to **preparing and signing tax returns** and claims for refund.

May represent taxpayers before revenue agents, customer service representatives, or similar officers and employees of the IRS if the RTRP signed the return or claim for refund.

An RTRP may not represent a client before appeals officers, revenue officers, Counsel or similar officers or employees of the IRS or Treasury Department.

Practice Before the IRS

Practice before the IRS includes all matters connected with a presentation to the IRS or any of its officers or employees related to a taxpayer's rights, privileges, or liabilities under laws or regulations administered by the IRS.

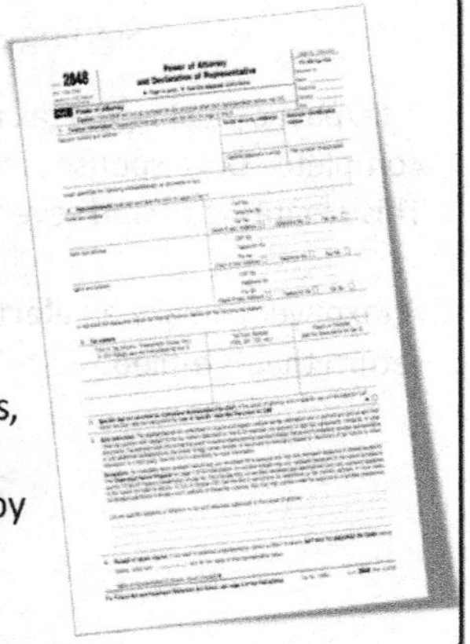

Practice Before the IRS

A power of attorney (**Form 2848**, Power of Attorney and Declaration of Representative) is required for an individual to represent a taxpayer before the IRS.

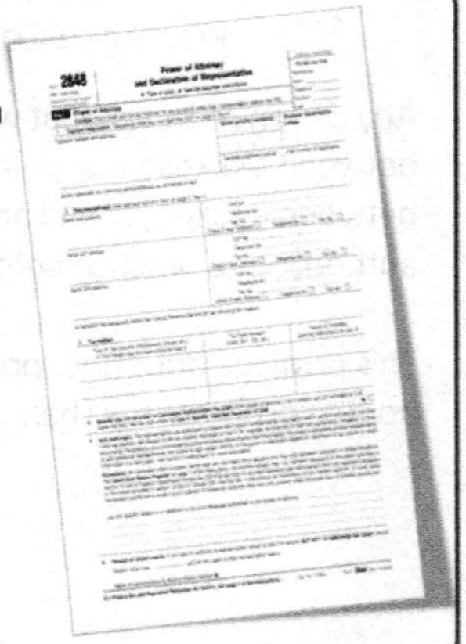

Other Professional Standards

CPAs are also subject to:

- AICPA's Code of Professional Conduct
- AICPA's Statements on Standards for Tax Services

Registration Requirements

As of January 1, 2011 any individual who prepares tax returns for compensation has to be registered with the IRS and pay a registration fee.

This includes attorneys, CPAs, and enrolled agents.

Individuals other than attorneys, CPAs, and enrolled agents must meet additional requirements such as passing examinations and maintaining continuing professional education.

COMPLIANCE RESPONSIBILITIES

Filing Requirements - Individuals

Form 1040 is due on April 15, unless that day falls on a weekend.

A taxpayer can receive an automatic extension of time to file until October 15 with the approval of the IRS.

Taxpayers must make estimated payments (on the **15th of April, June, September, and January**) if the amount of tax owed is **at least $1,000** after subtracting withholding and credits.

Payment Requirements - Individuals

There is **no underpayment penalty** if the total tax payments are at least equal to the lower of:

1. 90% of the current year's tax, or
2. 100% of the prior year's tax.

Also an annualization exception.

Underpayment penalty is the applicable interest rate times the underpayment until the earlier of April 15 or the time the tax is paid.

Filing Requirements - Entities

Corporate returns (regular and S) are due on the 15th day of the 3rd month after the close of the tax year. An automatic six-month extension is allowed.

Partnership returns are due on the 15th day of the 4th month after the close of the tax year. An automatic five-month extension is allowed.

Trust returns are due on the 15th day of the 4th month after the close of the tax year. An automatic five-month extension is allowed.

Payment Requirements - Corporations

Corporations must make estimated payments (on the **15th of April, June, September, and December**) if the amount of tax owed is **at least $500** after subtracting withholding and credits.

There is **no underpayment penalty** if the total tax payments are at least equal to the lower of:

- 100% of the current year's tax, or
- 100% of the prior year's tax.

There is also an annualized income exception for corporations.

Payment Requirements - Corporations

A corporation with **$1 million or more of taxable income in any of its three preceding tax years** can use the preceding year's tax exception only for its first installment.

For all taxpayers, if there was no tax liability in the preceding year, the preceding year exception method may not be used.

Review Question

Blink Corp., an accrual basis calendar year corporation, carried back a net operating loss for the tax year ended December 31, 2011. Blink's gross revenues have been under $500,000 since inception. Blink expects to have profits for the tax year ending December 31, 2012. **Which method(s) of estimated tax payment can Blink use for its quarterly payments during the 2012 tax year to avoid underpayment of federal estimated taxes?**

X I. 100% of the preceding tax year method

✓ II. Annualized income method

Failure to File Penalty

A nonfiling penalty is imposed on taxpayers if the return is not filed by the due date. The penalty for late filing is **5% per month** of the tax due.

The maximum penalty is 25% of the tax due.

If the failure to file is fraudulent (intentional), the penalty is increased to **15% per month** up to a maximum of 75% of the tax due with the return.

Failure to Pay Penalty

Any tax due must be paid at the time of filing, or else a penalty of **0.5% per month** of the underpayment is imposed (up to 25% in total).

Interest on late payments starts on the due date for filing and is calculated using Federal short-term interest rate.

Does not apply if failure to file penalty is imposed for a given month.

Taxpayer Penalties

A **20% accuracy-related penalty** applies to underpayments attributable to negligence or disregard of rules or regulations, substantial understatement of income tax, and substantial valuation overstatement.

An understatement is **substantial** if it exceeds the **greater of 10% of the tax required to be shown on the return, or $5,000.**

A **75% civil penalty**, and possible criminal penalties, can be imposed for **fraud**.

Taxpayer Penalties - Problem

A taxpayer filed his income tax return after the due date but neglected to file an extension form.

The return indicated a tax liability of $50,000 and taxes withheld of $45,000.

On what amount would the penalties for late filing and late payment be computed?

$50,000 − $45,000 = $5,000

Statute of Limitations

The IRS can assess additional tax up to **three years** from the later of:

- The date the return was filed, or
- The due date for the return, with two exceptions:
  1. The statute of limitations is 6 years if gross income omissions exceed 25% of the gross income stated on the return
  2. There is no statute of limitations if the taxpayer willfully evaded tax in a fraudulent manner.

Claims for Refund

Claims for refund must be filed by the later of:

1. Three years from the date the return was filed, or
2. Two years of the actual payment of the tax.

Tax Forms

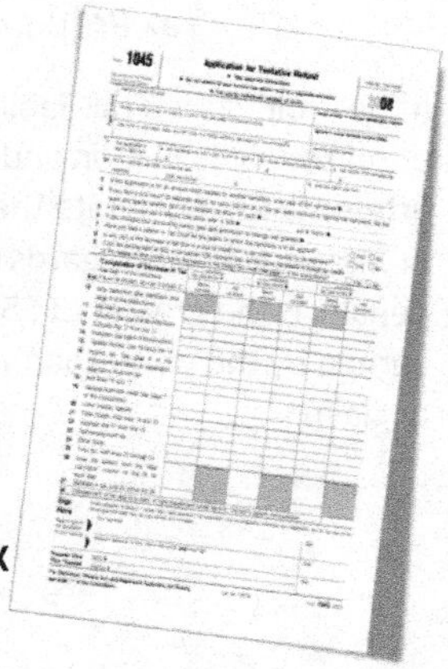

Form 1045 (Form 1139) is used by individuals (corporations) to claim refunds based on net operating losses, business credits or capital losses.

A claim for refund of erroneously paid income taxes must be submitted on Form **1040X**.

Corporations file Form **1120X** to amend a return.

Tax Preparer Penalties

These penalties apply to all tax return preparers, including preparers for estate, gift, employment, excise, and exempt organization returns.

Tax preparers are required to make reasonable inquiries if the taxpayer's information appears to be incorrect or incomplete.

Levels of Confidence for Tax Positions

Not frivolous = not patently improper

Reasonable basis = at least one authority that has not been overruled

Substantial authority = more than a reasonable basis

Realistic possibility = 1 in 3 chance of success

More likely than not = more than 50% chance of succeeding

Tax Preparer Penalties

For an "unreasonable position," the preparer must pay a penalty equal to the greater of $1,000 or 50% of the income derived by the preparer for preparing the return. A position is unreasonable if there is not **substantial authority** for it.

Tax Preparer Penalties

There is an exception to this rule if the position was **disclosed and there is a reasonable basis for it**. However, this exception applies to reportable transactions and tax shelters only if the position has a "more likely than not" chance of being sustained.

Tax Preparer Penalties

If the understated tax liability is due to an unreasonable position and the preparer **willfully attempts** to understate the tax liability or recklessly or intentionally disregards rules or regulations, the penalty is the greater of $5,000 or 50% of the income earned by the tax preparer for preparing the return or claim.

Other Penalties

Additional penalties for preparers are:

- Not signing returns done for compensation;
- Not providing a copy of the return for the taxpayer;
- Not keeping a list of returns filed;
- Endorsing or negotiating a refund check;
- Disclosing information from a tax return, unless for quality or peer review, or under an administrative order by a regulatory agency.

Tax Errors

A preparer should inform the taxpayer promptly (**but not the IRS**) upon becoming aware of an error in a previously filed return or of a taxpayer's failure to file a required return.

If a member is requested to prepare the current year's return and the taxpayer has not taken appropriate action to correct an error in a prior year's return, the member should consider whether to withdraw from preparing the return and whether to continue a professional or employment relationship with the taxpayer.

Chris Baker's adjusted gross income on her 2012 tax return was $160,000. The amount covered a 12-month period. For the 2012 tax year, Baker may avoid the penalty for the underpayment of estimated tax if the timely estimated tax payments equal the required annual amount of

I. 90% of the tax on the return for the current year paid in four equal installments.

II. 100% of prior year's tax liability paid in four equal installments.

- [ ] **A. I only.**
- [ ] **B. II only.**
- [ ] **C. Both I and II.**
- [ ] **D. Neither I nor II.**

REG 10-6

OTHER TAX ISSUES

Tax Planning

Business Entity Choice

Selected Questions (1)

TAX PLANNING

Marginal Tax Rate

Marginal tax rate is the rate that should be used for decision making.

Marginal tax rate is the amount of taxes that would be paid on the next dollar of taxable income, or that would be saved on the next dollar of deduction.

Tax Rates

Difference in tax rates over time:
- Moving between tax brackets
- Statutory changes in rates

If rates are increasing in the future, accelerate income and defer deductions.

If rates are decreasing in the future, accelerate deductions and defer income.

Tax Rates

Shift income to lower-bracket taxpayers.

Differences based on character of income (e.g., long-term capital gain vs. ordinary income).

Differences based on jurisdiction (e.g., U.S. tax rates versus foreign tax rates).

Tax Strategies

Avoid income by choosing nontaxable fringe benefits over taxable salary.

Defer income by meeting rules such as like-kind exchange rules.

Maximize contributions to retirement plans.

Recognize capital gains if capital losses have already been recognized which can offset the gains.

Tax Strategies

Generate passive income to offset unused passive losses.

Insure that carryforward amounts are used before they expire (e.g., charitable contributions, capital losses, net operating losses).

Alternative Minimum Tax

Taxpayers adopt planning strategies to avoid the individual AMT.

However, if the individual AMT cannot be avoided, it may be advantageous to accelerate income into the AMT year since it will be taxed at a maximum rate of 28%.

Recall that several itemized deductions are not allowed for AMT purposes.

Charitable Contributions

Gifting appreciated property to a charity avoids recognizing the appreciation as income.

Depreciated property should not be gifted because the loss is not recognized.

Rather, the asset should be sold so the loss can be recognized. The cash from the sale can then be contributed to a charity.

Cash Flows

Income taxes must be considered in analyzing cash flows. The marginal tax rate must be used when determining the after-tax cash flow from revenues or expenses.
Example: $1,000 charitable contribution; MTR = 25%

x25%
$250

1,000
(250)
750

The tax effect must also be considered when determining the cash flow from the sale or disposition of an asset.

Non-Tax Considerations

Tax effects should never be the only factors considered for a decision.

Non-tax factors must be considered also.

It is possible that the alternative with the best tax result increases costs in other areas for the company.

Goal is to maximize after-tax income, not minimize taxes.

BUSINESS ENTITY CHOICE

Common Business Entities

Tax classifications

- Corporations (C and S)
- Partnerships
- Trusts
- Disregarded entities

Legal forms

- Sole proprietorships (not a separate entity)
- Corporations
- General partnerships
- Limited partnerships
- Limited liability companies
- Limited liability partnerships
- Business trusts

Check-the-Box Regulations

Under entity classification rules, **per se corporations** include:

- Entities incorporated under state law
- Insurance companies
- Publicly-traded partnerships
- Specified foreign entities.

Other entities (such as REITs, tax-exempt organizations, and entities with S corporation election) are classified as corporations.

Check-the-Box Regulations

Default classification for business entities:

1. Corporation if on per se list
2. Unincorporated business entities
   - Partnership if two or more owners
   - Disregarded entity if one owner

Unincorporated business entities can elect to be taxed as an association/corporation if they prefer.

Check-the-Box Regulations

An election under the check-the-box regulations is effective for the tax year if made within the first 75 days of the year.

An election can be changed after 5 years or with IRS permission.

Comparison of Business Entities

Limited liability

Double taxation (income and on liquidation)

Ability to retain income at lower current tax cost

Tax-free contributions

Taxation of distributions

Owner tax basis for entity-level debt

Advantages/Disadvantages of Partnerships (and LLCs)

Advantages

- Single taxation
- Flexibility
- Basis increase for debt
- Tax-free contributions/admissions and distributions/withdrawals (generally)

Disadvantages

- Unlimited liability for general partners
- Limited partners have limited management rights

Which of the following is an advantage of forming a limited liability company (LLC) as opposed to a partnership?

- [ ] **A. The entity may avoid taxation.**
- [ ] **B. The entity may have any number of owners.**
- [ ] **C. The owner may participate in management while limiting personal liability.**
- [ ] **D. The entity may make disproportionate allocations and distributions to members.**

Made in the USA
Monee, IL
08 November 2026

68055351R00243